The
Enlightenment

PROBLEMS IN EUROPEAN CIVILIZATION SERIES

General Editor
Merry E. Wiesner

The Enlightenment

Edited with an introduction by
Dena Goodman
University of Michigan

Kathleen Wellman
Southern Methodist University

Houghton Mifflin Company   Boston   New York

Publisher: Charles Hartford
Editor-in-Chief: Jean Woy
Senior Sponsoring Editor: Nancy Blaine
Development Editor: Julie Dunn
Associate Project Editor: Lindsay Frost
Editorial Assistant: Teresa Huang
Production/Design Assistant: Bethany Schlegel
Manufacturing Coordinator: Renée Ostrowski
Senior Marketing Manager: Sandra McGuire

Cover image: Frontispiece to the *Encyclopedia* of Diderot and d'Alembert (1772). Engraved by Benoît-Louis Prévost from a drawing by Charles-Nicholas Cochin. Although engraved in 1772, this allegorical representation of the Enlightenment was intended to be inserted into volume one (1751) of the *Encyclopedia*. At the center, Reason is shown pulling the veils from Truth, as Imagination prepares to adorn her; the clouds are parted by the sun of Enlightenment that shines through them. Diderot tells us that the figure with her back to Truth is Theology, who seeks light elsewhere. (© *The Granger Collection, New York*)

Printed in the U.S.A.

Library of Congress Control Number: 2002109459

ISBN: 0-618-31296-X

23456789- EB -10 09 08 07 06

Contents

v

Preface

The intellectual and cultural movement that we call the Enlightenment shaped not only eighteenth-century Europe and its colonies, but also the modern world that emerged from it. This volume is intended to introduce students to this important movement and the continuing controversies over its interpretation and its legacies. What is distinctive about the Enlightenment is that the questions it raised for eighteenth-century readers about the nature and value of modernity have continued to resonate with readers in subsequent centuries. Indeed, as the readings in this volume make clear, the Enlightenment now serves as a site for both praise and blame of all that has unfolded since the French Revolution overtook it in 1789—that is to say, all that the modern world entails.

This volume not only attempts to demonstrate the richness of the Enlightenment and the historical scholarship that seeks to understand it, but also takes into account the central role the Enlightenment continues to play in contemporary cultural debates. In our selection of readings and topics, we have tried to keep the context of our readers in mind. We have asked ourselves: What issues have been and continue to be critical to understanding the Enlightenment in a contemporary context? How can we help students to think about their own relationship to the Enlightenment—its values, practices, and legacies?

The first two parts of the book, which introduce students to debates about what the Enlightenment was and who participated in it, open with brief selections from Enlightenment writers. We present the Enlightenment's own views of itself both to suggest where these debates originated and to suggest how the Enlightenment continues to shape our attitudes toward it. The answers constitute a dialogue among Enlightenment thinkers and between them and the historians who have tried to understand the Enlightenment as a phenomenon that has fundamentally shaped the modern world. Students will be able to consider the extent to which the twentieth-century understandings have been shaped by and diverge from those of the participants in the Enlightenment, as well as how particular historians portray the Enlightenment as an extension of the vision of particular philosophes, or in the light of later events.

The next two parts focus on specific aspects of the practice of Enlightenment. The articles in "Institutions of Enlightenment" introduce students to the media of Enlightenment through the institutions of print culture and intellectual sociability that furthered its projects and constituted some of its most important innovations. At the same time, they raise questions about the social location of the Enlightenment, its inclusiveness, and, thereby, its meaning. "Science and the Enlightenment" focuses on a key component of Enlightenment intellectual life. The philosophes consistently underscored their connections to science and the authority science conferred on them to challenge established social and intellectual traditions, and modern critics have often pointed to the scientific claims to knowledge associated with the Enlightenment as the basis of its power. This part asks how the Enlightenment understood science, how the science of the Enlightenment has been understood, and what were the practices of science in the Enlightenment.

The last two parts are meant to engage students with two of the most exciting debates that currently animate Enlightenment studies. "Did Women Have an Enlightenment?" raises the question of the relationship between women and the Enlightenment. Inspired by Joan Kelly-Gadol, who in 1977 posed the question: "Did Women Have a Renaissance?" historians continue to explore the question of the role of women in the Enlightenment and the meaning of the Enlightenment for women. In so doing, they have revived a debate on women that animated Enlightenment circles, as the selections from women and men of the day demonstrate.

"Critiques of the Enlightenment" is meant to engage students with the Enlightenment through the critiques currently mounted against it. Not only would it be irresponsible to pretend that the Enlightenment is not the object of serious criticism today, but the criticisms, rooted as they are in contemporary concerns, bring the Enlightenment alive by showing what is at stake in it. These critiques are mounted from within the critical practice broadly understood as postmodernism and take on what they consider to be the legacy of the Enlightenment. As this part reveals, because the Enlightenment has been associated with historical change and the modern world ushered in by it, it serves as a lightning rod for critics of all stripes, from political and religious conservatives to feminists and multiculturalists. In the true spirit of Enlightenment, we hope that the readings included in this volume will transform your classroom into a forum for passionate but civil and respectful debates about the Enlightenment through the study of its history and its legacies.

We should note that the selections from the writings of the philosophes included here are meant only to introduce the issues covered; they cannot begin to represent the richness of Enlightenment thought, which explored every conceivable topic. The philosophes themselves were a diverse group, and those represented here demonstrate that range of social and national backgrounds. At the end of the book you will find brief biographical sketches of the authors of the Enlightenment texts included in this volume, as well as suggestions for further reading about the Enlightenment and the men and women who contributed to it.

We would like to acknowledge the efforts of those who have made working on this project such a rewarding experience. We especially appreciate the support and encouragement of series editor Merry Wiesner, the care and attention of senior editor Nancy Blaine, and the helpfulness of development editor Julie Dunn and associate project editor Lindsay Frost in shepherding this project through the editorial and production processes. We would also like to thank the following reviewers who so enthusiastically endorsed this project:

Vincent P. Carey, State University of New York at Plattsburgh
Dale Lothrop Clifford, University of North Florida
Nancy Fitch, California State University, Fullerton
Oliver W. Holmes, Wesleyan University
Gerald L. Soliday, University of Texas, Dallas

Editor's Preface to Instructors

There are many ways to date ourselves as teachers and scholars of history: the questions that we regard as essential to ask about any historical development, the theorists whose words we quote and whose names appear in our footnotes, the price of the books that we purchased for courses and that are on our shelves. Looking over my own shelves, it struck me that another way we could be dated was by the color of the oldest books we owned in this series, which used to be published by D. C. Heath. I first used a "Heath series" book—green and white, as I recall—when I was a freshman in college and taking a modern European history course. That book, by Dwight E. Lee on the Munich crisis, has long since disappeared, but several Heath books that I acquired later as an undergraduate are still on my shelves. Those that I used in graduate school, including ones on the Renaissance and Reformation, are also there, as are several I assigned my students when I first started teaching or have used in the years since. As with any system of historical periodization, of course, this method of dating a historian is flawed and open to misinterpretation. When a colleague retired, he gave me some of his even older Heath series books, in red and black, which had actually appeared when I was still in elementary and junior high school, so that a glance at my shelves might make me seem ready for retirement.

The longevity of this series, despite its changing cover design and its transition from D. C. Heath to Houghton Mifflin, could serve as an indication of several things. One might be that historians are conservative, unwilling to change the way they approach the past or teach about it. The rest of the books on my shelves suggest that this conservatism is not the case, however, for many of the books discuss topics that were unheard of as subjects of historical investigation when I took that course as a freshman thirty years ago: memory, masculinity, visual culture, sexuality.

Another way to account for the longevity of this series is that several generations of teachers have found it a useful way for their students to approach historical subjects. As teachers, one of the first issues we confront in any course is what materials we will assign our students to read. (This decision is often, in fact, paramount for we have to order books months before the class begins.) We may include a textbook to provide an overview of the subject matter covered in the course and often have several from which to choose. We may use a reader of original sources, or several sources in their entirety, because we feel that it is important for our students to hear the voices of people of the past directly. We may add a novel from the period, for fictional works often give one details and insights that do not emerge from other types of sources. We may direct our students to visual materials, either in books or on the Web, for artifacts, objects, and art can give one access to aspects of life never mentioned in written sources.

Along with these types of assignments, we may also choose to assign books such as those in this series, which present the ideas and opinions of scholars on a particular topic. Textbooks are, of course, written by scholars with definite opinions, but they are designed to present material in a relatively bland manner. They may suggest areas about which there is historical debate (often couched in phrases such as "scholars disagree about . . .") but do not participate in those debates themselves. By contrast, the books in this series highlight points of dispute, and cover topics and developments about which historians often disagree vehemently. Students who are used to the textbook approach to history may be surprised at the range of opinion on certain matters, but we hope that the selections in each of these volumes will allow readers to understand why there is such a diversity. Each volume covers several issues of interpretive debate and highlights newer research directions.

Variety of interpretation in history is sometimes portrayed as a recent development, but the age of this series in its many cover styles indicates that this account is not accurate. Historians have long recognized that historical sources are produced by particular individuals with particular interests and biases that consciously and unconsciously shape their content. They have also long—one is tempted to say "always"—recognized that different people approach the past differently, making choices about which topics to study, which sources to use, which developments and individuals to highlight. This diversity in both sources and methodologies is part of what makes history exciting for those of us who study it, for new materials and new approaches allow us to see things that have never been seen before, in the same way that astronomers find new stars with better tools and new ways of looking.

The variety and innovation that is an essential part of good historical scholarship allow this series both to continue and to change. Some of the volumes now being prepared have the same titles as those I read as an undergraduate, but the scholarship on that topic has changed so much in the last several decades that they had to be completely redone, not simply revised. Some of the volumes now in print examine topics that were rarely covered in undergraduate courses when the series began publication, and a few former volumes are no longer in print because the topics they investigated now show up more rarely. We endeavor to keep the series up-to-date and welcome suggestions about volumes that would prove helpful for teaching undergraduate and graduate courses. You can contact us at http://college.hmco.com.

Merry E. Wiesner

Editor's Preface to Students

History is often presented as facts marching along a timeline, and historical research is often viewed as the unearthing of information so that more facts can be placed on the timeline. Like geologists in caves or physicists using elaborate microscopes, historians discover new bits of data, which allow them to recover more of the past.

To some degree, this model is accurate. Like laboratory scientists, historians do conduct primary research, using materials in archives, libraries, and many other places to discover new things about the past. Over the last thirty years, for example, the timeline of history has changed from a story that was largely political and military to one that includes the experiences of women, peasants, slaves, children, and workers. Even the political and military story has changed and now includes the experiences of ordinary soldiers and minority groups rather than simply those of generals, rulers, and political elites. This expansion of the timeline has come in part through intensive research in original sources, which has vastly increased what we know about people of the past.

Original research is only part of what historians do, however, in the same way that laboratory or field research is only part of science. Historical and scientific information is useless until someone tries to make sense of what is happening, tries to explain why and how things developed the way they did. In making these analyses and conclusions, however, both historians and scientists often come to disagree vehemently about the underlying reasons for what they have observed or discovered, and sometimes about the observations themselves. Certain elements of those observations are irrefutable—a substance either caught fire or it did not, a person lived and died or he or she did not—but many more of them are open to debate: Was the event (whether historical or scientific) significant? Why and how did it happen? Under what circumstances might it not have happened? What factors influenced the way that it happened? What larger consequences did it have?

The books in this series focus on just those types of questions. They take one particular event or development in European history and present you with the analyses of several historians and other authors regarding this issue. In some cases the authors may disagree about what actually happened—in the same way that eyewitnesses of a traffic accident or crime may all see different things—but more often they disagree about the interpretation. Was the Renaissance a continuation of earlier ideas, or did it represent a new way of looking at the world? Was nineteenth-century European imperialism primarily political and economic in its origins and impact, or were cultural and intellectual factors more significant? Was ancient Athens a democracy worthy of emulation, an expansionary state seeking to swallow its neighbors, or both? Within each volume are often more specific points of debate, which add complexity to the main question and introduce you to further points of disagreement.

Each of the volumes begins with an introduction by the editor, which you should read carefully before you turn to the selections themselves. This introduction sets out the *historical* context of the issue, adding depth to what you may have learned in a textbook account or other reading, and also explains the *historiographical* context, that is, how historians (including those excerpted in the volume) have viewed the issue over time. Many volumes also include a timeline of events and several reference maps that situate the issue chronologically and geographically. These may be more detailed than the timelines and maps in your textbook, and consulting them as you read will help deepen your understanding of the selections.

Some of the volumes in the series include historical analyses that are more than a century old, and all include writings stretching over several decades. The editors include this chronological range not only to allow you to see that interpretations change, but also to see how lines of argument and analysis develop. Every historian approaching an issue depends not only on his or her own original research, but also on the secondary analyses of those who have gone before, which he or she then accepts, rejects, modifies, or adapts. Thus, within the book as a whole or within each section, the selections are generally arranged in chronological order; reading them in the order they are presented will allow you to get a better sense of the historiographical development and to make comparisons among the selections more easily and appropriately.

The description of the scholarly process noted above is somewhat misleading, for in both science and history, research and analysis are not sequential but simultaneous. Historians do not wander around archives looking for interesting bits of information but turn to their sources with specific questions in mind, questions that have often been developed by reading earlier historians. These questions shape where they will look, what they will pay attention to, and therefore what conclusions they will make. Thus, the fact that we now know so much more about women, peasants, or workers than we did several decades ago did not result primarily from sources on these people suddenly appearing where there had been none, but from historians, with new questions in mind, going back to the same archives and libraries that had yielded information on kings and generals. The same is true in science, of course; scientists examining an issue begin with a hypothesis and then test it through the accumulation of information, reaching a conclusion that leads to further hypotheses.

In both history and science, one's hypotheses can sometimes be so powerful that one simply cannot see what the sources or experiments show, which is one reason there is always opportunity for more research or a re-analysis of data. A scholar's analysis may also be shaped by many other factors, and in this volume the editor may have provided you with information about individual authors, such as their national origin, intellectual background, or philosophical perspective, if these factors are judged important to your understanding of their writings or points of view. You might be tempted to view certain of these factors as creating "bias" on the part of an author and thus to reduce the value of his or her analysis. It is important to recognize, however, that every historian or commentator has a particular point of view and writes at a particular historical moment; very often what scholars view as complete objectivity on their own part is seen as subjective bias by those who disagree. The central aim of this series over its forty-plus years of publication has been to help you and other students understand how and why the analyses and judgments of historians have differed and changed over time, to see that scholarly controversy is at the heart of the historical enterprise.

The instructor in your course may have provided you with detailed directions for using this book, but here are some basic questions that you can ask yourself as you read the selections:

- What is the author's central argument?
- What evidence does the author put forward to support this argument?
- What is the significance of the author's argument?
- What other interpretation might there be of the evidence that the author presents?
- How does each author's argument intersect with the others in the part? In the rest of the book?
- How convincing do you find the author's interpretation?

These questions are exactly the same as those that professional historians ask themselves, and in analyzing and comparing the selections in this book, you, too, are engaged in the business of historical interpretation.

Merry E. Wiesner

The Enlightenment

Introduction

The Enlightenment, the predominant intellectual and cultural movement of the eighteenth century, attracted to its ranks many of the most significant intellectual figures of its day. Most students today are familiar with at least some of the names of the major contributors to the Enlightenment: Voltaire, Diderot, Rousseau, and Montesquieu in France; Gibbon and Bentham in England; Hume and Adam Smith in Scotland; Kant, Lessing, and Goethe in Germany; Beccaria in Italy; Jefferson and Franklin in America. In addition, most people are familiar with the major ideas associated with the Enlightenment: a faith in human nature and in human reason manifested in scientific inquiry; a belief in the fundamental equality of all individuals; and an assumption that human freedom is both natural and desirable. The ideas of unlimited human progress and religious toleration are also common Enlightenment currency. This rather safe list of unexceptionable ideals, however, does not take us very far toward understanding the passions unleashed by the Enlightenment and the controversies that continue to swirl around it.

It is important to remember, first, that the Age of Enlightenment was also an age in which religious and political authorities, as well as families and other social institutions, wielded great power at the expense of individuals. Thus the values and practices of the Enlightenment frequently came into conflict with the values, beliefs, customs, and laws of eighteenth-century societies. Books were censored and sometimes confiscated and burned; writers were thrown in prison for running afoul of political or religious authorities and often denounced as dangerous to social order. Although the levels of freedom and repression varied from country to country, nowhere was the principle of freedom of expression established. In fact, it is not even clear that all proponents of Enlightenment believed in such freedom, at least not unconditionally. In the eighteenth century, words—and especially written and printed words—were understood to be powerful. As a movement based on the dissemination of the printed word, the Enlightenment came into conflict with traditional authorities challenged by its medium as much as by its messages.

The messages of the Enlightenment were as varied as the people who articulated them, from the son of a provincial cutler to the wife of a marquis, from a professor of philosophy to a gentleman scholar. The biographical sketches at the end of this book suggest the variety of men and women who embraced the Enlightenment and dedicated them-selves to it. Collectively, they shared an adherence to a set of common values that constituted principles of critical debate rather than a dogma or doctrine. Indeed, the men and women of the Enlightenment tended to be suspicious of all dogmas, doctrines, authorities, and traditions. This skepticism led them to characterize others as being subject to pas-sion and enthusiasm, in contrast to their own rationality, and to write off many firmly held beliefs as mere superstitions.

Of course, the men and women of the Enlightenment had their own passions as well. They were passionate about justice, as campaigns against slavery and religious intolerance demonstrate, but they were also passionate about science. The Scientific Revolution, coupled with what Elizabeth Eisenstein has dubbed the "Print Revolution," brought the ex-citement of scientific experiment and discovery into the lives of anyone who could read a book or enroll in a public course. Empirical science represented the Enlightenment's passion for discovery, for novelty and the new in all its forms, from new species on newly explored continents to new diets to promote health. It spilled over into a love for novelty over tradition in everything—from literature to fashion to furniture. In both the arts and the sciences, the generations shaped by the Enlightenment tended to look forward rather than back.

Because what brought the men and women of the Enlightenment together was a critical spirit, rather than a set of shared beliefs, they de-veloped new practices and institutions of intellectual sociability that were at once more open to newcomers and structured to facilitate greater par-ticipation. From Masonic lodges and Parisian salons to book clubs and societies for the improvement of agriculture and the advancement of science and technology, what all of these institutions had in common was that they were voluntary, in stark contrast to the traditional social institu-tions of family and church. All were based on mutual respect, reciprocity, and exchange, rather than traditional hierarchies and authority based on social status, rank, or gender. In all cases, their goal was the improvement of society and individuals and, through it, their increased happiness.

To embrace the Enlightenment was to assert one's membership in an intellectual community committed to expanding its membership through print, reading, and other forms of discourse; a community that was both intellectual and social, critical and collective. To join the Enlightenment was to become part of a process of expansion, like light radiating from the sun. This process was also understood to be transformative, like spiritual enlightenment, both for the individual and for society and humanity as a whole. As the community of the Enlightenment grew over the course of the eighteenth century, its messages were carried throughout Europe and across the Atlantic in a rapidly expanding number of print publications, from books and pamphlets to magazines and newspapers whose authors constantly developed new ways to attract readers. The movement established itself as an alternative and a challenge to families, governments, and churches whose traditional values it threatened. Young women and men in particular were as attracted to the Enlightenment as they were to the urban spaces in which it flourished. Both promised them not only new opportunities and the freedom to pursue them, but a community of like-minded individuals with whom to question received wisdom, social constraints, and traditional authority.

While proponents of Enlightenment agreed on the broad principles that brought them together, they were less clear about how those concepts should be implemented. Thus the issues generated great internal debates about the nature and practices of the Enlightenment. The cultivation and promulgation of new ideas required new venues and institutions that would open doors to those with shared intellectual interest irrespective of rank. Enlightenment institutions included to some extent those usually barred from more traditional institutions—women and members of the commercial classes, for example. Because the Enlightenment was an open, self-defining, self-critical movement, there have been many "enlightenments" since its inception.

From the very beginning, the Enlightenment has been defined as much by those who opposed or feared it as by those who promoted or embraced it. Those whom historian Peter Gay has called "the party of humanity," and others have dubbed "the forces of reason," were often condemned in their own day as godless atheists and threats to society. Friends and foes of the French Revolution have given the Enlightenment a more political meaning. While the Revolutionaries were making heroes of Voltaire and Rousseau by ceremoniously transferring their remains to the Pantheon in a celebration of the first anniversary of the fall of the Bastille, counter-Revolutionaries proclaimed the Revolution to be the fruition of the Enlightenment conspiracy to destroy society. However the Revolution was interpreted, for a long time one of its main causes was assumed to be the Enlightenment.

Among European *intellectual* historians, however, only a few, such as Ernst Cassirer, saw the Enlightenment as a turning point in history; most tended to characterize it as the mere popularization of the new ideas that had emerged from the Scientific Revolution and the political and religious upheavals of the seventeenth century. American historians, however, cast the intellectual history of the Enlightenment into the social and political context out of which the United States would emerge from its own revolution as a modern, secular democracy dedicated to life, liberty, and the pursuit of individual happiness. Like most Americans, Peter Gay and others identified with the modernity of the Enlightenment, which challenged the traditional authority of the Old World just as America's founders did.

By and large, Americans have tended to take a more positive view of the Enlightenment than their European counterparts. Today, the Enlightenment represents for some Americans the progress of reason, humanity, liberty, equality, and justice for all—the very definition of fundamental American values. For others, who voice concern that America has lost touch with its religious origins and Christian moral values, the Enlightenment represents the height of human arrogance and the corrosion of the values that make social order and civil society possible—faith in God, respect for authority, and the primacy of community over the selfish individual. For still others, who see many of the present ills of the world as a result of the Enlightenment, this movement represents either a naive faith in human reason and virtue or a cynical guise for hidden inhumanities such as slavery, colonialism, and the oppression of women. Thus, although Americans continue to disagree as to whether the results of the Enlightenment were positive or negative, they tend not to question the importance of the Enlightenment in the formation of modern society and the entire world in which we live.

During much of the twentieth century, however, the consensus among academic historians in Europe and America was that economic forces—not ideas—were the primary agents of historical change. Influenced by the theories of Karl Marx, historians downplayed the role of the Enlightenment in shaping modernity and gave little attention to its study. And while most historians, especially those in the United States, were not Marxists, by the 1960s they overwhelmingly accepted the view that ideas were a product of historical change, not the driving force behind it. These social historians repudiated traditional political and intellectual history as the story of elite men (writers and artists, as well as kings and generals) and focused their attention instead on those who had been left out of previous historical accounts—notably, peasants, workers, and women. If for Marxist historians the Enlightenment was simply the ideology of the bourgeoisie that emerged in the eighteenth century and came to power in the nineteenth century, for most social historians it was entirely irrelevant to the lives of the people they studied.

This brief period of relative neglect of the Enlightenment has been redressed with a barrage of new work since the fall of the Marxist paradigm of historical change. Since the 1980s, historians have found the social and economic explanations of historical change unconvincing and turned instead to the study of language, and political language in particular, to try to understand how agents of change have been able to imagine a new social or political order and bring it into being. If, as proponents of this "linguistic turn" would say, an action must be thinkable for it to be doable, then forms of thought or "discourses" available at any given time must be viewed as crucial to our understanding of such events as the Atlantic Revolutions of the late eighteenth century, or the rise of domesticity in the nineteenth century. In this context, the Enlightenment has once again become an important object of study.

Some of this new work praises the Enlightenment and some of it condemns it; the debate it has provoked is the focus of this volume. Some recent scholarship, emerging from social history, broadens our view of the people associated with the Enlightenment and asks what their relationship was to the society they both criticized *and* belonged to. Other scholars expand our view of the Enlightenment beyond the ideas it produced to the modes of that production and the many ways in which the Enlightenment was "consumed" by readers. They take a cultural rather than an intellectual historical approach, as they try to understand the social world and worldview of the men and women who saw themselves as members of a community defined by the Enlightenment.

As a result of these studies, historians have come to understand the Enlightenment as a more diverse and inclusive movement and one that can less clearly be identified with either the history of philosophy or the single event of the French Revolution. Historical studies have revealed many diverse and popular manifestations of the Enlightenment and traced its influence far beyond the boundaries of continental Europe or any particular political formulation. Nevertheless, for good or ill, the Enlightenment continues to define the modern world. Today, social critics and intellectuals frequently articulate their stance toward the modern world as a position on the "Enlightenment project."

The end of the twentieth century was marked by a turning away from the principles that most intellectuals and social critics had identified as the Enlightenment foundations of the modern world, the philosophical underpinnings of modern ideology, society, and politics. Modernity, asserted these critics, is not a source of pride. From colonialism and slavery to the oppression of women and people of color; from the Holocaust to economic globalization, global poverty, and environmental destruction; the hallmark of the modern world has been the triumph not of civilization over barbarism or reason over ignorance, but of those who have claimed reason and civilization in an effort to oppress and exploit those they deem barbarous and ignorant. Such ideals as liberty, equality, and human rights may sound sweet to certain Western ears, but they turn sour when revealed as a justification for Western superiority, patriarchy, and racism. The conquest of nature through reason and technology is no longer a reason for pride but for shame, as resources dwindle, rain forests and wetlands disappear, and the planet warms. And it all begins with the Enlightenment—or at least, that's what the critics have claimed.

Historians of the Enlightenment have responded to this assault in part by defending the Enlightenment from its critics, and in part by acknowledging the legitimacy of some of their claims. As historians, though, their major concern has been to deepen the understanding of the Enlightenment, to rescue it from the catch phrases and caricatures to which the onslaught of criticism has reduced it. The current volume was undertaken in this spirit. On the one hand, we want to recognize the critiques that have been launched and to place the study of the Enlightenment in relation to the Western cultural context in which those criticisms have emerged and in which we, as teachers and students, live. On the other hand, as historians our aim is to introduce students to the richness of both the Enlightenment and the historical scholarship that seeks to understand it. For while the critics have been responding to a particular understanding of Enlightenment philosophy that places the focus on universal reason and individual autonomy, historians have been exploring a complex social and cultural world whose values go well beyond these abstractions.

Our aim is to present the Enlightenment as a site of contestation on two levels: as a lively community that nurtured debate about its own practices and about the world in which it operated; and as the very controversial site of current debates on the origins of modernity and its influence on the world in which we live. The Enlightenment was a vibrant community of inquiry. It was a community of men and women trying to make sense of their world and hoping to change it. They have left us with a legacy with which we must strive to come to grips, as the Enlightenment continues to inform our notions of who we are as modern men and women living in the twenty-first century.

ENCYCLOPÉDIE,

O U

DICTIONNAIRE RAISONNÉ

DES SCIENCES,

DES ARTS ET DES MÉTIERS,

PAR UNE SOCIÉTÉ DE GENS DE LETTRES.

Mis en ordre & publié par M. *DIDEROT*, de l'Académie Royale des Sciences & des Belles-Lettres de Prusse ; & quant à la PARTIE MATHÉMATIQUE, par M. *D'ALEMBERT*, de l'Académie Royale des Sciences de Paris, de celle de Prusse, & de la Société Royale de Londres.

Tantùm series juncturaque pollet,
Tantùm de medio sumptis accedit honoris ! HORAT.

TOME PREMIER.

A PARIS,

Chez {
BRIASSON, *rue Saint Jacques*, à la Science.
DAVID l'aîné, *rue Saint Jacques*, à la Plume d'or.
LE BRETON, Imprimeur ordinaire du Roy, *rue de la Harpe.*
DURAND, *rue Saint Jacques*, à Saint Landry, & au Griffon.
}

M. DCC. LI.

AVEC APPROBATION ET PRIVILEGE DU ROY.

Title page of volume one of the *Encyclopedia* of Diderot and d'Alembert (1751). Although the names and academic credentials of the two editors are prominently displayed here, the title page also proclaims this work to be the product of a larger, more inclusive, and less conventional "society of men of letters." The large number of publishers reveals the extensive financial commitment to the project, but the royal approval noted at the bottom of the page was often in jeopardy. The article "Encyclopedia" in this section may be read as amplifying the epigraph: "Such grace can order and connection give/ Such beauty may the commonplace receive." (*The Pierpont Morgan Library/Art Resource,* NY)

What Is the Enlightenment?

The purpose of an encyclopedia is to collect knowledge disseminated around the globe; to set forth its general system to the men with whom we live, and transmit it to those who will come after us.

Denis Diderot

Enlightenment is mankind's exit from its self-incurred immaturity.

Immanuel Kant

"Reason" becomes the unifying and central point of this century, expressing all that it longs and strives for, and all that it achieves.

Ernst Cassirer

All segments of society benefited from the new humanity; it became less fashionable to make victims than to succor them.

Peter Gay

The thread that may connect us with the Enlightenment is not faithfulness to doctrinal elements, but rather the permanent reactivation of an attitude—that is, of a philosophical ethos that could be described as a permanent critique of our historical era.

Michel Foucault

In its most basic historical sense, the Enlightenment was an intellectual movement that took place in Europe and its colonies in the eighteenth century. In this part we present first two key definitions of the Enlightenment by writers who participated in that movement: Denis Diderot and Immanuel Kant. For Diderot, the Enlightenment was an intellectual and political project for the benefit of posterity; for Kant, Enlightenment was an intellectual and historical process that began in his own century and would continue into the future. Later historians and philosophers, such as Ernst Cassirer, Peter Gay, and Michel Foucault, would draw upon the ideas of project and process to develop their own views of the Enlightenment and its legacy.

For Denis Diderot, the Enlightenment rested on a new, revolutionary approach to knowledge that would change not only *what* people thought, but also *how* they thought. In the 1740s, he and a friend, the mathematician Jean le Rond d'Alembert, proposed to a group of French publishers that they capitalize on the success in England of Ephraim Chamber's two-volume *Cyclopedia* by publishing a French version. This modest proposal by two men in their thirties ultimately produced the *Encyclopedia,* a work of 28 volumes, written by more than 150 contributors, which stands as a veritable monument to the Enlightenment. Diderot's article "Encyclopedia," which appeared in volume 5 of this colossal work, sets out its fundamental goals. In so doing, it also defines this document's role in a broadly conceived project of Enlightenment. An encyclopedia, Diderot explains, presents knowledge systematically and progressively and is intended as a gift to the next generation, which through the spread of knowledge will be both more virtuous and happier. An encyclopedia also "changes the common mode of thinking" by undermining superstition and other forms of false knowledge based only on faith or tradition. According to Diderot, the human being—not God—must be the organizing principle of knowledge; to be useful knowledge must be relevant to the human being, and to be valid it must originate in human experience rather than divine revelation.

As we will see, Diderot's article raises questions about the spread of knowledge that would preoccupy Enlightenment thinkers: How widely can and should knowledge be spread? How far can disciplines progress? What is the best way for an individual or a society to pursue and disseminate new knowledge? Today, we continue to ask these questions, but we also want to consider whether the advance of knowledge always leads to social improvement or more happiness for everyone. What effects do science and knowledge have on society, the individual, and particular social groups? Also, the corrosive effect of the critical approach on religion, tradition, and received wisdom has caused more conservative thinkers to wonder whether reason does more harm than good. Others have suggested that reason itself reflects only the power of the individuals or groups who claim to speak in its name, rather than the neutral or objective force they assume it to be.

In 1784, about 20 years after the last volume of the *Encyclopedia* was published, Immanuel Kant developed many of the points made by Diderot. In an essay written in response to the question "What is the Enlightenment?" posed by the editor of a German newspaper, Kant suggests that Enlightenment is a process that has just begun in his century, rather than an accomplished fact. For Kant, the realization of Enlightenment would mean that people have learned to think for themselves. This philosophical maturity can be achieved only through the advancement of knowledge, which in turn requires complete freedom of inquiry and expression. Thus freedom is an essential precondition of Enlightenment as well as its necessary consequence. But what does Kant mean by freedom? Like Diderot, Kant argues that Enlightenment depends on writers and thinkers (men of letters) being able to publish their research and ideas freely. However, he also maintains that this "public" use of reason must be balanced by one's "private" duty as a teacher, clergyman, or bureaucrat (government employee) to obey one's superiors. Kant confronts one of the most difficult political issues raised by the Enlightenment: Should the questioning of intellectual authority lead to the questioning of political and social authority? How can or should the advancement of knowledge or changes in thinking effect social and political change? Is freedom absolute, or must it be weighed against other considerations, such as the need for social order or the duty one owes to others? Can intellectual freedom and political liberty be pursued separately, or does one necessarily imply or entail the other?

Diderot defied political authority in publishing the *Encyclopedia* clandestinely, but his challenge to authority was still indirect. Kant was even more conflicted and circumspect in trying to resolve the dilemma of how to be a good citizen and member of society while pursuing truth and knowledge freely and honestly. This dilemma continues to challenge many intellectuals in the modern world.

In the final three selections in this part, two twentieth-century historians and one philosopher take up both the ideas and the concerns raised by Diderot and Kant about how to understand the Enlightenment and its role in society.

Ernst Cassirer shows that he shares Diderot's understanding of the Enlightenment as primarily an intellectual movement when he writes that the eighteenth century was the "century of philosophy par excellence." Like Diderot and Kant, he sharply distinguishes the Enlightenment's understanding of the use of reason from that of the seventeenth-century rationalists. Cassirer shares Diderot's belief that the scientific method associated with Newton was the model for the enlightened application of reason to a wide variety of disciplines. A lust for knowledge, as opposed to mere information, he insists, defines the Enlightenment.

Peter Gay emphasizes the social and political implications of the Enlightenment. Whereas Cassirer is concerned with showing the importance of the Enlightenment's contribution to the history of ideas, Gay argues that the significance of the Enlightenment lies in its humanitarian goals and its effects on the real world. He endorses the Enlightenment idea that the progress of knowledge leads to increased happiness and freedom. For Gay, as for Diderot, the advance of knowledge is inextricably linked to attacks on superstition and to a humanitarian approach to social issues. Voltaire, who challenged theological prejudices of his day by attacking their irrationality and championing their victims, embodied the spirit of Gay's Enlightenment. The project of Enlightenment was to change the world by stamping out irrational and inhumane thought and practice. But we might ask if Gay is himself sufficiently critical of the Enlightenment project so defined. Does he, for example, consider what may have motivated the men and women of the Enlightenment besides humanitarianism? How does he deal with the problem of negative or unintended consequences of their words and deeds? Most important, how does his own implicit acceptance of the ideals of American society—liberty, democracy, and happiness—shape his view of the Enlightenment?

The philosopher Michel Foucault returns to the question "What is the Enlightenment?" explicitly to revisit Kant's answer of 1784. Foucault contends that this is a perennial question but that Kant's answer to it, like our own, reflects the time in which he lived: we must see the Enlightenment differently than Kant did and, by extension, differently than Diderot, Cassirer, and Gay did. As Kant's response reflects the conflict between the desire for freedom and the concern for duty and order that marks the late Enlightenment, Foucault's answer, he maintains, must reflect his own historical position 200 years later. Right through the twentieth century, Foucault suggests, the Enlightenment way of thinking has shaped the modern worldview. Thus modern historians such as Cassirer and Gay could not have a critical perspective on it; only a postmodern perspective, Foucault's followers argue, allows sufficient critical distance. And yet, Foucault maintains, if there is an Enlightenment legacy that should be preserved, it is precisely the *critical* perspective toward knowledge, society, and politics that it championed. For Foucault, the essence of Enlightenment is this critical perspective, which must be turned on the Enlightenment itself, and the modern world that it ushered in—for better and for worse. Rather than simply taking a position for or against the Enlightenment, or for or against modernity, however, Foucault insists that we acknowledge our own historical position in relation to the Enlightenment if we are to understand it. For Foucault, Kant's text offers a foundation for reflecting on modernity as well as grounds for discussing the Enlightenment.

Denis Diderot

Encyclopedia

. . . The purpose of an *encyclopedia* is to collect knowledge disseminated around the globe; to set forth its general system to the men with whom we live, and transmit it to those who will come after us, so that the work of preceding centuries will not become useless to the centuries to come; and so that our offspring, becoming better instructed, will at the same time become more virtuous and happy, and that we should not die without having rendered a service to the human race. . . .

In a universal and analytical dictionary, in any work designed for the general instruction of men, one must therefore begin by framing one's object from the most extensive dimensions, understand the spirit of the nation, possess a sense of its direction, outpace it, so that it will not leave your work behind, but on the contrary meet up with it ahead; one must determine to work only for the following generations, because the moment of our existence passes, and a great enterprise will barely be completed before the present generation has passed on. . . .

Yet knowledge does not and cannot become common beyond a certain point. In truth, we do not know what this limit is. We do not know how far a given man can go. We know even less how far the human race would go, what it would be capable of, if it were not halted in its progress. But revolutions are necessary; there have always been revolutions, and always will be; the greatest interval from one revolution to another is known: this cause alone limits the extension of our work. There is a point in the sciences beyond which it is almost beyond their ability to go. When that point is reached, the achievements that remain of that advance are forever a marvel to the entire species. But if the species is limited in its efforts, how would the individual not be in his? The individual has only a certain amount of energy in his faculties, animal as well as intellectual; he only lasts for a time; he necessarily respects cycles of labor and rest; he has needs and passions to satisfy, and is exposed to endless distractions. Whenever all that is negative in these quantities adds up

Denis Diderot, "Encyclopedia (Philosophy)," trans. Philip Stewart, from *Encyclopedia of Diderot & d'Alembert Collaborative Translation Project*. Available at http://www.hti.umich.edu/d/did. Reprinted courtesy of Philip Stewart.

to the smallest possible sum, or all that is positive adds up to the largest, a man applying himself all alone to some branch of human science will take it as far as it can be taken by the efforts of a single individual. Add to the labor of that extraordinary individual that of another, and so forth, until you have filled the interval between one revolution and the one furthest removed, and you will have some notion of what the entire species could achieve, especially if you assume, as favoring its work, a certain number of auspicious circumstances that would have lessened the success had they gone against it. But the general mass of the species is able neither to follow nor to know this progress of the human mind. The highest point of instruction it can attain has its limits: whence it follows that there will be books that will forever be above the common ken of men; others will gradually drop beneath it, and still others will have both fates.

To whatever level of perfection an *encyclopedia* may be brought, it is evident from the nature of the work that it will necessarily be in the latter category. There are objects which are in the hands of the people, from which they draw their subsistence, the practical knowledge of which is their constant concern. Whatever treatise one may write about it, there will always come a moment when they know more about it than the book does. There are other objects about which they will remain almost entirely ignorant, because their gains in knowledge are too small and too slow, even if we assumed it is continuous, ever to amount to much enlightenment. Thus both the man of the people and the scientist will always have equally as much to desire and instruction to find in an *encyclopedia*. The most glorious moment for an opus of this nature would be that which immediately follows some great revolution which has suspended the progress of the sciences, interrupted the labors of the arts, and plunged a portion of our hemisphere back into darkness. What gratitude the next generation following such troubled times would feel for the men who had feared them from afar, and taken measures against their ravages by protecting the knowledge of centuries past! Then you would see (I say this without vainglory, because our *Encyclopedia* will perhaps never attain the perfection that would earn it such honors) that that great opus would be named along with the monarch under whom it was undertaken, the minister to whom it was dedicated, the powerful who favored its execution, the authors who devoted themselves to it, all the men of letters who took part in it. The same voice that recalled these supporters would not forget to evoke as well the burdens the authors had to bear and the affronts to which they were subjected; and the monument that would be elevated to them would have several sides, which would represent by turns the honors accorded their memory, and the marks of indignation attached to the memory of their enemies. . . .

Since the absolute perfection of a universal plan would not compensate for the weakness of our understanding, let us focus on what is appropriate to our human condition, and be content with going back to some very general notion. The higher the viewpoint from which we consider objects, the greater expanse it allows us to see, and the more the order we follow will be instructive and grand. Consequently it must be simple, because there is rarely grandeur without simplicity; it must be clear and accessible; it must not be a tortuous labyrinth where we might become lost, and in which we can perceive nothing from the point where we are; but a broad, vast avenue which extends into the distance, along which others are encountered at intervals, leading to remote and isolated objects via the easiest and shortest path.

One consideration above all must not be lost sight of, and that is that if man or the thinking, observing being is banished from the surface of the earth, this moving and sublime spectacle of nature is nothing but a sad and silent scene. The universe is dumb; silence and night overtake it. Everything changes into a vast solitude where unobserved phenomena occur in a manner dark and mute. It is the presence of man that gives interest to the existence of beings; and what could we better have in view in the history of those beings, than to yield to this consideration? Why not introduce man into our opus, as he is placed in the universe? Why not make of him a common center? Is there some point in infinite space from which we could more advantageously originate the immense lines which we propose to extend to all other points? What stirring and agreeable reaction of those beings towards man, and of man toward them, would not result?

This is what has led us to seek in the principal faculties of man, the general division to which we have subordinated our labors. One may follow some other path if he prefers, provided he not put in place of man some silent, insensitive and cold being. Man is the sole point from which to begin, and to which all must be brought back, if we are to please, engage, and affect the reader even in the most arid considerations and driest details. Aside from my existence and the happiness of my peers, what does the rest of nature matter? . . .

If I think there is a point beyond which it is dangerous to continue the argumentation, I also think one should not stop until one is sure it has been reached. Each science and each art has its metaphysics. This aspect is always abstract, lofty, and difficult. Yet that must be the principal aspect of a philosophical dictionary; and it could be said that as long as some such ground remains to be broken, there are unexplainable phenomena, and vice versa. Then the man of letters, the scientist, and the artist walk in darkness; if they make some progress, it is only thanks to chance; they arrive like a lost traveler who follows the right path without realizing it. It is therefore of the utmost importance to set forth the metaphysics of things, or their first and general reasons; the rest will be the more luminous for it and better assured in the mind. All the supposed mysteries for which some sciences are so criticized, and which some others so often cite to mitigate their own, when discussed metaphysically vanish like phantoms of the night on the approach of dawn. Art enlightened from the start will advance surely, rapidly, and always on the shortest path. We must thus take care to give the reasons of things, when there are some; assign the causes, when we know them; indicate the effects, when they are certain; resolve the conundrums through direct application of the principles; set forth truths; unmask errors; artfully discredit prejudices; teach men to doubt and wait; dispel ignorance; weigh the value of human knowledge; distinguish between true and false, true and plausible, plausible and miraculous or incredible, common phenomena from extraordinary phenomena, certain facts from doubtful facts, and those from facts absurd and counter to the natural order; become acquainted with the general course of events, and take each thing for what it is, and consequently inspire a desire for knowledge, a horror for lies and vice, and a love for virtue; for whatever has not happiness and virtue as its ultimate end is nought.

I cannot bear to see someone rely on the authority of authors in questions of reason; for what use is it in truth to look for the name of an author who is not infallible? . . .

In scientific treatises, it is the relations of ideas or phenomena which provide direction; as you advance, the subject matter develops, becoming either more general or more particular, according to the method chosen. The same will be true with respect to the general form of an article for the *Encyclopedia*, except that the dictionary or coordinated articles have advantages which in a scientific treatise can be achieved only at the expense of some quality; and it will owe these advantages to the [cross-]references, the most important aspect of encyclopedic ordering. . . .

[Cross-]references illuminate the object, indicate its closest connections to others immediately related to it, and its distant connections with others that might have seemed remote from it; recall to mind common notions and analogous principles; strengthen consequences; bind the branch to the trunk, and lend to the whole the unity that so favors the establishment of truth and persuasion. But when required, they will have the opposite effect: they will counter notions; bring principles into contrast; covertly attack, unsettle, or overturn some ridiculous opinions which one would not venture to disparage openly. If the author is impartial, they will always have the double function of confirming and refuting, disrupting and reconciling.

There would be much art and a considerable advantage in these latter references. The entire opus would gain from them internal force and unseen utility, the silent effects of which would necessarily be perceptible over time. Whenever a national prejudice commands respect, for example, that particular article ought to set it forth respectfully, and with its whole retinue of plausibility and persuasion; but at the same time it ought to overturn an edifice of muck, dispel a vain pile of dust, by referring to articles in which solid principles form a basis for contrary truths. This means of undeceiving men acts very quickly on good minds, and ineluctably and without any disagreeable consequence, silently and without scandal, on all minds. It is the art of tacitly deducing the boldest consequences. If such confirming and refuting references are foreseen well in advance, and skillfully prepared, they will give an *encyclopedia* the character which a good dictionary ought to possess: that of changing the common mode of thinking. . . .

Thanks to encyclopedic ordering, the universality of knowledge, and the frequency of references, the connections grow, the links go out in all directions, the demonstrative power is increased, the word list is complemented, fields of knowledge are drawn closer together and strengthened; we perceive either the continuity or the gaps in our system, its weak sides, its strong points, and at a glance on which objects it is important to work for one's own glory, or for the greater utility to humankind. If our dictionary is good, how many still better works it will produce! . . .

We think we are aware of all the advantages of an enterprise such as the one we pursue. We think we have had only too many opportunities to realize how difficult it was to emerge with some success from a first attempt, and how much the talents of a single man, whoever he be, were unequal to this project. . . . But we have seen that of all the difficulties, one of the most considerable was to produce it just once, however amorphous it be, and that no one could ever take from us the honor of having overcome that obstacle. We have seen that the *Encyclopedia* could only be the effort of a philosophical century; that that century had come; that fame, by conferring immortality on the names of those who would bring it to fruition, would perhaps not refuse to take up ours; and we have felt inspired by the pleasant and consoling thought that people would talk about us when we were gone; by the sensual whisper that made us hear, in the mouths of a few of our contemporaries, what men to whose instruction and happiness we were sacrificing ourselves would say about us, men we esteemed and loved, even though they did not yet exist. We have felt grow in ourselves the seed of emulation, which at death envies the best part of ourselves, and snatches from oblivion the only moments of our existence that were genuinely charmed. Indeed, man reveals himself to his contemporaries and sees himself as he is, a strange composite of sublime qualities and shameful weaknesses. But the weaknesses follow the mortal remains into the tomb, and disappear with them; the same earth covers them both: all that remains are the qualities made everlasting by the monuments he has raised to himself, or which he owes to public veneration and gratitude: honors of which the conscience of his own merit gives him advance delight; delight as pure, as strong, as real as any other delight, and in which nothing can be imaginary except the titles on which one grounds one's pretensions. Ours are deposited in this work; posterity will judge them.

I have said that only a philosophical century could attempt an *encyclopedia*; and I said this because this work everywhere requires more boldness of mind than is normally possessed in centuries of cowardly taste. One must examine and stir up everything, without exception and without cautiousness: one must dare to see, as we are beginning to be persuaded, that literary genres resemble the general compilation of laws, and the first formation of cities, in that they owe their birth to a singular chance, a strange circumstance, sometimes a flight of genius; that those who came after the first inventors, were for the most part merely their slaves; that productions that should be regarded as the first step, taken blindly as the final achievement, instead of advancing an art to its perfection, have served only to hold it back, reducing other men to the servile condition of imitators; that as soon as a name was given to a composition of a particular character, one had to model strictly upon that sketch all those that were made; that if there appeared from time to time a man of daring and original genius, who, weary of the yoke received, dared to shake it off, depart from the ordinary path, and give birth to some work to which the given name and prescribed laws were not exactly applicable, he dropped into oblivion, and remained there a very long time. We must trample under foot all that old foolishness; overturn barriers not put there by reason; restore to the sciences and arts their precious liberty. . . .

Immanuel Kant

An Answer to the Question: What Is Enlightenment?

Enlightenment is mankind's exit from its self-incurred immaturity. Immaturity is the inability to make use of one's own understanding without the guidance of another. Self-incurred is this inability if its cause lies not in the lack of understanding but rather in the lack of the resolution and the courage to use it without the guidance of another. Sapere aude! Have the courage to use your *own* understanding! is thus the motto of enlightenment.

Laziness and cowardice are the reasons why such a great part of mankind, long after nature has set them free from the guidance of others (*naturaliter majorennes*), still gladly remain immature for life and why it is so easy for others to set themselves up as guardians. It is so easy to be immature. If I have a book that has understanding for me, a pastor who has a conscience for me, a doctor who judges my diet for me, and so forth, surely I do not need to trouble myself. I have no need to think, if only I can pay; others will take over the tedious business for me. Those guardians, who have graciously taken up the oversight of mankind, take care that the far greater part of mankind (including the entire fairer sex)

Immanuel Kant, "An Answer to the Question: 'What Is Enlightenment?'" (1784), trans. James Schmidt, in *What Is Enlightenment? Eighteenth-Century Answers and Twentieth-Century Questions*, ed. James Schmidt (Berkeley: University of California Press, 1996), 58–63. Reprinted with permission of The University of California Press.

regard the step to maturity as not only difficult but also very dangerous. After they have first made their domestic animals stupid and carefully prevented these placid creatures from daring to take even one step out of the leading strings of the cart to which they are tethered, they show them the danger that threatens them if they attempt to proceed on their own. Now this danger is not so great, for by falling a few times they would indeed finally learn to walk; but an example of this sort makes them timid and usually frightens them away from all further attempts.

It is thus difficult for any individual man to work himself out of an immaturity that has become almost natural to him. He has become fond of it and, for the present, is truly incapable of making use of his own reason, because he has never been permitted to make the attempt. Rules and formulas, these mechanical instruments of a rational use (or rather misuse) of his natural gifts, are the fetters of an everlasting immaturity. Whoever casts them off would still take but an uncertain leap over the smallest ditch, because he is not accustomed to such free movement. Hence there are only a few who have managed to free themselves from immaturity through the exercise of their own minds, and yet proceed confidently.

But that a public [*Publikum*] should enlighten itself is more likely; indeed, it is nearly inevitable, if only it is granted freedom. For there will always be found some who think for themselves, even among the established guardians of the masses, and who, after they themselves have thrown off the yoke of immaturity, will spread among the herd the spirit of rational assessment of individual worth and the vocation of each man to think for himself. It is notable that the public, which had earlier been brought under this yoke by their guardians, may compel them to remain under it if they are incited to do so by some of their guardians who are incapable of any enlightenment. So it is harmful to implant prejudices, because they ultimately revenge themselves on those who originated them or on their descendents. Therefore a public can achieve enlightenment only gradually. A revolution may perhaps bring about the fall of an autocratic despotism and of an avaricious or overbearing oppression, but it can never bring about the true reform of a way of thinking. Rather, new prejudices will serve, like the old, as the leading strings of the thoughtless masses.

For this enlightenment, however, nothing more is required than *freedom*; and indeed the most harmless form of all the things that may be called freedom: namely, the freedom to make a *public use* of one's reason in all matters. But I hear from all sides the cry: *don't argue!* The officer says: "Don't argue, but rather march!" The tax collector says: "Don't argue, but rather pay!" The clergyman says: "Don't argue, but rather believe!" (Only one ruler in the world says: "*Argue*, as much as you want and about whatever you want, *but obey!*") Here freedom is restricted everywhere. Which restriction, however, hinders enlightenment? Which does not, but instead even promotes it? — I answer: the *public* use of reason must at all times be free, and it alone can bring about enlightenment among men; the *private* use of reason, however, may often be very narrowly restricted without the progress of enlightenment being particularly hindered. I understand, however, under the public use of his own reason, that use which anyone makes of it *as a scholar* [*Gelehrter*] before the entire public of the *reading world*. The private use I designate as that use which one makes of his reason in a certain *civil post* or office which is entrusted to him. Now a certain mechanism is necessary in many affairs which are run in the interest of the commonwealth by means of which some members of the commonwealth must conduct themselves passively in order that the government may direct them, through an artificial unanimity, to public ends, or at least restrain them from the destruction of these ends. Here one is certainly not allowed to argue; rather, one must obey. But insofar as this part of the machine considers himself at the same time as a member of the entire commonwealth, indeed even of a cosmopolitan society, who in the role of a scholar addresses a public in the proper sense through his writings, he can certainly argue, without thereby harming the affairs in which he is engaged in part as a passive member. So it would be very destructive, if an officer on duty should argue aloud about the suitability or the utility of a command given to him by his superior; he must obey. But he cannot fairly be forbidden as a scholar to make remarks on failings in the military service and to lay them before the public for judgment. The citizen cannot refuse to pay the taxes imposed on him; even an impudent complaint against such levies, when they should be paid by him, is punished as an outrage (which could lead to general insubordination). This same individual nevertheless does not act against the duty of a citizen if he, as a scholar, expresses his thoughts publicly on the inappropriateness or even the injustice of such taxes. In the same way, a clergyman is bound to lecture to his catechism students and his congregation according to the symbol of the church which he serves; for he has been accepted on this condition. But as a scholar he has the complete freedom, indeed it is his calling, to communicate to the public all his carefully tested and well-intentioned thoughts on the imperfections of that symbol and his proposals for a better arrangement of religious and ecclesiastical affairs. There is in this nothing that could burden his conscience. For what he teaches as a consequence of his office as an agent of his church, he presents as something about which he does not have free reign to teach according to his own discretion, but rather is engaged to expound according to another's precept and in another's name. He will say: our church teaches this or that; these are the arguments that it employs. He then draws out all the practical uses for his congregation from rules to which he himself may not subscribe with complete conviction, but to whose exposition he can nevertheless pledge himself, since it is not entirely impossible that truth may lie concealed within them, and, at least, in any case there is nothing in them that is in contradiction with what is intrinsic to religion. For if he believed he found such a contradiction in them, he could not in conscience conduct his office; he would have to resign. Thus the use that an appointed teacher makes of his reason before his congregation is merely a *private* use, because this is only a domestic assembly, no matter how large it is; and in this respect he is not and cannot be free, as a priest, because he conforms to the orders of another. In contrast, as a scholar, who through his writings speaks to his own public, namely the world, the clergyman enjoys, in the *public* use of his reason, an unrestricted freedom to employ his own reason and to speak in his own person. For that the guardian of the people (in spiritual matters) should be himself immature, is an absurdity that leads to the perpetuation of absurdities.

But would not a society of clergymen, such as a church synod or a venerable classis (as they call themselves among the Dutch), be justified in binding one another by oath to a certain unalterable symbol, in order to hold an unremitting superior guardianship over each of their members, and by this means over their people, and even to make this eternal? I say that this is completely impossible. Such a contract, concluded for the purpose of closing off forever all further enlightenment of the human race, is utterly null and void even if it should be confirmed by the highest power, by Imperial Diets, and by the most solemn peace treaties. One age cannot bind itself, and thus conspire, to place the succeeding age in a situation in which it becomes impossible for it to broaden its knowledge (particularly such pressing knowledge), to cleanse itself of errors, and generally to progress in enlightenment. That would be a crime against human nature, whose original destiny consists in this progress; and posterity would be fully justified to reject these resolutions as concluded in an unauthorized and outrageous manner. The touchstone of everything that can be concluded as a law for a people lies in the question: could a people have imposed such a law upon itself? Now this would be possible for a specified brief time period, in order to introduce a certain order, as it were, in expectation of something better. At the same time, all citizens, especially the clergy, would be left free, in their capacities as scholars — that is, through writings — to make remarks on the failings of the current institutions. This provisional order would continue until insight into the nature of these things became so public and so reliable that through uniting their voices (even if not unanimously) they could bring a resolution before the throne, to take those congregations into protection who had united into an altered religious organization according to their conception of better insight, without hindering those who wish to remain with the old. But it is absolutely forbidden to unite, even for the lifetime of a single man, in a permanent religious constitution that no one may publicly doubt, and thereby to negate a period of progress of mankind toward improvement and thus make it fruitless and even detrimental for posterity. One man may indeed postpone, for his own person and even then only for a short time, enlightenment in that which it is incumbent for him to know; but to renounce it, for his own person and even more for posterity, is to violate and to trample on the sacred rights of mankind. What even a people may not decide for itself can even less be decided for it by a monarch; for his lawgiving authority consists in his uniting the collective will of the people in his own. If only he sees to it that all true or alleged improvements are consistent with civil order, he can allow his subjects to do what they find necessary for the well-being of their souls. That does not concern him, though it is his concern to prevent one from forcibly hindering another from laboring with all his capacities to determine and to advance this well-being. It detracts from his own majesty if he meddles in this by finding the writings through which his subjects seek to put their insights into order worthy of governmental oversight. He does so if he acts out of his own exalted insight, where he exposes himself to the reproach *Caesar non est supra Grammaticos* [Caesar is not above the grammarians], and does so even more if he degrades his supreme power so far as to support the ecclesiastical despotism of a few tyrants in his state against the rest of his subjects.

If it is asked "Do we now live in an *enlightened* age?" the answer is "No, but we do live in an age of *enlightenment*." As matters now stand, much is still lacking for men to be completely able — or even to be placed in a situation where they would be able—to use their own reason confidently and properly in religious matters without the guidance of another. Yet we have clear indications that the field is now being opened for them to work freely toward this, and the obstacles to general enlightenment or to the exit out of their self-incurred immaturity become ever fewer. In this respect, this age is the age of enlightenment or the century of *Frederick*.

A prince who does not find it unworthy of himself to say that he regards it as a *duty* to prescribe nothing to men regarding religious matters but rather to allow them full freedom in this area—and who thus declines the haughty title of "tolerant"—is himself enlightened and deserves to be esteemed by the grateful world and by posterity as the first, with regard to government, who freed mankind from immaturity and left them free to use of their own reason in everything that is a matter of conscience. Under him venerable clergy, in their role as scholars and irrespective of their official duties, freely and publicly present their judgments and insights—which here or there diverge from the established symbol—to the world for examination. Those who are not restricted by the duties of office are even freer. This spirit of freedom spreads further, even where it must struggle with the external hindrances of a government which misunderstands itself. For it is an illuminating example to such a government that public peace and unity have little to fear from this freedom. Men work their way by themselves bit by bit out of barbarity if one does not intentionally contrive to hold them in it.

I have placed the main point of enlightenment—mankind's exit from its self-imposed immaturity—primarily on religious matters since our rulers have no interest in playing the role of guardian to their subjects with regard to the arts and sciences and because this type of immaturity is the most harmful as well as the most dishonorable. But the manner of thinking of a head of state who favors such enlightenment goes even further and sees that even with regard to his own legislation there is no danger in allowing his subjects to make *public* use of their reason and to lay publicly before the world their thoughts about a better formulation of this legislation as well as a candid criticism of laws already given. We have a shining example of this, in which no monarch has yet surpassed the one we honor.

But only a ruler who, himself enlightened, does not himself fear shadows, and at the same time has at hand a large, well-disciplined army as a guarantee of public peace, can say what a republic cannot dare: *argue, as much as you want and about whatever you want, only obey!* Here is displayed a strange and unexpected tendency in human affairs, so that, generally, when it is considered at large, almost everything in it is almost paradoxical. A high degree of civic freedom appears advantageous to the *spiritual* freedom [*Freiheit des Geistes*] of a people and yet it places before it insuperable restrictions; a lesser degree of civil freedom, in contrast, creates the room for spiritual freedom to spread to its full capacity. When nature has, under this hard shell, developed the seed for which she cares most tenderly—namely, the inclination and the vocation for *free thinking*—this works back upon the character of the people (who thereby become more and more capable of *acting freely*) and finally even on the principles of government, which finds it to its advantage to treat man, who is now *more than a machine*, in accord with his dignity.

Ernst Cassirer
_____

The Mind of the Enlightenment

D'Alembert begins his essay on the *Elements of Philosophy* with a general portrait of the mind of the mid-eighteenth century. He prefaces his portrait with the observation that in the intellectual life of the last three hundred years the mid-century mark has consistently been an important turning-point. The Renaissance commences in the middle of the fifteenth century; the Reformation reaches its climax in the middle of the sixteenth century; and in the middle of the seventeenth century the Cartesian philosophy triumphantly alters the entire world picture. Can an analogous movement be observed in the eighteenth century? If so, how can its direction and general tendency be characterized? Pursuing this thought further, d'Alembert writes:

"If one examines carefully the mid-point of the century in which we live, the events which excite us or at any rate occupy our minds, our

Ernst Cassirer, "The Mind of the Enlightenment," trans. Fritz C. A. Koelln and James P. Pettegrove, in *The Philosophy of the Enlightenment* (Boston: Beacon Press, 1955), 3–9, 12–14. Copyright © 1951 by Princeton University Press. Reprinted by permission of Princeton University Press.

customs, our achievements, and even our diversions, it is difficult not to see that in some respects a very remarkable change in our ideas is taking place, a change whose rapidity seems to promise an even greater transformation to come. Time alone will tell what will be the goal, the nature, and the limits of this revolution whose shortcomings and merits will be better known to posterity than to us. . . . Our century is called, accordingly, the century of philosophy par excellence. . . ."

For this age, knowledge of its own activity, intellectual self-examination, and foresight are the proper function and essential task of thought. Thought not only seeks new, hitherto unknown goals but it wants to know where it is going and to determine for itself the direction of its journey. It encounters the world with fresh joy and the courage of discovery, daily expecting new revelations. Yet its thirst for knowledge and intellectual curiosity are directed not only toward the external world; the thought of this age is even more passionately impelled by that other question of the nature and potentiality of thought itself. Time and again thought returns to its point of departure from its various journeys of exploration intended to broaden the horizon of objective reality. Pope gave brief and pregnant expression to this deep-seated feeling of the age in the line: "The proper study of mankind is man." The age senses that a new force is at work within it; but it is even more fascinated by the activity of this force than by the creations brought forth by that activity. It rejoices not only in results, but it inquires into, and attempts to explain, the form of the process leading to these results. The problem of intellectual "progress" throughout the eighteenth century appears in this light. Perhaps no other century is so completely permeated by the idea of intellectual progress as that of the Enlightenment. . . .

"Reason" becomes the unifying and central point of this century, expressing all that it longs and strives for, and all that it achieves. . . .

The eighteenth century is imbued with a belief in the unity and immutability of reason. Reason is the same for all thinking subjects, all nations, all epochs, and all cultures. From the changeability of religious creeds, of moral maxims and convictions, of theoretical opinions and judgments, a firm and lasting element can be extracted which is permanent in itself, and which in this identity and permanence expresses the real essence of reason. For us the word "reason" has long since lost its unequivocal simplicity even if we are in essential agreement with the basic aims of the philosophy of the Enlightenment. We can scarcely use this word any longer without being conscious of its history. . . .

The seventeenth century had seen the real task of philosophy in the construction of the philosophical "system." Truly "philosophical" knowledge had seemed attainable only when thought, starting from a highest being and from a highest, intuitively grasped certainty, succeeded in spreading the light of this certainty over all derived being and all derived knowledge. This was done by the method of proof and rigorous inference, which added other propositions to the first original certainty and in this way pieced out and linked together the whole chain of possible knowledge. No link of this chain could be removed from the whole; none was explicable by itself. The only real explanation possible consisted in its "derivation," in the strict, systematic deduction by which any link might be traced back to the source of being and certainty, by which its distance from this source might be determined, and by which the number of intermediate links separating a given link from this source might be specified. The eighteenth century abandons this kind of deduction and proof. It no longer vies with Descartes and Malebranche, with Leibniz and Spinoza for the prize of systematic rigor and completeness. It seeks another concept of truth and philosophy whose function is to extend the boundaries of both and make them more elastic, concrete, and vital. The Enlightenment does not take the ideal of this mode of thinking from the philosophical doctrines of the past; on the contrary, it constructs its ideal according to the model and pattern of contemporary natural science. . . .

This new methodological order characterizes all eighteenth century thought. The value of system, the *"esprit systématique,"* is neither underestimated nor neglected; but it is sharply distinguished from the love of system for its own sake, the *"esprit de système."* The whole theory of knowledge of the eighteenth century strives to confirm this distinction. D'Alembert in his "Preliminary Discourse" to the French *Encyclopedia* makes this distinction the central point of his argument, and Condillac in his *Treatise on Systems* gives it explicit form and justification. Condillac tries to subject the great systems of the seventeenth century to the test of historical criticism. He tries to show that each of them failed because, instead of sticking to the facts and developing its concepts from them, it raised some individual concept to the status of a dogma. In opposition to the "spirit of systems" a new alliance is now called for between the "positive" and the "rational" spirit. The positive and the rational are never in conflict, but their true synthesis can only be achieved by the right sort of mediation. One should not seek order, law, and "reason" as a rule that may be grasped and expressed prior to the phenomena, as their *a priori*;

one should rather discover such regularity in the phenomena themselves, as the form of their immanent connection. Nor should one attempt to anticipate from the outset such "reason" in the form of a closed system; one should rather permit this reason to unfold gradually, with ever increasing clarity and perfection, as knowledge of the facts progresses. The new logic that is now sought in the conviction that it is everywhere present on the path of knowledge is neither the logic of the scholastic nor of the purely mathematical concept; it is rather the "logic of facts." The mind must abandon itself to the abundance of phenomena and gauge itself constantly by them. For it may be sure that it will not get lost, but that instead it will find here its own real truth and standard. Only in this way can the genuine correlation of subject and object, of truth and reality, be achieved; only so can the correspondence between these concepts, which is the condition of all scientific knowledge, be brought about.

From the actual course of scientific thinking since its revival in modern times the Enlightenment derives its concrete, self-evident proof that this synthesis of the "positive" and the "rational" is not a mere postulate, but that the goal set up is attainable and the ideal fully realizable. In the progress of natural science and the various phases it has gone through, the philosophy of the Enlightenment believes it can, as it were, tangibly grasp its ideal. For here it can follow step by step the triumphal march of the modern analytical spirit. It had been this spirit that in the course of barely a century and a half had conquered all reality, and that now seemed finally to have accomplished its great task of reducing the multiplicity of natural phenomena to a single universal rule. And this cosmological formula, as contained in Newton's general law of attraction, was not found by accident, nor as the result of sporadic experimentation; its discovery shows the rigorous application of scientific method. . . .

The philosophy of the eighteenth century takes up this particular case, the methodological pattern of Newton's physics, though it immediately begins to generalize. It is not content to look upon analysis as the great intellectual tool of mathematico-physical knowledge; eighteenth century thought sees analysis rather as the necessary and indispensable instrument of all thinking in general. This view triumphs in the middle of the century. However much individual thinkers and schools differ in their results, they agree in this epistemological premise. . . .

We must, of course, abandon all hope of ever wresting from things their ultimate mystery, of ever penetrating to the absolute being of matter or of the human soul. If, however, we refer to empirical law and order, the "inner core of nature" proves by no means inaccessible. In this realm we can establish ourselves and proceed in every direction. The power of reason does not consist in enabling us to transcend the empirical world but rather in teaching us to feel at home in it. . . . The whole eighteenth century understands reason in this sense; not as a sound body of knowledge, principles, and truths, but as a kind of energy, a force which is fully comprehensible only in its agency and effects. What reason is, and what it can do, can never be known by its results but only by its function. And its most important function consists in its power to bind and to dissolve. It dissolves everything merely factual, all simple data of experience, and everything believed on the evidence of revelation, tradition and authority; and it does not rest content until it has analyzed all these things into their simplest component parts and into their last elements of belief and opinion. Following this work of dissolution begins the work of construction. Reason cannot stop with the dispersed parts; it has to build from them a new structure, a true whole. But since reason creates this whole and fits the parts together according to its own rule, it gains complete knowledge of the structure of its product. Reason understands this structure because it can reproduce it in its totality and in the ordered sequence of its individual elements. Only in this twofold intellectual movement can the concept of reason be fully characterized, namely, as a concept of agency, not of being.

This conviction gains a foothold in the most varied fields of eighteenth century culture. . . .

The lust for knowledge, the *libido sciendi*, which theological dogmatism had outlawed and branded as intellectual pride, is now called a necessary quality of the soul as such and restored to its original rights. The defense, reinforcement, and consolidation of this way of thinking is the cardinal aim of eighteenth century culture; and in this mode of thinking, not in the mere acquisition and extension of specific information, the century sees its major task. This fundamental tendency can also be traced unambiguously in the *Encyclopedia*, which became the arsenal of all such information. . . .

Peter Gay

The Spirit of the Age

Sometime in the course of his visits to England in 1726 or 1727, Voltaire observed in his notebook, in his newly acquired English: "Where there is not liberty of conscience, there is seldom liberty of trade, the same tyranny encroaching upon the commerce as upon Relligion." A few years later, probably not long after he had published *Lettres philosophiques*, his celebrated report on England, he noted, this time in French: "In a republic, toleration is the fruit of liberty and the basis of happiness and abundance." The *Lettres philosophiques* is many things— a critique of bigotry in France, a popular summary of Newton's thought, covert deist propaganda—but above all it is an extended commentary on the sociological aphorisms I have just quoted. "The commerce that has enriched the citizens of England," Voltaire concluded, "has helped to make them free, and that freedom in turn has encouraged commerce; this has produced the greatness of the state."

The point of these observations was not merely that England was rich, happy, and free, but that these characteristics depended upon and reinforced one another. Thus for Voltaire, as for the other philosophes, Anglomania and sociology were practically synonymous: besides embodying the recovery of nerve earlier and more completely than other countries, England exhibited the happy conjunctions that made this recovery possible. . . .

The lesson that England taught the philosophes, then, was that the recovery of nerve was infectious: progress in one sphere generated progress in others. The new sense of power seemed to be radiating out from scientists and physicians, merchants and civil servants, to civilization as a whole. There was nothing new in the philosophes' perception that society is a fabric with interdependent, interacting parts; what they did that was new was to take this perception as a justification for their own importance. After all, if progress is infectious, then to teach truth, expose error, and inculcate confidence—and all this, of course, the

Peter Gay, "The Spirit of the Age," in *The Enlightenment: An Interpretation, 2: The Science of Freedom* (New York: Norton, 1969), 24–27, 29, 32–33, 36–39, 45–46, 48–52. Reprinted with the permission of the author.

philosophes were sure they were doing—was to spread reason and shed light over large areas, even in unsuspected places. Thus the philosophes enlisted the enlightened atmosphere of their day in the service of their movement. . . . Every day men were instituting new, useful things and discarding old, outmoded ways. It is not extravagant to see the *Encyclopedia* itself—with its profusion of articles on arts and crafts, philosophy and politics, theology and language, and with its sly and informative cross references—as a striking display of the recovery of nerve, of the variety, wealth, and energy of eighteenth-century civilization. . . .

The advance of knowledge, whether devout Christians liked it or not, meant the advance of reason. In the course of the eighteenth century, the world, at least the world of the literate, was being emptied of mystery. Pseudo science was giving way to science, credence in the miraculous intervention of divine forces was being corroded by the acid of skepticism and overpowered by scientific cosmology. The sacred was being hollowed out from within by the drying up of religious fervor, the call for good sense, the retreat from Augustinian theology, the campaign against "enthusiasm," and the advance of rationalism among the clergy of all persuasions. . . .

The prosperity of reason in the eighteenth century was less the triumph of rationalism than of reasonableness. Reason and humanity were easily confounded, and an instance of one was often taken as an instance of the other. One of Diderot's spokesmen in his sentimental drama, *Fils naturel,* cheerfully pours rationality, refinement, and decency into the same container: "Certainly there are still barbarians. When won't there be? But the time of barbarism is past. The century has become enlightened. Reason has grown refined, and the nation's books are filled with its precepts. The books that inspire benevolence in men are practically the only ones read." . . .

This change was possible largely because freedom was safeguarded by reason. Rational love, the sober and well-considered mutual esteem of man and woman, was elevated to a social ideal. . . .

In consequence, marriage, which through the seventeenth century had been regarded as a sacred institution and as a legal device for the management of property and the regulation of inheritance, came to be spoken of in the age of the Enlightenment as a partnership, a contract, honorable and grave but secular in nature. Monogamy, long a Christian ideal, became for many a comfortable reality, and even those philosophes whose own marital experience was unhappy felt that they owed it to their philosophy to praise marriage as an institution. . . .

In this atmosphere, which was clearer and less oppressive than the atmosphere of preceding centuries, women and children secured new respect and new rights. . . .

The philosophes were at home with intelligent women—one thinks of Diderot's Sophie Volland, Voltaire's Madame du Châtelet, and the cultivated Parisian ladies who played hostess to philosophes from all over the world—and they made attempts to treat them as equals, as well as an item on the agenda of reform. But while the philosophes were feminists in their way, they were feminists with misgivings: the age-old fear of women, the antique superstition that women were vessels of wrath and sources of corruption, was too deeply rooted to be easily discarded. . . .

In general, humanity was acquiring the status of a practical virtue. The fashion of attending hangings or a good torture and the applause for brutal measures against religious dissenters or sexual deviates had been practically universal to the end of the seventeenth century. . . .

It became possible, and even stylish, to seek the causes of drunkenness and crime in social circumstances and to explain poverty neither as a divine dispensation nor as a just punishment for laziness, but as a stroke of misfortune or a failure of society. . . .

All segments of society benefited from the new humanity; it became less fashionable to make victims than to succor them. Even public servants found that the penalties for failure were less drastic than they had been in the past. Through the seventeenth century a fallen minister had generally been executed or imprisoned. In the eighteenth century he lost neither life nor property; he might be exiled to his estates, raised to the Peerage, or otherwise removed from active politics. . . .

Even the laboring poor came to be regarded as human beings with real feelings and a right to subsistence. Adam Smith's advocacy of "the liberal reward of labor" was radical but in no way revolutionary. Manufacturers like Josiah Wedgwood and David Dale organized model villages and provided a rudimentary form of social insurance for their workmen; and while their shrewd paternalist policies made humanity pay, they are hints at least of a new attitude toward a class of men traditionally beyond the bounds of humane concern. . . .

All over the West, in London as in Philadelphia, philosophers joined articulate businessmen in commending ceaseless activity and preached the postponement of immediate gratification for the sake of some higher and more enduring satisfaction. As preachers of practicality, the philosophes resorted to the virtue of action as a favorite text: it is significant that Locke, and Condillac after him, should regard restlessness or *inquiétude* as the mainspring of life. Other philosophes followed their lead. Hume regarded activity as essential to felicity: "There is no happiness without occupation." . . .

This doctrine has been sharply criticized as the ideology of a rising bourgeoisie complacently presiding over the exploitation of labor. There is some truth in this criticism. While facile allusions to "the rising bourgeoisie" have fallen into disfavor, it is undeniable that merchants, industrialists, bankers, attorneys, physicians, men of letters, respectable shopkeepers, and *rentiers*—that social congeries making up what we call, for short, the bourgeoisie—supplied the new industriousness with its most zealous troops and most single-minded advocates. Still, the term remains unsatisfactory: the philosophes applied the doctrine to themselves, and worked as hard as anyone. Furthermore, enterprising aristocrats and energetic members of the lower orders strove for success side by side with the most compulsive manufacturer. . . .

The celebration of industry, which is so prominent in eighteenth-century writings on morals and economic affairs, thus represents a radical criticism of the traditional ethical hierarchy. . . .

This was not simply, or not yet, the bourgeois spirit, which would merely rationalize the cowardice, the greed, and the philistinism typical of the trading mind. It was rather a spirit in which banker and squire, manufacturer, poet, and sensible aristocrat could participate. . . .

With the growing popularity of these sentiments, the way to the glorification of the merchant classes was open, and it was taken early in the eighteenth century by British publicists. . . .

In 1734 Voltaire appropriated this ideal for the Continent. The *Lettres philosophiques* is filled with tributes to the commercial spirit, which prefers peace to glory, opens high posts to men of talent, and converts the world into a market in which all traders tolerate one another. . . .

One of the most eloquent expressions of the new spirit at work, of reason, humanity, and industry celebrated by and for respectable Christians, was the periodical literature that began to flourish, first in Britain and then on the Continent at the beginning of the eighteenth century. . . .

It was, of course, precisely their blandness, their confounding of common sense with strenuous philosophizing, their concentration on improving manners and clarifying taste while avoiding political acrimony, that made these journals the civilizing agents they were. . . .

Michel Foucault

What Is Enlightenment?

I

Today when a periodical asks its readers a question, it does so in order to collect opinions on some subject about which everyone has an opinion already; there is not much likelihood of learning anything new. In the eighteenth century, editors preferred to question the public on problems that did not yet have solutions. I don't know whether or not that practice was more effective; it was unquestionably more entertaining.

In any event, in line with this custom, in November 1784 a German periodical, *Berlinische Monatschrift*, published a response to the question: *Was ist Aufklärung?* And the respondent was Kant.

A minor text, perhaps. But it seems to me that it marks the discreet entrance into the history of thought of a question that modern philosophy has not been capable of answering, but that it has never managed to get rid of, either. And one that has been repeated in various forms for two centuries now. From Hegel through Nietzsche or Max Weber to Horkheimer or Habermas, hardly any philosophy has failed to confront this same question, directly or indirectly. What, then, is this event that is called the *Aufklärung* and that has determined, at least in part, what we are, what we think, and what we do today? Let us imagine that the *Berlinische Monatschrift* still exists and that it is asking its readers the question: What is modern philosophy? Perhaps we could respond with an echo: modern

Michel Foucault, "What Is Enlightenment?," trans. Catherine Porter, in *The Foucault Reader*, ed. Paul Rabinow (New York: Pantheon, 1984), 32, 38–39, 42–45, 49–50. Copyright © 1984 by Paul Rabinow (Pantheon, New York). Reprinted by permission of Georges Borchardt, Inc.

philosophy is the philosophy that is attempting to answer the question raised so imprudently two centuries ago: *Was ist Aufklärung?*

*   *   *

... The hypothesis I should like to propose is that this little text is located in a sense at the crossroads of critical reflection and reflection on history. It is a reflection by Kant on the contemporary status of his own enterprise. No doubt it is not the first time that a philosopher has given his reasons for undertaking his work at a particular moment. But it seems to me that it is the first time that a philosopher has connected in this way, closely and from the inside, the significance of his work with respect to knowledge, a reflection on history and a particular analysis of the specific moment at which he is writing and because of which he is writing. It is in the reflection on "today" as difference in history and as motive for a particular philosophical task that the novelty of this text appears to me to lie.

And, by looking at it in this way, it seems to me we may recognize a point of departure: the outline of what one might call the attitude of modernity.

II

I know that modernity is often spoken of as an epoch, or at least as a set of features characteristic of an epoch; situated on a calendar, it would be preceded by a more or less naive or archaic premodernity, and followed by an enigmatic and troubling "postmodernity." And then we find ourselves asking whether modernity constitutes the sequel to the Enlightenment and its development, or whether we are to see it as a rupture or a deviation with respect to the basic principles of the eighteenth century.

Thinking back on Kant's text, I wonder whether we may not envisage modernity rather as an attitude than as a period of history. And by "attitude," I mean a mode of relating to contemporary reality; a voluntary choice made by certain people; in the end, a way of thinking and feeling; a way, too, of acting and behaving that at one and the same time marks a relation of belonging and presents itself as a task. A bit, no doubt, like what the Greeks called an *ethos*. And consequently, rather than seeking to distinguish the "modern era" from the "premodern" or "postmodern," I think it would be more useful to try to find out how the attitude of modernity, ever since its formation, has found itself struggling with attitudes of "countermodernity."

. . . I have been seeking, on the one hand, to emphasize the extent to which a type of philosophical interrogation—one that simultaneously problematizes man's relation to the present, man's historical mode of being, and the constitution of the self as an autonomous subject—is rooted in the Enlightenment. On the other hand, I have been seeking to stress that the thread that may connect us with the Enlightenment is not faithfulness to doctrinal elements, but rather the permanent reactivation of an attitude—that is, of a philosophical ethos that could be described as a permanent critique of our historical era. I should like to characterize this ethos very briefly.

1. This ethos implies, first, the refusal of what I like to call the "blackmail" of the Enlightenment. I think that the Enlightenment, as a set of political, economic, social, institutional, and cultural events on which we still depend in large part, constitutes a privileged domain for analysis. I also think that as an enterprise for linking the progress of truth and the history of liberty in a bond of direct relation, it formulated a philosophical question that remains for us to consider. I think, finally, as I have tried to show with reference to Kant's text, that it defined a certain manner of philosophizing.

But that does not mean that one has to be "for" or "against" the Enlightenment. It even means precisely that one has to refuse everything that might present itself in the form of a simplistic and authoritarian alternative: you either accept the Enlightenment and remain within the tradition of its rationalism (this is considered a positive term by some and used by others, on the contrary, as a reproach); or else you criticize the Enlightenment and then try to escape from its principles of rationality (which may be seen once again as good or bad). And we do not break free of this blackmail by introducing "dialectical" nuances while seeking to determine what good and bad elements there may have been in the Enlightenment.

We must try to proceed with the analysis of ourselves as beings who are historically determined, to a certain extent, by the Enlightenment. Such an analysis implies a series of historical inquiries that are as precise as possible; and these inquiries will not be oriented retrospectively toward the "essential kernel of rationality" that can be found in the Enlightenment and that would have to be preserved in any event; they will be oriented toward the "contemporary limits of the necessary," that is, toward what is not or is no longer indispensable for the constitution of ourselves as autonomous subjects.

2. This permanent critique of ourselves has to avoid the always too facile confusions between humanism and Enlightenment.

We must never forget that the Enlightenment is an event, or a set of events and complex historical processes, that is located at a certain point in the development of European societies. As such, it includes elements of social transformation, types of political institution, forms of knowledge, projects of rationalization of knowledge and practices, technological mutations that are very difficult to sum up in a word, even if many of these phenomena remain important today. The one I have pointed out and that seems to me to have been at the basis of an entire form of philosophical reflection concerns only the mode of reflective relation to the present.

Humanism is something entirely different. It is a theme or, rather, a set of themes that have reappeared on several occasions, over time, in European societies; these themes, always tied to value judgments, have obviously varied greatly in their content, as well as in the values they have preserved. Furthermore, they have served as a critical principle of differentiating. In the seventeenth century, there was a humanism that presented itself as a critique of Christianity or of religion in general; there was a Christian humanism opposed to an ascetic and much more theocentric humanism. In the nineteenth century, there was a suspicious humanism, hostile and critical toward science, and another that, to the contrary, placed its hope in that same science. Marxism has been a humanism; so have existentialism and personalism; there was a time when people supported the humanistic values represented by National Socialism, and when the Stalinists themselves said they were humanists.

From this, we must not conclude that everything that has ever been linked with humanism is to be rejected, but that the humanistic thematic is in itself too supple, too diverse, too inconsistent to serve as an axis for reflection. And it is a fact that, at least since the seventeenth century, what is called humanism has always been obliged to lean on certain conceptions of man borrowed from religion, science, or politics. Humanism serves to color and to justify the conceptions of man to which it is, after all, obliged to take recourse.

Now, in this connection, I believe that this thematic, which so often recurs and which always depends on humanism, can be opposed by the principle of a critique and a permanent creation of ourselves in our autonomy: that is, a principle that is at the heart of the historical consciousness that the Enlightenment has of itself. From this standpoint,

I am inclined to see Enlightenment and humanism in a state of tension rather than identity.

. . . In any case, I think that, just as we must free ourselves from the intellectual blackmail of "being for or against the Enlightenment," we must escape from the historical and moral confusionism that mixes the theme of humanism with the question of the Enlightenment. An analysis of their complex relations in the course of the last two centuries would be a worthwhile project, an important one if we are to bring some measure of clarity to the consciousness that we have of ourselves and of our past.

. . . A brief summary, to conclude and to come back to Kant.

I do not know whether we will ever reach mature adulthood. Many things in our experience convince us that the historical event of the Enlightenment did not make us mature adults, and we have not reached that stage yet. However, it seems to me that a meaning can be attributed to that critical interrogation on the present and on ourselves which Kant formulated by reflecting on the Enlightenment. It seems to me that Kant's reflection is even a way of philosophizing that has not been without its importance or effectiveness during the last two centuries. The critical ontology of ourselves has to be considered not, certainly, as a theory, a doctrine, nor even as a permanent body of knowledge that is accumulating; it has to be conceived as an attitude, an ethos, a philosophical life in which the critique of what we are is at one and the same time the historical analysis of the limits that are imposed on us and an experiment with the possibility of going beyond them.

This philosophical attitude has to be translated into the labor of diverse inquiries. These inquiries have their methodological coherence in the at once archaeological and genealogical study of practices envisaged simultaneously as a technological type of rationality and as strategic games of liberties; they have their theoretical coherence in the definition of the historically unique forms in which the generalities of our relations to things, to others, to ourselves, have been problematized. They have their practical coherence in the care brought to the process of putting historico-critical reflection to the test of concrete practices. I do not know whether it must be said today that the critical task still entails faith in Enlightenment; I continue to think that this task requires work on our limits, that is, a patient labor giving form to our impatience for liberty.

Sculpture of "Voltaire Nude" by Jean-Baptiste Pigalle (1776), discussed
by Roger Chartier in this section. Many contemporary viewers were
revolted by the sight of the great philosophe represented without clothes
to cover his aged body. However, the artist's vision, like that of the men
of letters who bought subscriptions to pay for the statue, was of a man
of genius who was nevertheless fully human and empowered by his
equality with his peers in the Republic of Letters. The sculpture is
now on display in the Louvre Museum (Paris). (*Art Resource*, NY)

PART

Who Were the Philosophes? Definitions of the Enlightenment Man of Letters

Universal knowledge is no longer within the grasp of one man, but true men of letters place themselves in a position to proceed into these different fields even if they cannot cultivate all of them.

Voltaire

The philosopher is thus an honorable man who acts in everything according to reason, and who joins to a spirit of reflection and precision, morals and sociable qualities.

Anonymous author of "Philosopher" from the Encyclopedia

I cannot but consider myself as a Kind of Resident or Ambassador from the Dominions of Learning to those of Conversation; and shall think it my constant Duty to promote a good Correspondence betwixt these two States, which have so great a Dependence on each other. *—David Hume*

The scientific intellectual was the model intellectual; the community of science the model for the republic of letters more generally.

Keith Michael Baker

As spokesmen for the writer's new estate . . . , Duclos, Voltaire, and d'Alembert urged their "brethren" to profit from the mobility available

to them in order to join the elite. Rather than challenge the social
order, they offered a prop to it.   —*Robert Darnton*

[Pigalle's] statue of Voltaire . . . was a perfect incarnation of the
contradictions that permeated both the definition and the status of
the man of letters in the age of the Enlightenment: privilege and
equality, protection and independence, prudent reformism and
utopian aspiration.   —*Roger Chartier*

Historians have typically studied the Enlightenment through those
considered to be its "great thinkers"—Voltaire, Diderot, Hume,
Rousseau, Kant, and a few others—because of their lasting contributions to intellectual history. In this part we ask not who the most
important thinkers of the Enlightenment were, but rather what characteristics or modes of inquiry define the Enlightenment man of
letters. This approach follows that of the philosophes themselves,
who tried to differentiate themselves from other intellectuals in their
approach to knowledge, their social relations, and their commitment
to improvement, and from nonintellectuals in their commitment to
reason and intellectual independence.

This section begins with two brief articles from Diderot's *Encyclopedia:* "Men of Letters," written by Voltaire, and "Philosopher," by
an unknown author. In his article, Voltaire distinguishes the modern
man of letters from previous generations of scholars by emphasizing
his wide-ranging philosophical spirit, in contrast to his predecessors'
narrow philological preoccupations. But Voltaire is also careful to
distinguish the Enlightenment man of letters from the mere wits who
shine in society, but whose knowledge is shallow. For Voltaire, what
is most important to the definition of a man of letters is not that he
writes books, but rather that he is an independent thinker who uses
his broad learning and his reason to "instruct and refine the nation"
through criticism of error and prejudice. Whereas Voltaire took up
the term "man of letters" to distinguish the intellectual of his day from
the traditional philosopher, the author of the article "Philosopher"
simply redefined that term such that today English-language historians tend to use the French word *philosophe* to refer to Enlightenment thinkers. Like Voltaire, the author of this article believes that
what distinguishes Enlightenment thinkers from earlier philosophers
is their independence and their dual commitment to the pursuit of
knowledge and the society in which they live. But this author also

emphasizes the ways in which the philosophe stands as a model human being, a moral exemplar for his age. These two articles thus call attention to the role of the Enlightenment in the development of the modern intellectual and raise the question of the legitimacy of claims to moral authority based on a person's standing as a man of letters, philosophe, or intellectual. Why, we must ask, should men of letters be "the judges, [while] the others are the judged," as Voltaire asserts.

In "Of Essay Writing," the Scottish man of letters, David Hume, focuses on the role of the man of letters as an ambassador from the world of learning to the "conversible" world of polite society. Conversation in this world depends on social skills as much as intellectual expertise, and the sovereigns or rulers of this new intellectual and social kingdom, he declares, are women. Hume thus brings women into the Enlightenment (albeit not into the definition of the philosophe or man of letters) and raises the issue of the role of gender in both contemporary and subsequent understandings of the Enlightenment and its participants.

Modern historians continue to discuss different aspects of the self-definition and the social character of the philosophes. The final three readings in this part address the issue of the roles that men of letters played in the broader world of eighteenth-century society.

Keith Baker finds in d'Alembert's "Essay on the Society of Men of Letters and the Great" a definition of the philosophe as a man of science committed to social reform. D'Alembert focuses on how the social order—and specifically the social order of science as practiced in royal academies—constrains the man of letters. For d'Alembert and those who followed his lead, Baker concludes, the practice of science required the reform of society to bring its norms into line with those of the Enlightenment. Through d'Alembert, Baker politicizes the social function of the man of letters, arguing that his commitment to the pursuit of knowledge requires him to be not just an ambassador to society, but also an agent of change within it.

Robert Darnton calls d'Alembert's essay "a declaration of independence for writers." However, he goes on to argue that the men of letters it liberated were "comfortable men" who spoke of an egalitarian Republic of Letters, but in practice constituted themselves as an elite. Their success depended upon social connections and moral compromises that made them a target of resentment and animosity for others who could not penetrate this circle. Darnton criticizes other historians for having looked at the Enlightenment only through the eyes of this elite and proposes that, instead, we examine it from the perspective of those who failed to break into this closed elite of "literary aristocrats." From this perspective, he concludes that, far from being revolutionaries, the philosophes formed another entrenched aristocracy that would fall in the French Revolution.

Roger Chartier sets out first to test Darnton's contention that the picture of the man of letters we get from Voltaire and others, of an independent thinker beholden to no one, is an idealized portrait. Chartier offers a sociological analysis of the man of letters based on two very different sources: a directory of French authors published in the eighteenth century and the files of a Parisian police inspector of the same era. He then compares the French situation to that of Germany and Italy. He concludes that men of letters were only rarely able to support themselves by their pens and thus maintain the intellectual independence they claimed. And yet, unlike Darnton, Chartier views the "aristocrats of literature" not as hypocrites, but as men caught in a set of contradictions perfectly represented in a statue of Voltaire commissioned in 1770.

Voltaire

Men of Letters

. . . This word corresponds exactly to "grammarians": the Greeks and Romans understood by the word "grammarian," not only a man versed in Grammar, properly speaking, which is the basis of all knowledge, but a man who was no stranger to Geometry, Philosophy, general and particular History; [a man] who above all studied Poetry and Eloquence. This is what our men of letters are today. This name is not given to a

Voltaire, "Men of Letters (Philosophy and Literature)," trans. Dena Goodman, from *Encyclopedia of Diderot & d'Alembert Collaborative Translation Project*. Available at http://www.hti.umich.edu/d/did/.

man with little knowledge who cultivates only a single genre. Someone who has read only novels will write only novels; a man who without any knowledge of literature may have composed by chance some plays, who, deprived of learning may have written some sermons, will not be counted among the men of letters. In our day this title has even greater breadth than the word "grammarian" had among the Greeks and the Romans. The Greeks contented themselves with their own language; the Romans learned only Greek; today, the man of letters often adds to the study of Greek and Latin that of Italian, Spanish, and above all English. The course of History is a hundred times more vast than it was for the ancients; and natural History has grown to the proportions of that of peoples. Men of letters are not expected to study all of these subjects in depth; universal knowledge is no longer within the reach of man. But true men of letters put themselves in a position to explore these different terrains, even if they cannot cultivate all of them.

Previously, in the sixteenth century, and well before the seventeenth, literary scholars spent a lot of their time on grammatical criticism of Greek and Latin authors; and it is to their labors that we owe the dictionaries, the accurate editions, the commentaries on the masterpieces of antiquity. Today this criticism is less necessary, and the philosophical spirit has succeeded it. It is the philosophical spirit that seems to constitute the character of men of letters; and when it is combined with good taste, it forms an accomplished literary scholar.

One of the great advantages of our century, is the number of educated men who [can] pass from the thorns of Mathematics to the flowers of Poetry, and who [can] judge equally well a book of Metaphysics and a play. The spirit of the century has rendered them for the most part as suitable for society as for the study; and this is what makes them superior to those of previous centuries. Up until the time of Balzac and Voiture they were kept out of society; since then they have become a necessary part of it. The deep and purified reason that several of them have spread through their writings and in their conversation, has contributed significantly to the instruction and polish of the nation. Their critical reason is no longer wasted on Greek and Latin words; rather, supported by a reasonable philosophy, it has destroyed the prejudices with which society was infected: the predictions of astrologers, divinations of magicians, spells of all sorts, false prodigies, false marvels, superstitious usages; it has relegated to the schools a thousand puerile disputes that were dangerous in the past and made them contemptible. In this way they have in fact served the state. It is sometimes astonishing that what in the past upset the world, no longer troubles it today; for this we are indebted to the true men of letters.

Ordinarily, they have more intellectual independence than other men; and those who are born without fortune easily find in the foundations of Louis XIV that with which to strengthen in them this independence; unlike in the past, one never sees these dedicatory epistles that interest and humility offered to vanity.

A man of letters is not what is called a "wit." Wit alone assumes less culture, less study, and requires no philosophy; it consists primarily of a brilliant imagination, pleasant conversation, assisted by general reading. A wit can easily not deserve the title of man of letters at all; and the man of letters may not at all claim the brilliance of the wit.

There are many men of letters who are not authors, and these are probably the happiest. They are sheltered from the distasteful things that the profession of author sometimes entails: quarrels to which competition gives rise, animosities of partisanship, and false judgments. They are more united among themselves; they enjoy society more; they are the judges, and the others are the judged.

Philosopher

Nothing is easier to acquire today than the name *philosopher*; an obscure and retired life, a few outward signs of wisdom, with a bit of reading, are enough to attract this name to people who are honored by it without deserving it.

Others, in whom freedom of thought takes the place of reasoning, regard themselves as the only true *philosophers* because they have dared to overturn the sacred boundaries established by religion, and have broken the shackles by which faith bound their reason. Proud of having undone the prejudices of education, in matters of religion, they regard others with disdain, as weak souls, servile geniuses, pusillanimous minds

"Philosopher," trans. Dena Goodman, from *Encyclopedia of Diderot & d'Alembert Collaborative Translation Project*. Available at http://www.hti.umich.edu/d/did/.

who allow themselves to be frightened by the consequences to which irreligion leads, and who, daring neither to depart for an instant from the circle of established truths, nor to walk in new paths, are lulled to sleep under the yoke of superstition.

But one ought to have a more just idea of the *philosopher*, and here is how we would characterize him.

Other men are determined to act without feeling, without knowing the causes that make them move, without even imagining that there are any. The *philosopher*, by contrast, brings causes to light to the degree that he is able, and often even anticipates them, and surrenders himself to them with full knowledge: he is, so to speak, a clock that sometimes winds itself. Thus he avoids those objects which could cause feelings that are suitable neither to well-being nor to a reasonable being, and seeks those which can excite in him affections suitable to the state in which he finds himself. Reason is to the *philosopher* what grace is to the Christian. Grace determines the action of the Christian; reason determines that of the *philosopher*.

Other men are carried away by their passions, without their actions being preceded by reflection: these are men who walk in the shadows; whereas the *philosopher*, even in his passions, acts only after reflection; he walks in the night, but he is preceded by a torch.

The *philosopher* forms his principles on the basis of an infinite number of discrete observations. The people adopt a principle without thinking about the observations that produced it: They believe that the maxim exists, so to speak, in itself; but the *philosopher* follows the maxim to its source; he examines its origin; he knows its true value, and only makes the use of it that is appropriate.

Truth is not for the *philosopher* a mistress who corrupts his imagination, and that he thinks he finds everywhere; he is satisfied to be able to bring it to light when he is able to perceive it. He certainly does not confuse it with probability; he takes as true that which is true, as false that which is false, as doubtful that which is doubtful, and as probable that which is only probable. He goes further—and here is a great perfection of the *philosopher*—when he has no proper motive for judging, he remains undecided.

The world is full of intelligent people and very intelligent people, who always judge; they always guess, because to judge without a sense of when one has a proper reason to judge is to guess. They do not know the extent of the human mind; they believe that everything can be known: thus they are ashamed not be able to pronounce judgment and imagine that intelligence consists in judging. The *philosopher* believes that it consists in judging well: he is more satisfied with himself when he has suspended that faculty of making a decision than he would be to have come to a decision before having a sense of the proper reason for a decision. Thus he judges and speaks less, but he judges more surely and speaks better; he does not avoid the bold strokes that are presented naturally to the mind by a swift assemblage of ideas that one is often surprised to see united. It is in this swift connection that what is commonly called *wit* consists; but this is also what he seeks least, and to this brilliance he prefers the care of distinguishing his ideas well, of knowing their proper extent and the precise connection between them, and of not allowing himself to be duped in taking too far some particular relationship there may be between ideas. It is in this discernment that what we call *judgment* and *precise thinking* consist: to this precision are then joined *flexibility* and *clarity*. The *philosopher* is not so attached to a system that he is unable to feel all the force of objections. The majority of men are so strongly attached to their opinions that they do not even take the trouble to penetrate those of others. The *philosopher* understands the sentiment that he rejects, to the same extent and with the same clarity that he understands the one he adopts.

The philosophic spirit is thus a spirit of observation and of precision, which relates all things to their true principles; but it is not the philosophic spirit alone which the *philosopher* cultivates, he carries his attention and his concerns further.

Man is not a monster who must live only in the abyss of the sea or in the depths of a forest: the very necessities of life make commerce with others necessary to him; and in whatever state he may find himself, his needs and well-being draw him to live in society. Thus reason compels him to know, to study, and to work to acquire sociable qualities.

Our *philosopher* does not find himself in exile in this world; he does not at all believe himself to be in enemy territory; he wants to enjoy like a wise housekeeper the goods that nature offers him; he wishes to find pleasure with others: and in order to do so, he must give it: thus he seeks to get along with those with whom he lives by chance or his own choice; and he finds at the same time those who suit him: he is an honorable man who wishes to please and to make himself useful.

The majority of the highborn, to whom dissipation leaves insufficient time to meditate, are ferocious towards those whom they do not consider their equals. Ordinary *philosophers* who meditate too much, or rather who meditate badly, are ferocious towards everyone; they flee men, and men avoid them. But our *philosopher*, who knows how to divide his time between retreat and the commerce of men, is full of humanity. He is Terence's Chremes, who feels that he is a man, and whose humanity alone makes him interested in the fortunes of his neighbor, good or bad. *Homo sum, humani a me nihil alienum puto* ["I am a man, and nothing human is alien to me"].

It would be useless to remark here how much the *philosopher* is zealous for all that is called *honor* and *probity*. For him, civil society is, as it were, a divinity on earth; he flatters it, he honors it by his probity, by an exact attention to his duties, and by a sincere desire not to be a useless or embarrassing member of it. Feelings of probity enter as much into the mechanical constitution of the *philosopher* as the enlightenment of the mind. The more reason you find in a man, the more probity you will find in him. In contrast, where fanaticism and superstition reign, there reign the passions and anger. The temperament of the *philosopher* is to act according to the spirit of order or by reason; as he loves society deeply, it is more important to him than to the rest of men to make sure that all of his actions produce only effects that conform to the idea of the honorable man. Have no fear that because no one is watching him, he will abandon himself to an action contrary to probity. No. Such an action does not conform to the mechanical disposition of the sage; he has grazed, as it were, on the leaven of order and rules; he is filled with the ideas of the good and of civil society; he knows its principles better than do other men. Crime would find in him too much opposition, he would have too many natural ideas and too many acquired ideas to destroy. His faculty of action is, as it were, like the string of a musical instrument tuned to a certain key; it would not be able to produce a contrary one. He is afraid to be off-key, to be out of harmony with himself; and this reminds me of what Velleius said of Cato of Utica. "Never," he said, "did he do good deeds in order to appear to have done them, but because it was not in him to do otherwise."

Moreover, in all the actions that men take, they seek only their own immediate satisfaction: it is the present good, or rather the present attraction, following the mechanical disposition where they find themselves, that makes them act. Now, the *philosopher* is disposed more than anyone else by his reflections to find more attraction and more pleasure in living with you, in attaining your confidence and your esteem, in acquitting himself of the duties of friendship and gratitude. These sentiments are still nourished at the bottom of his heart by religion, where the natural lights of his reason lead him. Once again, the idea of the dishonorable man is as antithetical to the idea of the *philosopher* as that of stupidity; and experience shows everyday that the more reason and enlightenment one has, the more one is steady and correct in the commerce of life. A fool, says La Rochefoucauld, does not have enough material to be good: one sins only because one's enlightenment is weaker than one's passions; and thus a theological maxim that is true in a certain sense, that every sinner is ignorant.

This love of society so essential to the *philosopher*, makes clear how true is the remark of the emperor Marcus Aurelius: "The people will be happy when kings are *philosophers*, or when *philosophers* are kings!"

The *philosopher* is thus an honorable man who acts in everything according to reason, and who joins to a spirit of reflection and precision, morals and sociable qualities. Graft a sovereign onto a *philosopher* of whatever stripe and you will have a perfect sovereign.

From this idea it is easy to conclude how far removed the insensitive sage of the stoics is from the perfection of our *philosopher*: such a *philosopher* is a man, and their sage was nothing but a phantom. Humanity would make them blush, and he glories in it; they wished foolishly to deny the passions, and to raise us above our nature by means of a chimerical insensitivity: as to him, he makes no claim to the chimerical honor of destroying the passions, because that is impossible; but he works at not being dominated by them, at benefiting from them, and at making reasonable use of them, because that is possible, and because reason directs him to do so.

What we have just said can still be seen everywhere, how far removed from the true idea of the *philosopher* are these idlers who, abandoning themselves to lazy meditations, neglect the care of their temporal affairs, and of everything that is called *fortune*. The true *philosopher* is not at all tormented by ambition, but he wishes to have the comforts of life; beyond what is strictly necessary, he requires an honest superfluity necessary to an honorable man, and by means of which alone he is happy: this is the basis of proprieties and pleasures. It is false *philosophers* who have given rise to this prejudice that the strictest necessity is sufficient, by their indolence and by their dazzling maxims.

David Hume

Of Essay Writing

The elegant Part of Mankind, who are not immers'd in the animal Life, but employ themselves in the Operations of the Mind, may be divided into the *learned* and *conversible*. The Learned are such as have chosen for their Portion the higher and more difficult Operations of the Mind, which require Leisure and Solitude, and cannot be brought to Perfection, without long Preparation and severe Labour. The conversible World join to a sociable Disposition, and a Taste of Pleasure, an Inclination to the easier and more gentle Exercises of the Understanding, to obvious Reflections on human Affairs, and the Duties of common Life, and to the Observation of the Blemishes or Perfections of the particular Objects, that surround them. Such Subjects of Thought furnish not sufficient Employment in Solitude, but require the Company and Conversation of our Fellow-Creatures, to render them a proper Exercise for the Mind: And this brings Mankind together in Society, where every one displays his Thoughts and Observations in the best Manner he is able, and mutually gives and receives Information, as well as Pleasure.

. . . 'Tis with great Pleasure I observe, That Men of Letters, in this Age, have lost, in a great Measure, that Shyness and Bashfulness of Temper, which kept them at a Distance from Mankind; and, at the same Time, That Men of the World are proud of borrowing from Books their most agreeable Topics of Conversation. 'Tis to be hop'd, that this League betwixt the learned and conversible Worlds, which is so happily begun, will be still farther improv'd, to their mutual Advantage; and to that End, I know nothing more advantageous than such *Essays* as these with which I endeavour to entertain the Public. In this View, I cannot but consider myself as a Kind of Resident or Ambassador from the Dominions of Learning to those of Conversation; and shall think it my constant Duty to promote a good Correspondence betwixt these two States, which have so great a Dependence on each other. I shall give Intelligence to the Learned of whatever passes in Company, and shall endeavour to import into Company whatever Commodities I find in my native Country

David Hume, "Of Essay Writing," in *Essays, Moral, Political and Literary*, vol. 2, ed. T. H. Green and T. H. Grose (London: Longmans, Green, 1898), 367–369.

proper for their Use and Entertainment. The Balance of Trade we need not be jealous of, nor will there be any Difficulty to preserve it on both Sides. The Materials of this Commerce must chiefly be furnish'd by Conversation and common Life: The manufacturing of them alone belongs to Learning.

As 'twou'd be an unpardonable Negligence in an Ambassador not to pay his Respects to the Sovereign of the State where he is commission'd to reside; so it wou'd be altogether inexcusable in me not to address myself, with a particular Respect, to the Fair Sex, who are the Sovereigns of the Empire of Conversation. I approach them with Reverence; and were not my Countrymen, the Learned, a stubborn independent Race of Mortals, extremely jealous of their Liberty, and unaccustom'd to Subjection, I shou'd resign into their fair Hands the sovereign Authority over the Republic of Letters. As the Case stands, my Commission extends no farther, than to desire a League, offensive and defensive, against our common Enemies, against the Enemies of Reason and Beauty, People of dull Heads and cold Hearts. From this Moment let us pursue them with the severest Vengeance: Let no Quarter be given, but to those of sound Understandings and delicate Affections; and these Characters, 'tis to be presum'd, we shall always find inseparable. . . .

Keith Michael Baker

The Passion for the Public Good

. . . It is immediately clear from its title that the *Essai sur la société des gens de lettres et des grands* is concerned not with the social role of scientists alone but with that of "men of letters" or "savants" more generally. This does not mean that d'Alembert made no distinction between the scientific intellectual and other "men of letters," for he constantly distinguished the exact sciences from other intellectual pursuits in his *Essai*

Keith Michael Baker, "The Passion for the Public Good," in *Condorcet: From Natural Philosophy to Social Mathematics* (Chicago: University of Chicago Press, 1975), 13–16. Reprinted with permission of The University of Chicago Press and the author.

and continuously held up the more highly developed norms of the former as a model for the latter. This, indeed, was one of his major purposes: for d'Alembert, as for Fontenelle before him, the scientific intellectual was the model intellectual; the community of science the model for the republic of letters more generally. What it does mean, however, is that he regarded the scientist as occupying a common social position with other intellectuals, a position in fact involving considerable dissonance with existing society. In other words, d'Alembert placed scientists in the common reforming stance developed for the intellectuals in the *Encyclopedia*, upon which his essay is in effect an extended commentary.

D'Alembert began the *Essai sur la société des gens de lettres et des grands* with a brief historical introduction, in some ways paralleling that of the preliminary discourse to the *Encyclopedia*. Fostered by kings for the close connection between public culture and social order—for it was an essential tactic of the philosophes to insist that public dissension was the work of fanaticism, to be soothed only by the healing breath of enlightenment—the germs of knowledge grew with the benevolent increase of royal power until they burst into full vigor under the rule of Louis XIV. As the esteem of the Sun King for knowledge gradually conquered the traditional predilection of the nobility for ignorance, intellectuals found themselves fashionable among "the great," whom d'Alembert defined as all those who by birth, personal resourcefulness, or wealth enjoyed a considerable position within society. "Snatched from their solitude, men of letters were swept up in a new social whirl in which they frequently found themselves out of place." It was this experience as a fashionable man of letters, d'Alembert insisted, that had prompted him to consider more fully the social role of the intellectual: a role which he described as the most difficult in the world after that of the clergy, "one of these two estates vacillating constantly between hypocrisy and scandal, the other between pride and grovelling."

At the heart of d'Alembert's concern, then, was the need to define the position of the man of letters in the social order of the old regime, transformed as it had been by Louis XIV's centralization of cultural patronage in a system of great academies. The cure for the pride and grovelling with which men of letters were by turns afflicted lay in their conscious acceptance of the independent public role their new institutional position offered them. No longer clients or courtiers, d'Alembert insisted, men of letters must exercise their public responsibility to "legislate for the rest of the nation in matters of philosophy and taste." To perform this role, they must above all be independent. D'Alembert's first concern was therefore to stress the autonomy of true intellectual activity, as contrasted with the slavishness of seeking to satisfy the desire for glory by winning the approval of those with prestige outside the intellectual community. This temptation to court the approval of the great, he argued, was strongest where the internal norms of the discipline were weakest: in literature, for example, as opposed to the stricter discipline of the mathematicians. The natural corollary of this argument was to contrast the empty flattery of nonprofessionals with the true meaning and value of professional recognition within the community of men of letters; and to claim for members of that community an independent position within society that would secure the benefits of the free exchange of professional recognition among them by emancipating them from dependence upon the great.

In order for the intellectual community to function effectively, however, certain internal norms and external conditions were also necessary. "LIBERTY, TRUTH, POVERTY (for if one fears the last, one is very far from the others), these are three words that men of letters must have constantly before their eyes, as kings the word POSTERITY." Externally, this liberty meant freedom of the press, freedom from the attempts of would-be protectors to direct the work of men of letters, and the independence of intellectual institutions from outside interference. Internally, it meant freedom to make judgments of a professional nature on the basis of no other criterion than that of the value of individual contributions to knowledge. "Anarchy, which destroys states," d'Alembert insisted, "on the contrary supports and maintains the republic of letters." Together with this requirement of liberty, commitment to knowledge also involved a strong bias towards equality: not as a goal in itself, but because only initial equality between men of knowledge—a willingness to dissociate a man's personal characteristics from the evaluation of his work—could make possible their ranking and reward in terms of a hierarchy of merit based on their contribution to truth. Finally there came the acceptance of poverty. While the man of letters is not obliged to be poor, d'Alembert maintained, he must nevertheless have no fear of poverty and no passion for wealth. For neither of these passions can be legitimately relieved without appealing beyond the intellectual community to the unprofessional world outside.

On all three of these cardinal points, d'Alembert found a clear contradiction between the norms of the intellectual community and those of the society of the old regime. But the most profound dissonance between his conception of the role of the man of knowledge and that of the society in which he found himself appears in his discussion of the relationship between equality and merit. All men, d'Alembert argued, are equal by natural right, that is, by their equal need of the society of their fellows. This natural equality gives way in society to a conventional inequality, which derives from the necessary division of labor among the different ranks of society. Three principal characteristics distinguish men in society: birth, wealth, and talent, of which only the latter is in effect a true or natural difference among men. Why then, d'Alembert demanded, if talent is the only true source of distinction among men, does it rank far behind birth and wealth in terms of external consideration? Bizarre and unjust as it is, he replied, there are perhaps reasons for this. If men cannot be equal, it is better that inequality be based on advantages that cannot be disputed or denied by the common run of men. And since it is much easier to decide the status of titles and incomes than to evaluate merit correctly, "it was therefore accepted that birth and fortune would be the most palpable criteria of inequality among men, for the same reason that collective decisions are made by a majority vote, although the opinion of the majority is often not the best one." It follows, then, that the man of knowledge, conscious that his position in the natural hierarchy of merit is freely accorded by his fellows, finds his own evaluation of his role constantly at odds with the prevailing values of a society that attributes more importance to the factitious qualities of birth and wealth.

> *In rendering to birth and wealth the obligations that society imposes upon him, the wise man is in a sense niggardly with these duties; he limits them to external forms, for the philosopher deals carefully with the prejudices of his nation without burning incense to them, and he salutes the idols of the people when necessary without seeking to do so of his own accord. What if he finds himself in the very rare situation, which powerful and laudable reasons sometimes make necessary in which he is obliged to pay his court? Secure in his talents and his virtue, he laughs without anger and without contempt at the role that he is then obliged to play. . . . Above all, the sage never forgets that if there is an external homage that talent owes to title, there is another and more real respect that title owes to talent.*

For d'Alembert, therefore, there was clearly a profound dissonance between the values of the intellectual (particularly the scientific intellectual) and those of eighteenth-century French society at large. How then was the man of knowledge to react? He was to withdraw from the humiliating posture he had assumed before the great, acknowledging that the true values of his profession are to be found in the independent functioning of the intellectual community. He was to realize that the idea of a philosopher-king is a myth, that the true philosopher flees the court, where he either forgets his profession or finds himself constantly out of place. But this acceptance of a professional role within an independent community of men of letters was by no means a passive one in d'Alembert's view. That community was still far from independent and its professional norms were far from being fully institutionalized in the academies which had fostered its growth. It was necessary, then, to close this gap between professional norms and institutional practice, which d'Alembert bitterly denounced in the passages of his *Essai* describing "the spirit of despotism" that prevailed in some of the academies of Europe. He made an important but unsuccessful attempt to achieve this aim in the Academy of Sciences in 1769 (the year in which Condorcet entered the academy) when he presented a project of reform that would give the academicians greater equality, especially in decisions affecting their immediate scientific concerns. Despite the failure of this scheme, d'Alembert remained an academic reformer: a statesman of organized science to whom Lagrange appealed (unsuccessfully) from Berlin "as the only person who can re-establish [our academy] on a sound basis and serve the sciences and those who cultivate them at the same time."

To close the gap between intellectual norms and institutional practice, however, it was also necessary to narrow that between intellectual values and those of existing society by exercising the independent function of the man of letters: that of criticism and definition. If science required freedom of the press at a time when the power to control the censorship was at the heart of the political and institutional struggles of eighteenth-century France; if science required academic reform at a time when the academies were closely bound to the hierarchical structure of the old regime; if science valued a hierarchy of merit profoundly at odds with the existing social structure: then to accept the norms of the scientific profession as d'Alembert defined them was at the same time to adopt an orientation toward social reform. The reforming stance developed for men of letters in the *Encyclopedia* was an essential concomitant of the definition of the intellectual's role elaborated by d'Alembert in the *Essai sur la société des gens de lettres et des grands*. . . .

Robert Darnton

The High Enlightenment and the Low-Life of Literature

The summit view of eighteenth-century intellectual history has been described so often and so well that it might be useful to strike out in a new direction, to try to get to the bottom of the Enlightenment, and even to penetrate into its underworld, where the Enlightenment may be examined as the Revolution has been studied recently—from below.

Digging downward in intellectual history calls for new methods and new materials, for grubbing in archives instead of contemplating philosophical treatises. As an example of the dirt that such digging can turn up, consider the following letter from a bookseller in Poitiers to his supplier in Switzerland: "Here is a short list of philosophical books that I want. Please send the invoice in advance: *Venus in the Cloister or the Nun in a Nightgown, Christianity unveiled, Memoirs of Mme la marquise de Pompadour, Inquiry on the Origin of Oriental Despotism, The System of Nature, Theresa the Philosopher, Margot the Campfollower.*" . . . Perhaps the Enlightenment was a more down-to-earth affair than the rarefied climate of opinion described by textbook writers, and we should question the overly highbrow, overly metaphysical view of intellectual life in the eighteenth century. One way to bring the Enlightenment down to earth is to see it from the viewpoint of eighteenth-century authors. After all, they were men of flesh and blood, who wanted to fill their bellies, house their families, and make their way in the world. Of course, the study of authors does not solve all the problems connected with the study of ideas, but it does suggest the nature of their social context, and it can draw enough from conventional literary history for one to hazard a few hypotheses.

A favorite hypothesis in histories of literature is the rise in the writer's status throughout the eighteenth century. By the time of the

Robert Darnton, "The High Enlightenment and the Low-Life of Literature," in *The Literary Underground of the Old Regime* (Cambridge, Mass.: Harvard University Press, 1982), 1–21, 39–40. Reprinted by permission of Past & Present Society.

High Enlightenment, during the last twenty-five years of the Old Regime, the prestige of French authors had risen to such an extent that a visiting Englishman described them exactly as Voltaire had described English men of letters during the early Enlightenment: "Authors have a kind of nobility." Voltaire's own career testifies to the transformation of values among the upper orders of French society. . . . The last twenty years of his correspondence read like a continuous campaign to proselytize for his "church," as he called it, and to protect the "brothers" and the "faithful" composing it. How many youths in the late eighteenth century must have dreamt of joining the initiates, of lecturing monarchs, rescuing outraged innocence, and ruling the republic of letters from the Académie Française or a château like Ferney. To become a Voltaire or d'Alembert, that was the sort of glory to tempt young men on the make. But how did one make it as a philosophe?

Consider the career of Jean-Baptiste-Antoine Suard, a typical philosophe of the High Enlightenment. Others—Marmontel, Morellet, La Harpe, Thomas, Arnaud, Delille, Chamfort, Roucher, Garat, Target, Maury, Dorat, Cubières, Rulhière, Cailhava—might do just as well. The advantage of Suard's case is that it was written up by his wife. A philosophe's rise to the top is indeed revealing when seen from his wife's viewpoint, and especially when, as in the case of Mme. Suard, the wife had an eye for domestic detail and the importance of balancing the family accounts.

Suard left the provinces at the age of twenty and arrived in Paris just in time to participate in the excitement over the *Encyclopedia* in the 1750s. He had three assets: good looks, good manners, and a Parisian uncle, as well as letters of introduction to friends of friends. His contacts kept him going for a few months while he learned enough English to support himself as a translator. Then he met and captivated the Abbé Raynal, who functioned as a sort of recruiting agent for the sociocultural elite known as *le monde*. Raynal got Suard jobs tutoring the well-born, encouraged him to write little essays on the heroes of the day—Voltaire, Montesquieu, Buffon—and guided him through the salons. Suard competed for the essay prizes offered by provincial academies. He published literary snippets in the *Mercure*; and having passed at Mme. Geoffrin's, he began to make frequent appearances in *le monde*—a phrase that recurs with the regularity of a leitmotif in all descriptions of Suard. With doors opening for him in the salons of d'Holbach, Mme. d'Houdetot, Mlle. de Lespinasse, Mme. Necker, and Mme. Saurin, Suard walked into a job at the *Gazette de France:* lodging, heating, lighting, and 2,500 livres a year for putting polish on the materials provided every week by the ministry of foreign affairs.

At this point Suard took his first unorthodox step: he got married. Philosophes did not generally marry. The great figures of the early Enlightenment—Fontenelle, Duclos, Voltaire, d'Alembert—remained bachelors; or, if they fell into matrimony, as in the case of Diderot and Rousseau, it was with someone of their own station—shop girls and servants. But the elevated status of the philosophe in Suard's time made marriage conceivable. Suard picked a girl of good bourgeois stock like himself; overcame the objections of her brother, the publisher Panckoucke, and of Mme. Geoffrin, who held old-fashioned ideas about the incompatibility of professional writing and family life; and set up house in the apartment that went with his job on the *Gazette de France.* Mme. Suard trimmed her wardrobe to fit their tight budget. Friends like the Prince de Beauvau and the Marquis de Chastellux sent them game from the hunts every week. And princely patrons like Mme. de Marchais sent carriages to carry the couple off to dinners, where the bride marveled at "the rank and the merit of the guests." This was something new: Madame Philosophe had not accompanied her husband on his forays into *le monde* before. Mme. Suard followed her husband everywhere and even began to form a salon of her own, at first a modest supper for literary friends. The friends and patrons responded so enthusiastically that something of a cult grew up around the *petit ménage,* as it was known from a poem celebrating it by Saurin. Formerly a fringe character picked up for amusement by the salons and readily turned out into the street for drubbings, begging, and *embastillement,* the philosophe was becoming respectable, domesticated, and assimilated into that most conservative of institutions, the family.

Having made it into *le monde,* Suard began to make money. By taking over the entire administration of the *Gazette de France,* he and his collaborator, the Abbé Arnaud, boosted their income from 2,500 to 10,000 livres apiece. They succeeded by appealing over the head of a bureaucrat in the ministry of foreign affairs, who was "astonished that men of letters shouldn't consider themselves rich enough with 2,500 livres of revenue," to the foreign minister, the Duc de Choiseul, whose sister, the Duchesse de Grammont, was an intimate of the Princesse de Beauvau, who was a friend of the Suards and of Mme. de Tessé, who was the protector of Arnaud. Such obliging noblesse was vulnerable to the vagaries of court politics, however, and when d'Aiguillon replaced Choiseul, the Suards were turned out of their *Gazette* apartment. Once again *le monde* rallied to the defense of its *petit ménage*. Suard received a compensatory pension of 2,500 livres from d'Aiguillon, who was persuaded by Mme. de Maurepas, who was moved by the Duc de Nivernais, who was touched by the sight of Mme. Suard weeping in the Académie Française and by the prodding of d'Alembert and La Harpe. Then a gift of 800 livres in *rentes perpétuelles* arrived from the Neckers. The Suards rented a house in the rue Louis-le-Grand. Suard managed to get the lucrative post of literary correspondent to the Margrave of Bayreuth. His friends arranged a pension for him of 1,200 livres on the income from the *Almanach Royal*. He sold his collection of English books to the Duc de Coigny for 12,000 livres and bought a country house. He became a royal censor. Election to the Académie Française came next, bringing an income of up to 900 livres in *jetons* (doubled in 1786) and far more in indirect benefits, such as a position as censor of all plays and spectacles, worth 2,400 livres and later 3,700 livres a year. When the *Journal de Paris* was suspended for printing an irreverent verse about a foreign princess, the keeper of the seals called in Suard, who agreed to purge all future copy and to share the profits: another 1,200 livres. "He took a cabriolet, which transported him after he fulfilled the duties of his posts, to the lovely house he had given to me," Mme. Suard reminisced. They had reached the top, enjoying an income of 10,000, perhaps over 20,000, livres a year and all the delights of the Old Regime in its last days. The Suards had arrived.

The most striking aspect of the Suard success story is its dependence on "protection"—not the old court variety of patronage, but a new kind, which involved knowing the right people, pulling the right strings, and "cultivating," as it was known in the eighteenth century. Older, established writers, wealthy bourgeois, and nobles all participated in this process of co-opting young men with the right style, the perfect pitch of bon ton, into the salons, academies, privileged journals, and honorific posts. The missing element was the market: Suard lived on sinecures and pensions, not on sales of books. In fact, he wrote little and had little to say—nothing, it need hardly be added, that would offend the regime. He toed the party line of the philosophes and collected his reward.

But how many rewards of that kind were there, and how typical was Suard's *cas typique*? Part of the answer to those questions lies in a box in the Archives Nationales containing a list of 147 "Men of Letters Who

Request Pensions" and ten dossiers crammed with material on writers and their sources of support. . . . The pension list . . . shows a strong bias in favor of established writers, especially academicians. . . .

In some cases the government subsidized writers who had produced propaganda for it. It looked favorably on the Abbé Soulavie, because "he has submitted some manuscripts on financial matters to M. le Contrôleur Général." Conversely, the government avoided making payments to anyone whose loyalties were in doubt. It turned down J.-C.-N. Dumont de Sainte-Croix, a minor author on jurisprudence, because, according to the marginal note next to his name, "All the new systems of this genre would merit some encouragement, if they were made only to be known by the government and not by the public, which is incited to rebel against the established laws instead of becoming enlightened as to the means of making them better." Then, in another hand: "Nothing." . . .

Of course it always helped to be a member of the Académie Française.

The dozens of volumes about the history . . . of the academy in the eighteenth century, whether written in love or in hatred, reveal a dominant theme: the Enlightenment's successful campaign to win over the French elite. After the *chasse aux Pompignans* of 1760, the election of Marmontel in 1763, and d'Alembert's elevation to the perpetual secretaryship in 1772, the academy fell to the philosophes. It became a sort of clubhouse for them, an ideal forum for launching attacks against *l'infâme*, proclaiming the advent of reason, and co-opting new philosophes as fast as the old-guard academicians would die off. This last function, virtually a monopoly of the philosophic salons, assured that only party men would make it to the top. And so Voltaire's church was besieged by converts. The spectacle of a new generation taking up the torch warmed the old man's heart. When he congratulated Suard on his election, Voltaire exulted, "Voilà, God be thanked, a new career assured. . . . At last I see the real fruits of philosophy, and I begin to believe that I shall die content." Thus Suard and his circle, the high priests of the High Enlightenment, took over the summit of the literary world, while the mid-century philosophes declined and died. The new men included both writers like Thomas, Marmontel, Gaillard, La Harpe, Delille, Arnaud, Lemierre, Chamfort, and Rulhière, and philosophically minded *grands*, powerful courtiers and clergymen, like the Marquis de Chastellux; the Maréchal de Duras; Boisgelin, Archbishop of Aix; and Loménie de Brienne, Archbishop of Sens.

The fusion of *gens de lettres* and *grands* had been a favorite theme of philosophic writing since the mid-century. Duclos had proclaimed it triumphantly in his *Considérations sur les moeurs de ce siècle* (1750). Writing had become a new "profession," which conferred a distinguished "estate" upon men of great talent but modest birth, he explained. Such writers became integrated into a society of courtiers and wealthy patrons, and everyone benefited from the process: the *gens du monde* gained amusement and instruction, and the *gens de lettres* acquired polish and standing. It went without saying that promotion into high society produced some commitment to the social hierarchy. Duclos had a keen eye for all the subtleties of status and rank; and although he took pride in the man of letters' ability to rise by sheer talent, he showed equal respect for what made a man of *le monde*: "One is an *homme du monde* by birth and by position."

Voltaire, the archapologist for *le mondain*, shared the same attitudes. His article entitled "Gens de lettres" in the *Encyclopedia* emphasized that in the eighteenth century "the spirit of the age made them [men of letters] for the most part as suitable for *le monde* as for the study. They were kept out of society until the time of Balzac and Voiture. Since then they have become a necessary part of it." And his article "Goût" in the *Dictionnaire philosophique* revealed the elitist bias in his conception of culture: "Taste is like philosophy. It belongs to a very small number of privileged souls. . . . It is unknown in bourgeois families, where one is constantly occupied with the care of one's fortune." Voltaire—who incessantly cultivated courtiers, tried to become one himself, and at least managed to buy his way into the nobility—thought that the Enlightenment should begin with the *grands*: once it had captured society's commanding heights, it could concern itself with the masses—but it should take care to prevent them from learning to read.

D'Alembert believed in essentially the same strategy, but he did not share his "master's" taste for the court. His *Essai sur les gens de lettres et les grands* (1752), published two years before his election to the Académie Française, amounted to a declaration of independence for writers and writing as a proud new profession. . . . Yet despite some strong language advocating a "democratic" republic of letters in contrast to the humiliating practices of patronage, d'Alembert stressed that society was and ought to be hierarchical and that the *grands* belonged on top. By the time he wrote his *Histoire des membres de l'Académie française* (1787), when he ruled the academy as Duclos's successor in the perpetual secretaryship, d'Alembert reformulated Duclos's theme in a conservative vein. He casti-gated the "horde of literary rebels" (*frondeurs littéraires*) for venting their frustrated ambitions in attacks on the academy. He defended the acad-emy's mixture of *grands seigneurs* and writers. And he emphasized the role of courtiers, as experts in the realm of taste and language, in a very elitist Enlightenment—a process of gradual, downward diffusion of knowledge, in which the principle of social equality could play no part.

> *Is a great effort of philosophy necessary to understand that in society, and especially in a large state, it is indispensable to have rank defined by clear distinctions, that if virtue and talent alone have a claim to our true homage, the superiority of birth and position commands our defer-ence and our respect . . . ? And how could men of letters envy or miscon-strue the so legitimate prerogatives of other estates?*

As spokesmen for the writer's new estate (but not for the brand of philosophe represented by Diderot and d'Holbach), Duclos, Voltaire, and d'Alembert urged their "brethren" to profit from the mobility avail-able to them in order to join the elite. Rather than challenge the social order, they offered a prop to it.

But what was the meaning of this process? Was the establishment becoming enlightened or the Enlightenment established? Probably both, although it might be best to avoid the overworked term "estab-lishment" and to fall back on the eighteenth-century expression already cited, *le monde*. After fighting for their principles in the mid-century and consolidating their victories during the last years of Louis XV's reign, the great philosophes faced the problem that has plagued every victorious ideology: they needed to find acolytes worthy of the cause among the next generation. Admittedly, "generation" is a vague concept. Perhaps there are no real generations but only demographic "classes." Still, the great philosophes form a fairly neat demographic unit: Mon-tesquieu 1689–1755, Voltaire 1694–1778; and then Buffon 1707–1788, Mably 1709–1785, Rousseau 1712–1778, Diderot 1713–1784, Condillac 1715–1780, and d'Alembert 1717–1783. Contemporaries were naturally struck by the deaths, not the births, of great men. Voltaire, Rousseau, Diderot, Condillac, d'Alembert, and Mably all died between 1778 and 1785; and their deaths left important places to be filled by younger men, who were born, for the most part, in the 1720s and 1730s.

As age overcame them, the great philosophes made the rounds of the salons, searching for successors. . . . But it was no use. . . . [T]he

Enlightenment passed into the hands of nonentities like Suard: it lost its fire and became a mere tranquil diffusion of light, a comfortable ascent toward progress. The transition from the heroic to the High Enlightenment domesticated the movement, integrating it with *le monde* and bathing it in the *douceur de vivre* of the Old Regime's dying years. As Mme. Suard remarked after reporting the receipt of their last pension, "I have no more events to recount, other than the continuation of a soft and varied life, until that horrible and disastrous epoch [the Revolution]." Her husband, turned censor, refused to approve Beaumarchais's not so very revolutionary play, *Le Mariage de Figaro*. And Beaumarchais put most of his energy into speculation, and ultimately into building the biggest townhouse in Paris—"a house that is talked about"—the arriviste's dream. . . .

J. J. Garnier, a writer with a highly developed sense of professionalism, noted that by 1764 many men of letters were moved by "the hope of gaining reputation, influence, wealth, etc. The avenues of advancement having been closed to them because of their humble birth and modest fortunes, they observed that the career of letters, open to everyone, offered another outlet for their ambition." Mercier agreed that the immigrant from the provinces could hope to shake off his humble origins and climb to the top in Paris. But the top of Paris, the *tout Paris*, had little room for ambitious young men on the make, perhaps because, as sociologists claim, rising status groups tend to become exclusive; perhaps because of a literary version of the Malthusian crush; perhaps because France suffered from a common ailment of developing countries: a surplus population of overeducated and underemployed littérateurs and lawyers. In any case, it seems that the attractiveness of the new career celebrated by Duclos and the new church proclaimed by Voltaire resulted in a record crop of potential philosophes, far more than could be absorbed under the archaic system of protections. Of course the lack of statistics and the confusion of social categories in prerevolutionary France (how does one define a "man of letters"?—someone with a literary reputation, someone who has published a book, or someone who lives by his pen?) make these hypotheses unverifiable. But there is no need for a complete census of eighteenth-century writers in order to make sense of the tension between the men of Grub Street and the men of *le monde* on the eve of the Revolution. The facts of literary life at that time speak for themselves.

The most salient fact is that the marketplace could not support many more writers than in the days when Prévost and Le Sage proved that it was possible—barely possible—to live from the pen instead of pensions. Although publishers offered somewhat better terms than earlier in the century, authors were caught between the masters of the publishing-bookselling guilds, who paid little for manuscripts, and pirate publishers, who paid nothing at all. None of the great mid-century philosophes relied much on sales except for Diderot, who never fully extricated himself from Grub Street. Mercier claimed that in his day only thirty hard-core "professionals" supported themselves by writing. The open, "democratic" market that could feed large numbers of enterprising authors did not appear in France until well into the nineteenth century. Before the day of the steam press and the mass reading public, writers lived by the kind of scavenging along the road to riches that worked so well for Suard—or they dropped by the wayside, in the gutter.

Once he had fallen into Grub Street, the provincial youth who had dreamt of storming Parnassus never extricated himself. As Mercier put it, "He falls and weeps at the foot of an invincible barrier. . . . Forced to renounce the glory for which he so long has sighed, he stops and shudders before the door that closes the career to him." The nephews and grand-nephews of Rameau really faced a double barrier, both social and economic; for after Grub Street had left its mark on them, they could not penetrate into polite society where the plums were passed around. So they cursed the closed world of culture. They survived by doing the dirty work of society—spying for the police and peddling pornography and they filled their writings with imprecations against the *monde* that humiliated and corrupted them. The prerevolutionary works of men like Marat, Brissot, and Carra do not express some vague, "anti-Establishment" feeling; they seethe with hatred of the literary "aristocrats" who had taken over the egalitarian "republic of letters" and made it into a "despotism." It was in the depths of the intellectual underworld that these men became revolutionaries and that the Jacobinical determination to wipe out the aristocracy of the mind was born. . . .

It would seem to be necessary, therefore, in looking for the connection between the Enlightenment and the Revolution, to examine the structure of the cultural world under the Old Regime, to descend from the heights of metaphysics and to enter Grub Street. At this low level of analysis, the High Enlightenment looks relatively tame. Voltaire's *Lettres philosophiques* may have exploded like a "bomb" in 1734, but by the time of Voltaire's apotheosis in 1778, France had absorbed the shock. There was nothing shocking at all in the works of his successors, for *they* had been absorbed, fully integrated into *le monde*. Of course one must allow for exceptions like Condorcet, but the Suard generation of philosophes had remarkably little to say. They argued over Gluck and Piccini, dabbled in pre-Romanticism, chanted the old litanies about legal reform and *l'infâme*, and collected their tithes. And while they grew fat in Voltaire's church, the revolutionary spirit passed to the lean and hungry men of Grub Street, to the cultural pariahs who, through poverty and humiliation, produced the Jacobinical version of Rousseauism. The crude pamphleteering of Grub Street was revolutionary in feeling as well as in message. It expressed the passion of men who hated the Old Regime in their guts, who ached with hatred of it. It was from such visceral hatred, not from the refined abstractions of the contented cultural elite, that the extreme Jacobin revolution found its authentic voice.

Roger Chartier

The Man of Letters

. . . The ideal of the man of letters, the negative image of which was given in Voltaire's scathing description of *la canaille de la littérature*, incontrovertibly associated the sovereign's protection and the philosophical spirit. Because it liberated the writer from the obligations of clientage, protected him from the perversions of the market, and recognized true scholars, monarchical patronage as it was instituted by Louis XIV, was a prime condition for men of letters worthy of the name to exercise the independence of their minds freely and without constraint or censorship. Voltaire noted in the 1765 edition of the *Dictionnaire philosophique*: "The literary man is without aid; he resembles the flying fish; if he rises a little, the birds devour him; if he dives, the fishes eat him up." His only recourse lay in the magnanimity of an enlightened prince.

Roger Chartier, "The Man of Letters," trans. Lydia G. Cochrane, in *Enlightenment Portraits*, ed. Michel Vovelle (Chicago: University of Chicago Press, 1997), 146–152, 178–183. Reprinted by permission of The University of Chicago Press.

Men of Letters, Academicians, and Pamphleteers

Did the real social world confirm this ideal figure of an independent, well-protected man of letters? . . .

Two groups emerge from the sociological description of authors provided by *La France littéraire* [a literary almanac published starting in 1755, which offered information on "all the men of letters who have lived in France from the beginning of the century to the present."] In the first, which was traditional and might be called Voltairean, we can see the coexistence, in unequal measure, of some people whose status and wealth sheltered them from need and others who benefited from the positions and remunerations offered by service to the great. In the second, which shows that the century was evolving, we can see the affirmation of a *bourgeoisie à talents* that rooted its writing activities in the exercise of an intellectual profession.

. . . The reports drafted between 1748 and 1751 by a police officer who was inspector of the book trade, Joseph d'Hémery, about the authors living in Paris show a different balance. D'Hémery's criteria were more demanding than those of *La France littéraire:* he included only writers who had written a genuine work, and, as might be imagined, he gave special attention to those whom he held to be "dangerous." If we take the 333 authors whose social identity d'Hémery provides and divide them according to the three sociological groups that we have seen in connection with *La France littéraire,* we see that the first category (clerics, nobles, and commoner officials and administrators) is of equal proportion in the two listings, accounting here for 40 percent of the total. The differences lie in the smaller proportion of clergy (12 percent as opposed to 20 percent in *La France littéraire*) and the greater proportion of commoners in the service of the judicial system or the royal administration (12 percent compared with 6 percent). But in Inspector d'Hémery's files there were many more men who held positions that depended on patronage than men in the liberal professions: 33 percent of the authors he describes served a protector in some capacity (twenty-five were secretaries; thirty-five were tutors), whereas only 13 percent were lawyers, professors, or physicians. At midcentury and for the literary figures most involved in the book trade, we must agree with Robert Darnton that "protection functioned as the basic principle of literary life."

Was the social world of *La France littéraire* closer to the society of the provincial academicians, as reconstructed by Daniel Roche, than to the Parisian Republic of Letters that fell under police surveillance? The sociology of men of letters and that of the academicians both reserved a prominent place for the traditional elites, and although the clergy was present in nearly equal proportion (22 percent of ordinary members of the academies instituted in thirty-two provincial French cities were clerics, as were 20 percent of authors), the proportion of nobles was quite different, with 40 percent of academicians in the second order, as compared to only 14 percent of authors. Within the third estate the two listings are quite similar, showing nearly identical percentages for physicians (28 percent of academicians who were commoners; 28 percent of authors) and for merchants and manufacturers (8 percent of academicians; 7 percent of authors). There is only one gap but it is a significant one: the world of the robe—officials, lawyers, administrators—accounted for 51 percent of the commoners who were ordinary members of the academies and for only 25 percent among men of letters. Inversely, the intellectual professions, in the strong minority among commoner academicians (only 13 percent), account for 32 percent of the commoner authors listed by the editors of *La France littéraire*. The world of authors in its broadest interpretation (as in *La France littéraire*) thus fairly closely resembled the society of provincial literati who made up the academic network.

But what was the situation of Voltaire's "unhappy class who write in order to live"—those who hoped to survive on the "commercial value" of their works, which meant ceding what they produced to the bookseller-publishers? Was there a sizable number of people who hoped to cover the better part of their expenses from revenues from the sale of their manuscripts? Diderot justified their hopes in his *Lettre sur le commerce de la librairie* when he pointed out that the affirmation that the bookseller-publisher's "privilege" was inalienable implied a recognition of the author's full rights of ownership to the work that he ceded in exchange for just remuneration. Rousseau set them an example by entering into negotiations for the same work several times, selling it, after making a few changes or additions, to different publishers inside and outside of France. He sold rights to *La nouvelle Héloïse* three times: Marc-Michel Rey acquired the original manuscript for 2,160 livres; Robin and Grangé paid 1,000 livres for an expurgated version that would be sure of authorization by the French authorities; and Duchesne spent 1,200 livres to buy the text augmented by the "Préface de Julie, ou, Entretien sur les Romans." . . .

In Inspector d'Hémery's reports as in the listings of *La France littéraire*, no profession or "estate" is given for a number of authors. The proportion of these men of letters with no employment listed or otherwise ascertainable increases from one source to another. This is the case of 101 out of the 434 writers described by d'Hémery between 1748 and 1753 (23 percent of the total), but it is also true of 1,326 out of the 2,819 authors (47 percent) listed in *La France littéraire* in 1784. In the 1757 edition of that publication, this was true of 27 percent of the authors listed; in the 1769 edition, of 33 percent. It would of course be extremely hazardous to conclude from this that these growing numbers of literati with neither a title nor a craft were all professional writers. Nonetheless, one might reasonably suppose that many among those with no post or sinecure tried to live by their pens. But they weren't all Rousseau. The first resource for such men lay in the large publishing enterprises — encyclopedias, dictionaries, collections, abridgements, translations — that required a number of collaborators. As Louis-Sébastien Mercier observed, it was these initiatives that gave a living to the writers whom he scornfully calls *demi-littérateurs* and *écrivailleurs*. . . .

It was from the ranks of such writers that the various factions recruited pamphleteers to carry on the pamphlet wars attacking other factions or the ministers, the court, or the queen. Propaganda campaigns of this sort always sprang out of divisions among the elites, each *parti* attempting to put public opinion on its side. As Jeremy Popkin writes: "The collusion of important members of the Court, the ministerial elite or wealthy financiers was necessary for the publication and circulation of almost all the controversial pamphlet literature of the period up to the crisis of 1788." This was a new type of patronage that enrolled the most impecunious men of letters in the service of the interests of the people who commissioned their writings. Obviously, not all libelists were "gutter Rousseaus." Pidansat de Mairobert was secretary to the king, *secrétaire des commandements* to the duc de Chartres, royal censor, and a shareholder in the Compagnie des Indes; Théveneau de Morande was engaged by the French government to publish a periodical financed by Versailles, *Le Courrier de l'Europe*. Still, a good many pamphleteers came from the world of writers who had no "estate" or fortune and who fulfilled their needs by entering into a clientage relationship. This was true of Brissot: after his stay in the Bastille and financial ruin, he wrote a number of pamphlets (not necessarily published in his own name but often under Mirabeau's) for the Geneva banker Clavière, who was attempting to manipulate the stock market. This made Brissot the perfect example of a "typical hack, making compromises and writing for money."

Comparisons

Did the characteristics of the French man of letters hold true everywhere in Europe? Two points of comparison may be of help. In the German states, authors seem to have increased markedly in number during the last third of the eighteenth century. The annual published by Johann Georg Meusels entitled *Das gelehrte Teutschland oder Lexicon der Letzt lebenden teutschen Schriftsteller* lists 3,000 authors in 1766, 4,300 in 1776, 6,200 in 1788, about 8,000 in 1795, and nearly 11,000 in 1806, or a four-fold increase in four decades. During the 1780s, the population of men of letters in German lands was thus twice as large as it was in France.

Comparison between France and Italy is of another order, since in Italy it is based on a sample of 219 authors born between 1720 and 1780. The definition of the man of letters in this sample is narrow because it does not include philosophers, theologians, economists, men of science, or scholars, and lists only authors of works of fiction, critics and historians of literature, and editors of ancient texts. The milieu of men of letters in Italy, circumscribed in this manner, shows, first, a decline in the number of clerics, who made up 51 percent of the authors born between 1720 and 1740, 37 percent of those born between 1741 and 1760, and 35 percent of those born between 1761 and 1780. This is a sizable reduction, but it should be noted that clergy accounted for a much higher proportion of authors than in *La France littéraire* (20 percent in 1784). We have to wait for the generation born between 1781 and 1800 to see a real reduction in clerical authors in Italy, when they account for only 15 percent of all authors.

Second, in the Italian states as in France, writing was nearly always a secondary activity made possible because the writer belonged to a privileged elite or exercised a profession. In the first case, the condition of man of letters fitted into an aristocratic and lordly existence of financial ease and leisure. This happened frequently in Italy, where 27 percent of the authors born between 1720 and 1780 were nobles and members of the laity (compared with 14 percent in *La France littéraire* in 1784). In the second case, literary production depended upon profitable use of the time left

over from the writer's principal occupation, which might be a teaching
position, an intellectual responsibility (as secretary, librarian, etc.), an ad-
ministrative office, or the exercise of a liberal profession. These various activities, practiced by clerics, nobles, and laymen, account, respectively, for
25, 17, 17, and 8 percent of the population of the 219 authors examined.
This means that, all in all, there were few "professional" men of letters:
"The case of 'professional' writers—that is, of writers for whom writing
was not a second profession—is objectively rare: a court poet here and
there or a dramatic poet (who might also be an actor)." If we add the few
journalists of the age, the figure rises to 13 percent of the sample.

Although the notion of literary property had been asserted and
various legislative bodies had recognized it in one form or another, the
men of letters whose material existence did not depend upon a situation, a profession, or on state or private patronage remained a very small
minority. . . .

From the Glories of Parnassus to the Citizen of the Republic of Letters

The image that men of letters gave of themselves provides the last group
of representations that we need to consider here. These representations
are inscribed in a great variety of literary genres—*éloges, anas, extraits,
mélanges,* and more—that aimed at perpetuating the memory of one
particular author (by gathering together his writings or his witticisms or
by giving an account of his actions) and, beyond the individual portrait,
at tracing the ideal image of the man of letters.

On exceptional occasions those representations took the form of a
monument. This happened in 1718 and again in 1776. In 1718, the
sculptor Louis Garnier finished a bronze statue representing the French
Parnassus, a work commissioned and paid for by Titon du Tillet. . . . His
intention was "to raise to the Famous Poets and Musicians a Monument
that I have called *The French Parnassus,* presided over by Louis the Great,
the August Protector of the Sciences and of the Fine Arts." Parnassus was
"represented by an isolated Mountain, somewhat steep and of handsome
form, on which are scattered Laurels, Palms, Myrtle branches, and
trunks of Oak covered with Ivy." On the slopes of the mountain Louis
Garnier, the sculptor, placed thirty-six figures. The fourteen principal
statues represented Apollo (that is, Louis XIV), the three graces (Mes-
dames de La Suze and Deshoulières and Mademoiselle de Scudéry),

the nymph of the Seine, and, in imitation of the nine muses, eight poets (Pierre Corneille, Molière, Racan, Segrais, La Fontaine, Chapelle, Racine, and Boileau) and one musician, Lully, who carried on one arm a medallion with a portrait of Quinault. Twenty-two smaller figures held either medallions showing the effigies of other poets and musicians or three scrolls on which their names were inscribed—ninety-one persons in all, including eleven women. Titon du Tillet had thought to leave room so that new writers or composers could be admitted to his Parnassus on their death: their pictures or names could figure on a fourth scroll, on new medallions, or, if one of them should prove worthy of the honor, in a tenth authorial figure.

Titon du Tillet's monument was realized in a reduced format that could be placed in a salon or a gallery. . . . The monument, which was conceived to be installed in a public place in Paris or in the courtyard of the Louvre, was to have figures of "at least natural size" and to be placed on a pedestal of white marble. At its base there was to be "a heap of stones and rocks, thrown there as if by chance" and it was to be enlivened by cascading waters falling into a basin of fine marble. The project was never executed, but as Titon du Tillet imagined it, the monument nonetheless bears witness to a representation using an allegorical and analogical language to construct a pantheon of literary figures whose talents had blossomed thanks to the protection of the prince who governed them.

Fifty years later, Pigalle made a statue of a totally different sort. This one was realistic rather than allegorical; it neither exalted the sovereign's munificence nor celebrated past literary glories. Instead, it offered a true likeness, in the nude, of a contemporary—Voltaire. In a letter to Galiani dated 13 April 1770, Madame d'Épinay tells how the project got started:

> *The Sunday gatherings of the rue Royale [the salon of Baron d'Holbach], the Thursdays of the rue Sainte-Anne [at the house of Helvétius, who lived on the same street as Madame d'Épinay], and the Fridays of the rue de Cléry [Madame Necker's salon] got the idea of taking up a collection to erect a statue to Voltaire and of placing it in the new hall of the Comédie Française, which is under construction. Pigalle has been asked to do it; he is asking 10,000 livres and [it will take] two years. Panurge [Abbé Morellet] immediately took charge of the project, and he has drawn up a financial prospectus for its execution. The first rule is that one must be a man of letters whose works have appeared in print in order to subscribe, and he set the subscription levels at 2 louis, 10 louis, and 2,000 livres. D'Alembert will act as treasurer and hold the requests and the money,*

*and Panurge insists that the amounts and the name of each subscriber be
kept secret. And to cap his despotism, he has drawn up a list prescribing,
without consulting them, what all the associates must contribute.*

A week later, Madame d'Épinay informed her correspondent that the
subscription conditions had been broadened so that it was no longer
necessary to have published to participate: "A plurality of votes went
against Panurge, and all *gens de lettres* or amateurs can subscribe for the
statue erected to Voltaire. The epigraph says, 'A Voltaire de son vivant
par les gens de lettres ses compatriotes.'"

. . . This initiative, which *La Correspondance Littéraire* attributed to
"an assembly of seventeen venerable philosophers, at which, after they
had duly invoked the Holy Spirit, copiously dined, and talked at random,
it was unanimously decided to erect a statue to Monsieur de Voltaire,"
created a scandal. No man of letters had as yet received an homage of this
sort during his lifetime. That honor was customarily reserved to sovereigns, a principle that had been respected in the *Parnasse Français*, which
celebrated only dead poets. By commissioning a statue of Voltaire, the
"House of Lords of literature" (as *La Correspondance Littéraire* wrote)
that gathered at Madame Necker's house intended not only to exalt the
merits of a man but also to present a representation of the new definition
of the man of letters. The subscription, which emanated from the nar-
rowest circle among the literary folk who made up the intellectual sociability of Paris, offered a broader milieu not only an opportunity to declare
its candidacy as participants in the Republic of Letters but also a chance
to be recognized by the sponsors of the enterprise. As Dena Goodman
writes, "By subscribing to the statue of Voltaire, one thus made a political
statement: one asserted oneself as a citizen of the Republic of Letters."

Notified of the project by private correspondence . . . and by . . .
manuscript newsletters, eighty persons subscribed. They represented
the two aspects of the Enlightenment in its most legitimate definition:
within the kingdom of France, wealthy men of letters who had "arrived"
(the average age of subscribers was high: forty-five), many of whom held
offices or charges in the royal administration or were members of academies, and one-fourth of whom were occasional or regular correspondents of Voltaire's; outside France, the princes of enlightened Europe.
Morellet recalled in his memoirs the importance of this princely participation—which was political more than financial, since the size of
the contributions was limited to preserve at least the fiction of equality

among the subscribers: "What put the final touch on determining the execution of the project was the part played by the king of Denmark, the empress of Russia, Frederick the Great, and several German princes."

Pigalle's statue of Voltaire . . . showed the writer nude but for an unrolled scroll held in one hand and a quill pen in the other. As a representation of the man of letters it was less than fully appreciated by contemporaries. Morellet declared: "Persons of taste generally criticized the execution. In order to demonstrate his knowledge of anatomy, Pigalle has made a nude, fleshless old man, a skeleton—a defect barely remedied by the verity and the life to be admired in the physiognomy and the oldster's attitude."

Nonetheless, when he sculpted Voltaire in his full humanity, without monumentality and without aestheticizing him, Pigalle displayed the fundamental and necessary equality among all citizens of the Republic of Letters, but also the dignity inherent in all citizens. The statue of Voltaire—sponsored by the very aristocratic and very exclusive society of the Paris salons, supported by the literary milieus that were both the wealthiest and the most solidly established within a society of orders and bodies, supported by the enlightened (if despotic) princes of northern Europe—nevertheless offered a representation of the values of a new literary and political order. It was a perfect incarnation of the contradictions that permeated both the definition and the status of the man of letters in the age of the Enlightenment: privilege and equality, protection and independence, prudent reformism and utopian aspiration.

Detail of "At the Sign of Minerva," by Léonard de France (1735–1805). Posters announcing the works of French philosophes, as well as the Edict of Toleration issued in 1781 by Hapsburg Emperor Joseph II, are pasted to the walls of a Flemish bookseller's shop. A young woman reads in the doorway, while off to the side, clerics of different Christian denominations converse civilly and even shake hands. Bundles of books piled up in front of the shop suggest how the works of the philosophes, written in Catholic France, were published in the Protestant Low Countries and shipped out to areas of Catholic Europe under more repressive regimes (Spain, Portugal, Rome) in order to spread Enlightenment. (*Erich Lessing/Art Resource, NY*)

Institutions of Enlightenment

Bearing out the Baconian dictum that knowledge is power, print proved the great engine for the spread of enlightened views and values.

Roy Porter

Together with their editors, booksellers, and publishers, they [the philosophes] formed a relatively autonomous pressure group and used an expanding communications network for ends of their own.

Elizabeth L. Eisenstein

For a collective project of Enlightenment, the salons were not simply diversions; nor were the women who ran them simply an audience whose social demands undermined the seriousness of male work. What the salons provided the philosophes was a serious social environment that established a structure for their discourse.

Dena Goodman

The importance of the musées derives in part from the work of their founders in repackaging and commodifying scientific knowledge, an effort that led to the formation of a popular scientific culture and contributed to the general commerce of Enlightenment ideas.

Michael R. Lynn

The traditional approach to the Enlightenment that focused on the books and ideas of a few "great" thinkers not only ignored debates about what characterized the philosophes as a group, but also tended to ignore the institutions in and through which the Enlightenment, as a project, was carried out. In this part, we explore two kinds of institutions of Enlightenment: institutions of print culture and institutions of sociability. We will see how, according to different historians, print media and forms of association were important both to the spread of Enlightenment ideas and to the social and intellectual practices of the philosophes. By looking at the institutions of Enlightenment, we can start to explore several relationships central to the Enlightenment: those between the philosophes and the reading public; between printers and writers; between men of letters and women; between popular and elite culture; between the sale of goods and the commerce of ideas; and between the society of the Enlightenment and the political world of the Old Regime. If the institutions of Enlightenment were responsible for the expansion of knowledge that would, as the philosophes believed, lead to the improvement of society, they also forged the link between the ideas of the Enlightenment and the material worlds of commerce and sociability from which some of the contradictions in the position of the man of letters explored in "Who Were the Philosophes? Definitions of the Enlightenment Man of Letters" derived.

Printing was essential to the Enlightenment, but Roy Porter and Elizabeth Eisenstein interpret its significance differently. Porter gives us an idea of great variety of forms of literature and literary culture circulating in mid-eighteenth century England, the country with the freest press and the least onerous censorship, and the only one in which authors enjoyed the protection of copyright. Porter shows how the expansion of printing led to the development of new roles for men of letters: the critic became an established figure and authorship became a profession and a business. Porter stresses how the author's need for buyers as well as readers raised concerns about how to use the power of the printed word to shape an expanding reading public that could be harnessed as a force for Enlightenment. Men of letters had to consider not only how to reach the public with their new ideas, but also how to train and flatter their new audience.

In contrast to Porter, who focuses on the new liberties of the English book trade, Eisenstein emphasizes the importance of Protestant printers located just outside the borders of Catholic France. These descendants of religious refugees expelled by Louis XIV used their presses to publish in French for a French readership all sorts of things considered subversive to the French state and the Catholic Church. In doing so, Eisenstein argues, they established French as a new universal language of Enlightenment, gave the Enlightenment its cosmopolitan and oppositional character, and led the way in disseminating new ideas and inventions. In her view, the institutions of the French Enlightenment must include the print shops located outside France's borders both because they made it more subversive and more cosmopolitan, and because they help to explain why the Enlightenment looked to many of its critics like a conspiracy to overthrow church and state.

Porter and Eisenstein introduce us to the wide range of print media and literary genres that the men and women of the Enlightenment developed and exploited in pursuit of their complicated aims of increasing knowledge, improving society, and advancing themselves. Periodicals (from scholarly journals to newspapers and magazines), novels, encyclopedias, dictionaries, atlases, and compendia of all sorts, along with mathematical treatises, science textbooks, and self-help and how-to books, were all media and vehicles of Enlightenment that we take for granted today. Just as varied were the institutions of Enlightenment sociability that were often sources of civic pride in cities and towns throughout Europe and its colonies. These included royal and provincial academies, reading societies and lending libraries, societies for the improvement of agriculture and the trades, and masonic lodges. The American Philosophical Society, founded by Benjamin Franklin in 1743, is an Enlightenment institution that still exists today.

The next two selections focus closely on two very different institutions of Enlightenment that suggest the richness of the terrain of sociability that historians have only recently begun to explore: the Parisian salon and the science club. Dena Goodman argues for the central role of the Parisian salon in the Enlightenment Republic of Letters. She sees the salon as a social base and a center of communications for men of letters whose aim was to enlighten an expanding reading public. But she credits the transformation of the salon from a venue for literary games into a serious institution of Enlightenment to the women we now call *salonnières:* the hostesses who, to further their own education and participate in the project of Enlightenment, created the working spaces in which men of letters could meet and exchange ideas on a footing of equality. Goodman concludes that, in contrast to the anarchic world of print, the salon provided a model for a new social and political order based on Enlightenment values that included women as well as men.

 Michael Lynn focuses on one of the many clubs that were founded throughout Europe and the Americas in the 1780s to promote useful knowledge and give a broad segment of the urban population direct access to the Enlightenment. As the case of the Musée de Monsieur reveals, these clubs sought to cultivate a taste for science by combining education andentertainment—while making money for the entrepreneurs who founded them. Like Roy Porter, Lynn emphasizes the commercial dimension of Enlightenment; like Robert Darnton, he criticizes those historians whose vision of the Enlightenment focuses too narrowly on the Parisian elite. For Lynn, it is important to understand not only how the Enlightenment was practiced by a small elite, but also how it was commodified and packaged for the public. To appreciate the scientific dimension of the Enlightenment in particular, he argues, we must study those institutions that "sold" the new knowledge to large numbers of the curious and taught them how science could improve their lives.

Roy Porter

Print Culture

 . . . Literature became a commodity circulating in all shapes and sizes. John Wesley turned out fourpenney pocket-sized abridgements of classics like *Paradise Lost*—Milton for the masses—as well as a dictionary and a nine-page English grammar. New packages were also pioneered, for instance publishing by parts. The first edition of Johnson's *Dictionary*

(1755), of which 2,000 copies were printed, cost £4 10s.; hard on its heels came a second, brought out in 165 weekly sections at sixpence each. Smollett's *Complete History of England* (1757–8) sold 10,000 copies in sixpenny weekly numbers.

In addition, enterprising publishers began to market cheap sets of the standard English poets and playwrights at the knock-down price of a shilling or so—in effect, paperbacks. This was made possible by a 1774 copyright ruling which established that after the expiry of the protected period (a maximum of twenty-eight years), a text entered the public domain. The old cartels could now be smashed. John Bell launched his *Poets of Great Britain Complete from Chaucer to Churchill* series, which came out between 1776 and 1792 in 109 volumes, at 1s. 6d. each— or just 6d. on tatty paper. Soon John Cooke was competing, with his editions of the British poets, prose writers and dramatists, in sixpenny weekly numbers. Young William Hazlitt gobbled up English literature through Cooke's books which regularly arrived by mail order at his parental home ('a perpetual gala-day'). Another 1770s innovation was William Lane's Minerva Press and Library, notorious for its salacious and sentimental novels.

Thus, more made its way into print, more cheaply. Books also became easier of access, particularly as provincial publishing brought a bookshops boom. Under the Licensing Acts printing had been a London monopoly and provincials had had to make do without printed broadsides and handbills, advertisements, theatre programmes, tickets, receipts or other trade items. In 1700 Birmingham had no bookseller, while as late as the 1720s Lincoln had a towncrier but no newspaper or printer. All that changed fast. By 1740, there were about 400 printing outlets in nearly 200 towns, and, by the 1790s, this had risen to nearly 1,000 in more than 300 centres. In 1800, Newcastle-upon-Tyne could boast not only twenty printers but twelve booksellers and three engravers as well. 'There are now as many Booksellers as there are Butchers,' observed the Londoner William Blake.

Nor was it even necessary to buy, as hosts of book clubs and libraries— circulating, proprietary and subscription—came into being. By 1800 there were about a hundred in the metropolis and a thousand in the provinces. Some were huge: in 1793 Bell's London circulating library claimed to hold 150,000 volumes—including the kinds of *belles lettres* and Minerva Press fiction which drove Sir Anthony Absolute to apoplexy.

Though most libraries kept large stocks of history, travel and the like, it was the novels, play texts and light reading which were seized off the shelves.

The print boom bred new varieties of men of letters. 'In opulent or commercial society,' observed Adam Smith, theorist of the division of labour, 'to think or reason comes to be, like every other employment, a particular business, which is carried on by a very few people.' Among the emergent breeds was the critic, that self-appointed judge, censor and reformer of the republic of letters. . . . [T]he critic was enlightened man incarnate, the caustic Restoration wit purified into the more civilized character required in the age of politeness, standing for freedom of speech and rational argument against dogmatism and absolutism.

Mr Critic overlapped somewhat with the satirist for, especially in the early Enlightenment, the burlesque, the spoof and the parody formed ideal vehicles for free-thinking, opposition and subversion. And his younger brother was Mr Reviewer. . . . [R]eviewing, like criticism, filled the sails of the ship of print. It told readers what to think and say, while nurturing a much-desired (if despised) cultural narcissism in circles eager to hear themselves talked about and liking the sound of their own voices.

The crony of them all was Mr Spectator, arbiter of standards and ubiquitous commentator. Hinting that there was no coffee house which he did not frequent, that Addisonian persona assumed a universal status, transcending the particular identities of the individual members of his club—the cleric, man of fashion, merchant, country gentleman and soldier—to become the cosmopolite, the very epitome of sweet reason, composure and tolerant pluralism.

These literary identities were part and parcel of the key Enlightenment reinvention of the persona of the thinker, signalled by Adam Smith's remark about the trade of thinking. Proposing to bring 'Philosophy out of Closets and Libraries, Schools and Colleges, to dwell in Clubs and Assemblies, at Tea-Tables and in Coffee Houses,' Joseph Addison, the first great media man, sought to turn the philosopher into a man of letters and thus a man of the world. Thinking was not for academics alone and must be rescued from the 'monkish' seminaries which bred arcane pomposity; what was needed was discussion not disputation, conversation not controversy, politeness not pedantry. 'If Philosophy be, as we take it, the Study of Happiness,' remarked the 3rd Earl of Shaftesbury, 'must not everyone, in some manner or other, either skilfully or unskilfully philosophize?' It was not thus a matter of metaphysics but of *savoir vivre:* 'The

Taste of Beauty, and the Relish of what is decent, just, and amiable, perfects the Character of the Gentleman and the Philosopher.'

David Hume concurred in urging a reincarnation for the philosopher: 'The separation of the learned from the conversable world,' he maintained, had been 'the great defect of the last age' . . . Where lay the fault? Thinking had been monopolized by self-absorbed academics 'who never consulted experience in any of their reasonings, or who never searched for that experience, where alone it is to be found, in common life and conversation.' Things, however, were on the mend. 'It is with great pleasure I observe,' he noted,

> *that men of letters in this age have lost in a great measure that shyness and bashfulness of temper, which kept them at a distance from mankind; and, at the same time, that men of the world are proud of borrowing from books their most agreeable topics of conversation.*

. . . In his vastly influential *Lectures on Rhetoric and Belles Lettres* (1783), Hugh Blair approached the question of the thinker and his public from a further angle. What did readers of serious books want? Doubtless they hoped 'for instruction, not for entertainment,' but readability must be a plus: 'The same truths, and reasonings, delivered in a dry and cold manner, or with a proper measure of elegance and beauty, will make very different impressions on the minds of men.' Indeed, Blair extolled 'good Writing.' Particularly valuable were illustrations from history and the affairs of great men, 'for they take Philosophy out of the abstract, and give weight to Speculation, by shewing its connection with real life, and the actions of mankind.'

Moreover, it was now insisted, unlike its monkish ancestor, enlightened philosophy should and would be useful. . . . [T]he true philosopher was no armchair daydreamer—James Watt of steam-engine fame, for example, amply deserved the accolade. . . . [I]t was to be that rational understanding of the real world which would drive the Enlightenment.

Bearing out the Baconian dictum that knowledge is power, print proved the great engine for the spread of enlightened views and values. . . . Alongside chapbooks, prayer books, jest books and what have you, the presses spewed forth improving teach-yourself guides, educational treatises and advice manuals by the score, from gardening to gymnastics, carpentry to cookery. . . .

Monumental reference works appeared, including Johnson's *Dictionary of the English Language* (1755). John Harris's *Lexicon Technicum* (1704) was the first modern English encyclopaedia, weighted on the scientific and technical side. Inspired by Harris, Ephraim Chambers compiled a more comprehensive work, entitled *Cyclopaedia: or, An Universal Dictionary of Arts and Sciences*, published in 1728 in two folio volumes, with plates, at four guineas. Chambers was to be honoured by election to the Royal Society of London and burial in Westminster Abbey. In 1778 the Dissenting minister Abraham Rees re-edited Chambers in four volumes—it appeared in 418 weekly numbers—and he later cranked out a further edition, before planning his *Cyclopaedia, Or an Universal Dictionary of Arts and Sciences . . . Biography, Geography and History*, a vast undertaking completed in 1819 in thirty-nine quarto volumes.

Meanwhile, the *Encyclopaedia Britannica* had appeared, also in parts (the first appearing in 1768), at a cost of 6d. each on plain paper, with over a hundred parts in all. Its 2,670 quarto pages with 160 copperplate engravings cost just £12. Ten thousand copies were printed of the third edition (1787–97)—France, with three times the population of Britain, had a mere 4,500 subscribers for its *Encyclopedia*. All human knowledge was thus made readily available, for the first time, in English and within reach of middle-class pockets.

Though far from every title flew under the 'enlightened' ensign—mountains of devotional literature were published—print became indelibly linked in the public mind with progress. And, through the printed word, a specifically national culture was crystallizing, aided by works that taught what every educated Briton should know, particularly about home-bred achievements. Horace Walpole's *Anecdotes of Painting in England*, published from 1762, was the first history of English art; Thomas Warton's *History of English Poetry* (1774–81) complemented Dr Johnson's *Lives of the Poets* (1779–81); Sir Joshua Reynolds's *Discourses*, on matters of taste, came out between 1769 and 1791, while in music Sir John Hawkins's *A General History of the Science and Practice of Music* (1776) was counterpointed in the same year by Charles Burney's polished *A General History of Music*.

Early in the century, Shaftesbury had protested that 'the British Muses' were 'yet in their mere infant-state.' But critical and popular editions of British writers and biographical dictionaries of native worthies, like the *Biographia Britannica* (1747–66), allayed cultural anxieties and boosted national pride. Bardolatry boomed, especially after David

Garrick's Shakespeare jubilee staged in 1769 at Stratford-upon-Avon. Anthologized in works of the 'beauties of Shakespeare' genre, the Bard became the national saint—chips of his chair were on sale as relics: 'Shakespear,' mused the playwright-scholar Arthur Murphy, 'is a kind of establish'd Religion in Poetry.' Poets' Corner in Westminster Abbey became a tourist must . . . Voltaire was impressed: 'The English have so great a Veneration for exalted Talents, that a Man of Merit in their Country is always sure of making his Fortune. Mr Addison was rais'd to the Post of Secretary of State in England. Sir Isaac Newton was made Warden of the Royal Mint. Mr Congreve had a considerable Employment.' Writers and thinkers had become national assets.

'Meantime, the pamphlets and half-sheets grow so upon our hands,' groaned Swift in 1710, 'it will very well employ a man every day from morning till night to read them.' His solution? Never to open any! The doctor Thomas Beddoes was another who grumbled about the welter of print—all those endless pamphlets and periodicals befuddling the brain. . . . The consequence? 'You must needs hang your heavy head, and roll your bloodshot eyes over thousands of pages weekly. . . .' Yet that didn't sap his ardour for enlightenment, or still his quill.

Be they reactionaries like Swift or radicals like Beddoes, many feared truth was being buried in the avalanche of textual production. . . . Old fogeys feared what Johnson memorably and approvingly called 'a nation of readers'—for his part, however, the lexicographer never doubted the benefits of literacy, even if he also muttered that 'this teeming of the press in modern times . . . obliges us to read so much of what is of inferior value, in order to be in the fashion.'

What made critical reactions to the diffusion of knowledge, and the culture industry sustaining it, so caustic was that this cornucopia of secular information, instant opinion and urbane values, purveyed by the *Monthly Mess*, was new and unprecedented. People seemed to be picking up beliefs from their reading like apples from a barrel. Moreover, amid the welter of essays, *belles lettres* and novels, life and letters seemingly mirrored each other in a looking-glass world—no accident, surely, that the prime Scottish periodical was actually titled the *Mirror*.

It was a turning point. The print boom was bringing into being an intelligentsia, separate from (though overlapping with) the clergy, a 'commonwealth of polite letters' linked to the public at large via the publishing industry. Print technologies and surplus wealth were supporting cultural performers who became established as self-appointed tribunes of the people, sustained by infrastructures created by impresarios, critics and capitalists. The writer's status became irrevocably bound up with his relations to the public—indeed, his public relations—as he projected himself as the nation's eyes, ears and voice, a figure commanding public presence, notoriety even. The business of writing and the reading public were two sides of the coin of print capitalism. . . .

Elizabeth L. Eisenstein

Print Culture and Enlightenment Thought

. . . When considering the relationship between activities pursued in printing shops and the development of Enlightenment thought, one must deal with two rather different special fields, cultivated on the one hand by intellectual historians and on the other by social historians. First are developments in the history of ideas that may be related to changes affecting the transmission of texts, the collecting of data, and the workings of the knowledge industry. Second are the new occupations and institutions, new forms of patronage and of censorship, and other aspects of the printed book trade that are usually allocated to the field of social history. The rest of this paper is divided into two sections that deal with selected issues bearing on each of these two fields.

Let me start in the field of intellectual history and consider first of all the increasingly rich orchestration of ideas of progress. Here our point of departure would be different from that taken by the genealogist of ideas, who tries to trace back as far as possible the rejection of traditional "decay of nature" themes. Instead of beginning with the first writers who

Elizabeth L. Eisenstein, *Print Culture and Enlightenment Thought* (Chapel Hill: Hanes Foundation, Rare Book Collection/University Library, University of North Carolina at Chapel Hill, 1986), 3–11, 13–14, 19–22. Reprinted by permission of Elizabeth L. Eisenstein.

celebrated an "advancement of learning," why not consider how learning was in fact advanced when a variety of reference works underwent the shift from script to print? This strategy brings to the fore materials such as maps, gazetteers, atlases, and lexicons, which are generally passed over by intellectual historians and which are indeed often ignored by historians at large. Yet the activities of lexicographers, map publishers, and globe makers during the first centuries after printing reverberated throughout the learned world. The production of a multi-volume world atlas, such as Abraham Ortelius's sixteenth-century *Theatrum* or Joan Blaeu's seventeenth-century *Grand Atlas*, represented just the sort of large-scale collaborative venture in data collecting that made optimism about the advancement of learning seem increasingly irresistible. The Age of Enlightenment was an age when geography was undergoing a major reform; maps of the coastline of France itself were being corrected, and many distant lands with "dark interiors" still remained to be explored. Yet by then there was well-founded confidence that all major land masses and bodies of water would eventually be completely and accurately charted.

The acquisition of precise, detailed information about the world that lay beyond the Pillars of Hercules—beyond limits set to earthly knowledge heretofore—provided early proponents of progress with one of their chief figures of speech. But of course the advantage of using a new information technology was not confined to cartography. The replacement of a sequence of corrupted copies by a sequence of ever-augmented and often-corrected editions affected a vast variety of learned disciplines, ranging from bibliography to zoology. Moreover themes of perfectibility and improvement were sounded repeatedly each time a new title or new edition was introduced. In his preface to the first edition of his *Dictionnaire philosophique*, for example, Pierre Bayle referred to the usefulness of the emendations and addenda in successive editions of a previous reference work. He wrote about casting light into dark corners and took note of the success of cartographers in pinpointing small details. Similarly the 1750 prospectus for the *Encyclopedia* marveled over "the progress that had been made in the sciences and arts" in order to push yet another improved book of knowledge upon a public that had already been provided with over thirty different encyclopedias in the previous seventy-five years.

No doubt very few if any printed reference works completely lived up to their advance billings. More data were copied, and less were checked and corrected than optimistic blurbs and prefaces implied. Yet the very fact that so many optimistic reports were being issued helps to explain why a new "spirit" of optimism seemed to be abroad. Furthermore, readers were not invariably disappointed.

Even the most responsible editors and publishers borrowed a great deal from earlier compendia. But they also created vast networks of correspondents and enlisted help from readers who sent in notice of the errors that they spotted or the new information they could provide. In the sixteenth century, Ortelius's correspondents ranged from Muscovy to Wales. Two centuries later Linnaeus received reports, seed packets, and specimens from readers scattered over the entire world. Not every edition incorporated new data; few eliminated *all* errors that were spotted. Yet the very publication of errata contributed to cognitive advance. Moreover the requests of some editors inspired some readers to launch their own research projects and to undertake field trips that resulted in additional publication programs. By such means the six hundred plants described in Pliny's *Natural History* (which was first printed in 1469) had grown to six thousand by Francis Bacon's day and continued to multiply thereafter.

Not only did later editions improve on earlier ones in a manner that led to the gradual eclipse of the authority of certain ancient authors—such as Pliny—but the sequence of improved versions and ever-expanding reference guides was without limits, in marked contrast to the abortive sequences initiated by men of learning in the age of scribes. When Conrad Gesner called his path-breaking bibliography *Biblioteca Universalis,* he was deliberately drawing a contrast with earlier manuscript libraries that were contained within four walls and were destined to be dispersed or destroyed. Gesner's bibliography, his so-called "universal library," was not destroyed; it was simply outdated. It pointed to the future development of a library without walls, one which was capable of infinite expansion. Printing initiated a new kind of sequence in the world of books: a cumulative sequence entailing unlimited growth.

That continuous incremental sequences were ushered in by printing needs to be considered when trying to account for the new outlook that Ernst Cassirer and others attribute to the "mind of the Enlightenment." In the age of scribes, men of learning had served primarily as the transmitters of an inherited corpus of texts that had to be guarded against loss and contamination. After printing, less effort was required to preserve and pass on what was known; more energy could be spent on exploration and investigation—on the search for what Sir Thomas

Browne called the "untravelled parts of truth." Successive generations began to pride themselves on knowing more than had their forebears and to speculate about what remained for their descendants to explore. Human history itself acquired the character of an indefinitely extended unfolding sequence, as we can see by comparing Enlightenment views of printing with those of earlier days. Condorcet agreed with Luther that Gutenberg's invention inaugurated a new epoch that ended the Dark Ages and papal rule. But unlike Luther, who saw it as the "last flame before the extinction of the world," Condorcet's eighth stage was followed by a ninth and tenth—with prospects for continuous improvement extended into an indefinite future.

Print culture also contributed in a paradoxical way to the discarding of the narrow limits once assigned to human history, by endowing precise dates with a great fixity. In the age of scribes, there had always been a considerable margin for uncertainty in Western Christendom about just when the Creation or the birth of Christ had occurred and about just when to begin the New Year after the first millennium A.D. had ended. But by the seventeenth century round numbers that were vague and approximate (such as 800 for the year of Charlemagne's coronation or 1000 for that of the Last Judgment) gave way to more precise calculations that could be fixed in print. For example, there is the date 4004 B.C., assigned to Creation by Bishop Ussher and placed in the margins of countless English Bibles, or the date 1694 A.D., assigned in all copies of Alsted's encyclopedia, to the Last Judgment. In Bayle's *Dictionnaire*, first published in 1697, there is skepticism about many aspects of sacred history. But a new tone of certitude accompanies Bayle's declaration that "we can state with absolute confidence that Alsted's date of 1694 for the end of the world is in error."

The sense of participation in an indefinitely extended, continuous historic process was reinforced by the resort to serial publication that began several decades before the date Alsted set for the end of the world. Indeed periodical journalism may well be related to the sense of "modernity" that is attributed to Enlightenment culture by writers such as Peter Gay. The expectation of learning about the latest findings and sensations every month (not to mention weekly or thrice-weekly or daily) needs to be considered in connection with the development of a new "mentalité" among literate elites in early modern times.

At first the new journals fell into two main categories, described by Jean Sgard as *Mercures* and *Bibliothèques*. The latter, which focused on literary news, are of special interest for our purposes. These literary journals may be regarded partly as promotional ventures serving to advertise the recent output of publishers, much as had earlier booksellers' catalogs. In addition to bookish news, many carried reports of new instruments and experiments as described in published treatises. Just as map publishers and naturalists had elicited contributions from unknown readers, so too did the journal editors ask for help from the public at large, appealing to readers as potential collaborators.

> *I entreat the assistance of all those who wish well to the progress of learning and beg they will favor me . . . with extracts of curious books with such original pieces and accounts of new inventions and machines and any other improvements . . . as are fit to be communicated to the public. In which case I shall either mention their names or observe a religious silence as they shall desire.*

The quotation comes from the first issue (January 1728) of *The Present State of the Republick of Letters,* an English journal that was imitating its more celebrated French precursor. In his *Nouvelles de la République des lettres,* Pierre Bayle had been no less assiduous in soliciting the opinions of his readers.

. . . I am going to curtail further discussion of how printing entered into ideas of progress in order to take up one other intellectual development, well summarized by Ernst Cassirer's discussion of the new concept of truth proclaimed by Galileo: "a truth of nature which was revealed not in God's words but in His works; which was not based on testimony of Scripture but was visible at all times." This truth of nature, writes Cassirer, "cannot be expressed in mere words . . . but only in mathematical constructions, figures and numbers. In these symbols, nature presents itself in perfect form and clarity. Revelation by means of the sacred word can never achieve . . . such precision, for words are always . . . ambiguous."

This passage describes a major intellectual transformation but stops short of explaining why it happened when it did. It needs to be supplemented by noting that "mathematical constructions, figures and numbers" had not always presented themselves "in perfect form and clarity." "To discover the truth of propositions in Euclid," wrote John Locke, "there is little need or use of revelation, God having furnished us with a natural and surer means to arrive at knowledge of them." In the eleventh century, however, God had not furnished Western scholars with a natural or sure means of grasping a Euclidean theorem. Instead the most learned men in Western Christendom engaged in a fruitless search to discover what Euclid meant when referring to interior angles. During the age of scribes diagrams, tables, charts, and fresh drawings were particularly vulnerable to corruption by copying. Text translated from Greek into Arabic and then into Latin suffered from problems posed by "ambiguous words," and this was true even of works by Euclid and Archimedes.

After printing, however, the language of nature increasingly departed from that of Scripture. A new confidence in the accuracy of mathematical construction, figures, and numbers was generated by the new method of duplication. Printed charts, logarithm tables, equations, and uniform grids made it possible to present identical data in an identical form to readers who were otherwise divided by linguistic frontiers. A similar confidence was generated by pictorial statements and visual aids such as the engravings made from drawings of soil, rocks, and plants collected on Captain Cook's expedition. These engravings provided "a common measure which speaks universally to all mankind," in the words of Joseph Banks. The same thing could be said of the magnificent plates (approximately 2,900) appended to the *Encyclopedia*, some of which were borrowed from earlier works. New improved editions of star maps, atlases, and globes also inspired growing confidence that a universal consensus on natural phenomena—whether celestial or terrestrial—could be obtained.

But even while the study of nature was being increasingly freed from translation problems by the use of printing, the study of Scripture became more ensnared. In a succession of polyglot editions of the Bible, scholars were presented with a print-made sequence that spurred cognitive advance but at the same time enormously complicated the study of the revealed word of God. The first of these, printed in Acalá in 1517, showed Greek, Vulgate (Latin), and Hebrew text in parallel columns ("Christ crucified between the two thieves," gibed Spanish theologians who opposed the project). By the time the London *Polyglotte* of 1657 had been completed, the number of ancient languages had increased to nine. The English publication was undoubtedly a masterpiece of Baroque erudition. The vast apparatus accompanying it testified to the advancement of learning. But these magnificent volumes did more to complicate than to simplify efforts to decipher God's words. Of course, there are many other ways in which printing changed the character of scriptural texts and changed the way Western scholars viewed their sacred book. The multilingual problems posed by polyglot Bibles have been noted here because they seem especially pertinent to the new concept of truth discussed by Cassirer. By the end of the seventeenth century, God's "works" were appearing in an ever more uniform guise, His "words" in an ever more multiform one. Surely this needs to be taken into account when attempting to set the stage for Enlightenment thought.

Now let me turn from ideas to institutions and also focus more specifically on the French Enlightenment. Once again my point of departure is unconventional, for I shall pass over the institutions of *ancien régime* France. I agree with the editors of a recent essay collection, entitled *The Enlightenment in National Context*, that social context is too often absent from treatments of the Enlightenment and that we should pay more attention to its "geographical, social, and political *location* as a cultural movement." But I do not think this purpose is best accomplished by looking for roots in diverse "national soils." A more cosmopolitan context is needed for what was after all a cosmopolitan movement.

Obviously the outlook of the French philosophes owed much to the teachings of Jesuits, Jansenists, and Oratorians, to the clubs, cafés, and salons of Paris, to the court of Versailles, to the parlements, academies, and to other French institutions that have all been examined in many careful studies. But to understand the French Enlightenment we must also make room for the difference between the French press that operated within the Bourbon realm and the Francophone press that served a far-flung Republic of Letters from printing centers outside the borders of France.

By the end of the seventeenth century, the *respublica litterarum* had been transformed into the *République des lettres*. Although Latin continued to be used for scientific and scholarly interchange, eighteenth-century literati by and large accepted French as *the* cosmopolitan language of their day. . . .

From the 1680s down to the 1780s the printing firms that supported the cause of Enlightenment were almost all located outside the Bourbon realm. A "fertile crescent of printing houses . . . arched around

France from Amsterdam to Avignon." These firms did not merely supply books and journals to French book dealers and readers. They also offered publication outlets to French writers. The clandestine traffic went in two directions: while bales of books were being smuggled into France (in a manner carefully researched and brilliantly described by Robert Darnton), manuscripts were also being smuggled out of France. This second aspect tends to be relatively neglected, perhaps partly because some transactions were so covert that they left few records behind. Yet "the flight of French manuscripts" abroad was by no means a minor or insignificant trend. During the second half of the eighteenth century, it has been estimated, one out of every two French books was published outside France. It is thus a mistake to make too much of conditions peculiar to Paris when depicting the lot of prerevolutionary French men of letters. The provincials who flocked to the great city did not all end as "prisoners" trapped in a Grub Street that "had no exit." Foreign firms offered a wide range of job opportunities to writers who had good command of French. . . .

Amsterdam was the central city of the eighteenth-century French-language press, but other Dutch towns such as Rotterdam, Leiden, Utrecht, and the Hague continued to attract considerable business. It should be noted that Dutch authorities did not exhibit the same liberality toward Dutch-language publications intended for home markets as they did toward French work aimed at an export trade. The same point applies to Swiss authorities.

This brings me to an often neglected distinction that needs to be drawn between the privileged printers who served domestic markets under official supervision and the more freewheeling entrepreneurs who aimed at foreign markets. Most histories of early printing adopt the framework supplied by nineteenth-century nation-states and structure their narratives to take up in successive chapters German printing, Italian printing, French printing, English printing, Spanish printing, and so forth. But some of the most interesting developments fall outside these categories. They occurred under the aegis of merchant publishers who took advantage of late medieval political fragmentation to extend far-flung trade networks from the shelter supplied by numerous petty principalities, relatively autonomous city-states, republics, bishoprics, and walled towns. It is not in the major political centers such as Paris, Madrid, Vienna, Berlin, Rome, and London, but rather in commercial centers and quasi-autonomous "free cities" like Venice, Lyon, Strasbourg, Basel, Antwerp, and Frankfurt that one will find early print culture flourishing, so to speak, in its native habitat. And there also are located the printing shops that served as the earliest seedplots for Enlightenment thought.

Many of the elements that later entered into the outlook of the philosophes were already present in embryonic form in certain celebrated sixteenth-century printing houses. A recent study entitled *The Cosmopolitan Ideal in Enlightenment Thought* commences by discussing the eighteenth-century Grand Tour. But the cosmopolitan ideal described in that book was already well articulated by the master printers and merchant publishers who served the Commonwealth of Learning during the religious wars. Indeed Cosmopolis may be found (along with Utopia, Eleuthera, Philadelphia, and Irenopolis) among the false addresses used by sixteenth-century printers.

This tendency toward cosmopolitanism was based, in part, on needs that enterprising master printers shared with other wholesale merchants and early capitalists, namely the securing of credit and trade outlets in diverse regions. But there was also a special need, peculiar to the new occupational culture, for foreign scholars to serve as translators, editors, and correctors. In these capacities, emigrés and refugees, even schismatics and infidels (such as Greeks and Jews), might be given room and board for weeks on end, becoming part of their employers' extended family households. Domestic peace thus hinged on toleration of diverse views. As the mention of Greeks and Jews suggests, heterodoxy often accompanied cosmopolitanism. . . .

Advantages accrued to those who were neither orthodox Catholic nor zealous Calvinist but willing to serve either creed when the chance arose. As a result they are often portrayed as cynical opportunists who took only Mammon as their God. Yet an absence of genuine piety should not be assumed. To fight over dogma was not simply unprofitable; in some circles it was viewed as unchristian as well. Whether they were God-fearing or not, these seemingly opportunistic publishers were among the first men of substance in many European towns to sponsor an irenic, tolerant, and ecumenical approach to Christian dogma. . . .

It seems to me little wonder that a conspiratorial hypothesis developed around the victory of Enlightenment in France, not only because a foreign, largely Protestant, book trade played such a significant role but also because the spread of printing shops entailed double-dealing of so many different kinds. Voltaire once complained that he was forced to lie and then punished because he didn't lie enough. But it is difficult to imagine lying more than Voltaire did. His correspondence with Marc-Michel Rey is incredibly duplicitous. He used more than two hundred pseudonyms and denied authorship of almost every work he wrote.

The conspiratorial thesis, however, goes beyond merely demonstrating that men of letters, publishers, printers, and engravers engaged in clandestine operations and often acted in bad faith. It coordinates all forms of double-dealing and points them all to the one goal of bringing down the Old Regime. The philosophes are thus equated with those old-fashioned plotters who contrived to assassinate a ruler or put a usurper on the throne. Here as elsewhere, inadequate allowance is made for the effects of a new medium that no one group controlled or fully understood.

Authors are often surprised by what is read into their works, and a wide margin for uncertainty has to be left when speculating about what goes on in the minds of other readers. The conspiratorial thesis leaves no room for uncertainty. It fails to allow for the distance between author and public that was produced by print. Instead men of letters are endowed with power to manipulate the minds of readers and to know in advance how the latter will react.

It seems foolish to thus endow eighteenth-century men of letters with superhuman powers. But it is equally mistaken to cast them as mere hired hands who must serve every cause save their own. The French philosophes were not ghostwriters for bourgeois interests, nor were they disembodied spirits who have to be materialized to be believed. Together with their editors, booksellers, and publishers, they formed a relatively autonomous pressure group and used an expanding communications network for ends of their own. As I have tried to suggest in this paper, to understand their interests and aspirations and some of the basic postulates of their thought, we need to supplement study of institutions within *ancien régime* France with a closer look at a long-lived, cosmopolitan printed book trade and especially at a Francophone press that cut across so many traditional frontiers. . . .

Dena Goodman

Enlightenment Salons: The Convergence of Female and Philosophic Ambitions

1. The Enlightenment Republic of Letters

A republic of letters in any age is a community of discourse and in discourse. The Republic of Letters of the French Enlightenment was a highly developed community of discourse based on a network of intellectual exchanges centered in the salons of Paris. In the 1760s, the cosmopolitan Republic of Letters that went back as far as the *Respublica Litterarum* of Erasmus and his contemporaries was taking shape in Paris as a community of discourse that took itself seriously in new ways. For the philosophes of the French Enlightenment, both the political and the literary dimensions of their citizenship in this republic were crucial to their self-conception. This new sense of community and of collective purpose was shaped by the collective experience of making an *Encyclopedia* whose purpose, according to its editor, was "to change the common way of thinking." The success of the Enlightenment as a project to change the common way of thinking depended upon the expansion of the Republic of Letters beyond a small elite. It required a more permanent institutional base than the *Encyclopedia*, as a single project, could afford, one that would continue to promote and support an expanding Republic of Letters. This meant a social base and network of communications that was broader, deeper, and more institutionalized than the *Encyclopedia*; one that was regular and which could expand as the Republic of Letters itself expanded with the spread of Enlightenment. The philosophes found their institutional base in the Parisian salon. . . .

Dena Goodman, "Enlightenment Salons: The Convergence of Female and Philosophic Ambitions," *Eighteenth-Century Studies* 22 (Spring 1989): 329–340. Copyright © American Society for Eighteenth-Century Studies. Reprinted with permission of The Johns Hopkins University Press.

The cosmopolitan basis and higher ideals of the old Republic of Letters gave this new, French one, the independent ground from which to criticize the monarchy; a republic in name, it was already a formal challenge to both the monarchy and the aristocracy that supported it socially. What it needed was a continuing, regular, institutional base in order to establish itself in the real, social, and political world. For the Republic of Letters to become the place from which France would be transformed socially and politically, it had to be more than an ideal republic, more than the conceptual space in which to live the life of the mind. It also had to be independent in a way that the old Republic of Letters, based in royal academies, could not be.

By the 1760s, the Parisian salons, already at the center of Parisian social and intellectual life, had become centers of Enlightenment. Seventeenth-century women had created the salon as an undifferentiated social space that valued ideas and fostered discussion of them. The seventeenth-century salon was the very symbol of urbanity that challenged the closed court and courtly ideals as they were being glorified and exploited by Louis XIV at Versailles. The challenge was not to nobility itself or even to the monarchy's cooptation of it, but to birth as the basis of nobility. These salons and the women who led them actively asserted the idea that nobility could be acquired, and that the salonnières were instrumental in helping the initiate to do so.

In the eighteenth century, under the guidance of Mme Geoffrin, Mlle de Lespinasse, and Mme Necker, the salon was transformed from a noble, leisure institution into an institution of Enlightenment. In the salons, nobles and non-nobles were brought together on a footing of equality. "The *politesse* of an equality founded on the value of the person was imposed little by little against the ritual of hierarchies," writes Jürgen Habermas. The salon became an institution of Enlightenment not only by embodying a new set of values, but by using those values to shape a serious working space for the women who led them and for the men who frequented them, engaged together in the project of Enlightenment.

. . . To understand their project of Enlightenment requires an understanding of how eighteenth-century salon women transformed a noble, leisure form of social gathering into a serious working space, and in so doing created the ground on which such a collective project could be carried out.

2.   The Salon in the Eighteenth Century

Why did women form salons? Not, I think, because they sought fame and power through their association with brilliant and powerful men. This is the sort of explanation that assumes the centrality of men in understanding the actions of women. It is what the men who frequented the salons thought and what historians of the salon have continued to write. It is embedded in all the books on the salons that are little more than collections of anecdotes and *bon mots* of these same brilliant and powerful men. Abbé Morellet, for example, in his praise of Mme Geoffrin, wrote that her purpose in forming a salon was to achieve celebrity by "procuring the means to serve men of letters and artists, to whom her ambition was to be useful in bringing them together with men of power and position." While Mme Geoffrin did aim to be useful, just as it is clear that she did achieve celebrity through doing so, the noble "service ideal," so often attributed to women, does not provide a satisfactory explanation of her actions. Fame and glory were dubious goals for a woman such as Mme Geoffrin, who would have had a hard time aspiring to these virtues of the old male nobility. Fame and glory were the by-products of more complex and individual ambitions at a time when, according to Elisabeth Badinter, ambition itself was a dubious quality in a woman. Rather than social climbers, the salonnières of the Enlightenment must be viewed as intelligent, self-educated, and educating women who reshaped the social forms of their day to their own social, intellectual, and educational needs. The initial and primary purpose behind salons was to satisfy the self-determined educational needs of the women who started them.

In an age when women did not have or aspire to careers, the salon was just that: a career based on a long apprenticeship and careful study, resulting in the independence of a mastership. It was a career open to talents, but also one which required significant capital both to launch and support it. Unlike the men who shaped themselves and made their mark in the world through careers, the salonnière reaped no material rewards from her labor. Hers was a career, but it provided no income and its economic side was pure outlay.

The women who led the Parisian salons always apprenticed in an established salon before breaking out on their own. The primary relationship that underlay the salon as a continuing social institution was thus between female mentors and students, rather than between a single woman and a group of men. Such is the case of Mme du Deffand who, in her youth, according to one observer, practically lived at the private court of Sceaux dominated by the Duchesse de Maine. Mme Geoffrin, the most important of eighteenth-century salonnières, frequented the salon of Mme de Tencin for almost twenty years. Only at the older woman's death in 1749 did she formalize her own salon. Mme Necker, in turn, "studied" under Mme Geoffrin, and Julie de Lespinasse, who served as Mme du Deffand's companion for twelve years, also dined regularly at Mme Geoffrin's.

I can only suggest here the variety and complexity of motivations that might explain why particular women in the eighteenth century established salons. Mme de Lambert, for example, sought to provide for herself a social space and time free from gambling, which had taken on epidemic proportions by the early years of the century. As an alternative to this form of social life, she regularly invited a wide assortment of men and women to her home, where they were enjoined to "speak to one another reasonably and even wittily, when the occasion merited."

A different sort of motivation must be ascribed to Mme Geoffrin, who was moving in the opposite direction when she attended Mme de Tencin's salon and eventually established her own. Whereas Mme de Lambert was trying to upgrade a social life characterized by dissipation, Mme Geoffrin made a daring step for a devout girl when, at the age of eighteen, but already a wife and mother, she began to frequent the afternoon gatherings at the home of Mme de Tencin. For Mme de Tencin's reputation featured a youthful escape from a convent and forced vows, and the production of an illegitimate child who grew up to be the philosophe, d'Alembert. By the time she moved into Mme Geoffrin's neighborhood in 1730, Mme de Tencin was considerably more sober, but still dazzling to a young girl who had been raised by her grandmother and married off at fourteen to a man literally five times her age. However, the enticement of Mme de Tencin's salon for this girl was not the titillation of the older woman's past, but the stimulation of her present intellectual company: men such as Fontenelle, Marivaux, and Montesquieu. For Mme Geoffrin was not only young and devout, she was also ignorant. As she wrote later to Catherine the Great of the grandmother who had raised her: "She was so happy with her lot that she regarded knowledge as superfluous for a woman. She said: 'I've gotten along so well that I've never felt the need for it.'" Following these principles, Mme Chemineau taught her granddaughter to read but not to write, trusted her to neither a convent nor a tutor, and personally gave her an education that was for the most part religious.

Two years after her grandmother's death, Mme Geoffrin began her own course of studies with the men who gathered at the home of Mme de Tencin, a course which she continued for the rest of her life. For Mme Geoffrin, the salon was a socially acceptable substitute for a formal education denied her not just by her grandmother, but more generally by a society that agreed with Mme Chemineau's position. Years later, Mme de Genlis wrote that as a child she had had the opportunity to attend regularly her brother's Latin lessons for seven months, but when he went back to school and she asked to continue the lessons herself, her mother said no. The problem was not simply that parents did not want to educate their female children, but that there were not even institutions available in which to do so. The convents to which young girls were often sent performed primarily a social and moral function, and only secondarily a pedagogical one. Mme du Châtelet's father had had to provide her with a battery of tutors in the early years of the century, and fifty years later Diderot was struggling to do the same on a much more limited budget for his daughter, Angélique.

. . . It was a talent for and dedication to organization that not only made salonnières successful at what they did, but made of their joint creation a structured institution of Enlightenment. Abbé Morellet wrote of Mme Geoffrin that the regularity of her life contributed significantly to her ability to attract guests. Like Mme du Deffand and Julie de Lespinasse, she was always at home at the hours set aside for regular social gatherings and she travelled rarely, in contrast to the almost frenetic movement that characterized her contemporaries, of whom Mme de Genlis was more typical. But this regularity was part of a greater sense of organization that defined all aspects of Mme Geoffrin's life and every hour of her day, from a 5 a.m. rising, through a morning of domestic duties, letterwriting, and errands, to the afternoons she devoted twice a week to her salon. For twelve years, Julie de Lespinasse was home every evening from five until nine o'clock to receive.

Mme Necker has left evidence of her preparations for the gatherings she planned. The Chevalier de Chastellux is said to have once leafed through a notebook in which she had written: "Preparation for today's dinner: I will speak to the Chevalier de Chastellux about [his books] *Félicité publique* and *Agathe*, to Mme d'Angiviller about love." She had also noted her intention to start a literary discussion between Marmontel and the Comte de Guibert. The development of such an agenda is not surprising in a woman who wrote in her journal: "One must take care of one's cleaning, one's toilette, and above all the maintenance of order in one's domestic interior before going into society; but once one is in the world, one must not think about all these little things, nor let them penetrate that which occupies one." And in contrast to Mme Geoffrin's grandmother, who believed that conversation could be a substitute for learning in a world where women could and should get along on wit rather than knowledge, Mme Necker prepared herself thoroughly for her weekly performances. "One is most ready for conversation when one has written and thought about things before going into society," she wrote in her journal.

In case there can be any doubt as to the seriousness with which these women took themselves, here again is Mme Necker: "[Catherine the Great] never had a taste for pleasure, and this characteristic was one of the causes of her greatness; it is the taste for pleasure which undermines the consideration of all women." In one way or another, all these women, from Mme de Lambert to Mme Necker, were trying to establish centers of seriousness in a society and an age generally characterized, then and now, as frivolous and licentious. Furthermore, it was a society characterized in this way because of the perceived dominance of salon women. Jacques-Joseph Duguet wrote of women in the seventeenth century:

> *Gradually, the court, where they have power, as serious as it may have been originally, degenerates into a court full of amusements, pleasures, frivolous occupations. Luxury, revelry, gambling, love, and all the consequences of these passions reign there. The city soon imitates the court; and the province soon follows these pernicious examples. Thus, the entire nation, formerly full of courage, grows soft and becomes effeminate, and the love of pleasure and money succeeds that of virtue.*

And in the eighteenth century Jean-Jacques Rousseau expressed the same fears in his *Letter to d'Alembert on the Theatre*. Again, it is pleasure and its identification with salon women that Rousseau sees as the basis of corruption in society. In the salons, men try to please women, and in so doing they become womanish, effeminate. "Unable to make themselves into men, the women make us into women," Rousseau complained. The result was a corrupt society that contrasted with the serious, virtuous, male societies of Sparta and Geneva.

. . . Rousseau, who was increasingly alienated from the philosophes, remained out of step here as well. It is not coincidental that his most violent attack on salons and salonnières appears in a public letter to d'Alembert, editor of the *Encyclopedia* and leading citizen of the Republic of Letters that was developing in the salons.

Each for her own reasons, Mme Geoffrin, Mlle de Lespinasse, and Mme Necker gathered around them people willing and eager to socialize in a serious fashion, and set up regular, structured occasions for doing so. It was the seriousness and regularity of these salons that distinguished them from seventeenth-century salons and other social gatherings of their own time, not their lightness. Abbé Galiani thought often about the difference between these Parisian salons and the gatherings available to him in Naples. In 1771 he wrote to Mme d'Epinay, thanking her for a manuscript she had sent him and noting that he would present it on one of the "Fridays" when he met with friends who were trying to recreate their Parisian experience. "But our Fridays are becoming Neopolitan Fridays," he wrote, "and are getting farther away from the character and tone of those of France, despite all [our] efforts. . . . There is no way to make Naples resemble Paris unless we find a woman to guide us, organize us, *Geoffrinise* us."

3.   From Education to Enlightenment: Enter the Philosophes

In using the social gathering and transforming it to meet their own needs, Mme Geoffrin and salonnières like her created a certain kind of social and intellectual space that could be exploited by the expanding group of intellectuals who were beginning to call themselves "philosophes." As Raymond Picard has written:

> There was forming, little by little in France, a "Republic of Letters," which had its own laws and unwritten customs, its loyal citizens and its international alliances . . . It was in the salons, the circles, and also the cafés where the vogue began, that this Republic held its sessions, where its members met in order to unite or at times to oppose one another, but to create, above their quarrels or their differences, passing or durable, a true esprit de corps and to assure the dominance of thought in society.

The salon offered the philosophes a social space that valued ideas and fostered discussion of them. Whereas other social gatherings were organized around the goal of passing time, Enlightenment salons were never conceived of as a means simply to while away the hours. They were to be useful to those who directed and attended them, and, eventually, to the society at large beyond them. Like the philosophes they gathered around them, the salonnières were practical people who kept busy at tasks they considered productive and useful. Pleasant as salon gatherings certainly were, they were not mere leisure activities created to while away the hours or as relaxation from serious work or business. The relationship between work and leisure which marks our twentieth-century existence cannot be written back into this eighteenth-century world without misrepresenting it. Under the Old Regime, work and leisure were dominant activities of distinct social groups.

What the eighteenth-century salonnières did was to transform a noble and thus leisure form of social gathering into a serious working space. They did this by regularizing such gatherings, and by encouraging and organizing the intellectual activity that took place in them. Most importantly, they redefined such activity from pastime to work. They no longer conceived of intellectual activity as games to amuse them, but as work to instruct them.

In addition to sponsoring serious and productive intellectual activity, the salons were also crucial in establishing an undifferentiated social space in which such activity could take place. What distinguished salons from courts and the dominant society they represented was not only their conception of intellectual activity as useful work, but also the mixing of ranks and orders, the absence of hierarchy and marks of social distinction that took place in them. The kind of conversation fostered in the salons depended upon a recognized equality among the speakers which allowed for the very activity of criticism and judgment that characterized their speech. This breaking down of social barriers for the facilitation of discourse was conducive both to the expansion of Parisian intellectual life and to the development of an ideology reflecting it. As Habermas writes of the new institutions of the café in England and the salon in France between the Regency and the Revolution: "They were centers where criticism developed, first of a literary order, then of a political order later on, and which started to promote a sort of equality among cultivated people, putting on the same footing aristocratic society and certain bourgeois intellectuals."

The philosophes' understanding both of intellectual activity and of progress as the collective action of equals, evident in their adoption of a Baconian scientific method and in their creation of the *Encyclopedia* based on it, found a social base in these salons. For they provided a regular meeting place and center of intellectual exchanges upon which such collective activity could grow. A significant development in epistemology and in intellectual history more generally here intersects the social and institutional development of the salon. Each strengthened the other as they became two complementary aspects of the project of Enlightenment that gained strength through this union in the 1760s and '70s.

The philosophes captured the salons from the aristocracy, "liberating themselves from the authority of their noble hosts," according to Habermas, "and reaching that autonomy which would transform conversation into criticism and *bon mots* into arguments."

With this capture of the salons in a period of growing collaboration, the philosophes created for themselves a social base which facilitated their work and made possible its expansion. This development was in no way extrinsic to the intellectual activity of the Enlightenment when it is understood as a collective project, rather than as a collection of texts. For a collective project of Enlightenment, the salons were not simply diversions; nor were the women who ran them simply an audience whose social demands undermined the seriousness of male work. What the salons provided the philosophes was a serious social environment that established a structure for their discourse: a structure that, although it did have limits, was highly elastic and allowed for the growth of speakers and of speech. And because intrinsic to the project of Enlightenment was the expansion of the audience, the creation of an enlightened public, the composition of salon society, and especially the inclusion of women in it, made it a model for that general public that was to be enlightened even as it was created. As Habermas argues, the public constituted itself in the eighteenth century from these circles of interlocutors, considering itself simply as an extension of that core which set the tone for the public at large.

By the 1760s, the philosophes not only dominated the guest lists of the major salons, but had even begun their own. In 1764, d'Alembert and his friends took advantage of a break between Mme du Deffand and Julie de Lespinasse to start their own salon. Here it was not the philosophes who served the ends of the salonnière, but the salonnière who was selected to fulfill a necessary function for the philosophes. Viewed in this way, Julie de Lespinasse's salon was a parody of a Parisian salon, and she a parody of a salonnière, a woman formed by men. As she herself wrote: "Look at what an education I've received"; and as she named the regular guests of Mme du Deffand she added: "Voilà the men who have taught me to speak, to think, and who have deigned to think of me as somebody." Formed entirely in the salon, Julie de Lespinasse was a philosophic by-product of other women's aspirations, perfectly suited to serve the men who now realized the need for female direction, as a previous generation of women had realized an equally important need for male learning. The salon of Julie de Lespinasse met all the formal requirements of that new institution, but it did so with the even newer collective aims and purposes of the philosophes, rather than with the older individual ones of the salonnières. Perhaps this is why Julie de Lespinasse, whose life had never been happy, did not find happiness or fulfillment even in her own salon. As her letters to the Comte de Guibert reveal, she led a double life: a public life in the salon that was empty, and a private one in her love letters that was meant to but could not fill this emotional void.

In setting up Julie de Lespinasse's salon, the philosophes were both acknowledging the salon itself as an important institution of Enlightenment and identifying the functions of the salon that could be put into the service of Enlightenment. Even as new salons were opened by women to serve their own needs, they became additional centers of the growing Enlightenment Republic of Letters. The activities carried out in salons merged with the social and intellectual activity of Enlightenment. The ambitions of female salonnières and male philosophes came together in the daily life of the Parisian salons. To complete our understanding of Enlightenment salons, I would now like to turn from the aims of the salonnières to the functions the salon came to serve for the Republic of Letters and the project of Enlightenment in which its members were engaged.

First, the salon served as a central clearing house for news, information, ideas, discourse broadly understood; as a communications center, into and out of which discourse (and thus Enlightenment, as a function of discourse) flowed. Secondly, it was a space for people to make contact, to meet each other, to come to know one another; where they could join together for common purposes, conceive and collaborate on common projects; a space where new people could be introduced, brought in; an expanding space for an expanding Republic. Third, it provided a model for French society as a whole, a model on the basis of which that greater society could be transformed. The common thread which runs through all these functions, which weaves together salonnières, philosophes, and the public they sought to shape and serve, is the epistolary exchange. If salons were the heart of the Enlightenment, letters circulated through them like its life blood. . . .

Michael R. Lynn

Enlightenment in the Public Sphere: The Musée de Monsieur and Scientific Culture in Late-Eighteenth-Century Paris

Eighteenth-century Parisians witnessed the creation of numerous social and cultural institutions, all competing for their attention, patronage, and financial support. Many of these organizations sought to attract members by facilitating access to the Enlightenment and acting as centers for the dissemination of useful knowledge. In the last decades of the eighteenth century one type of club, usually called *musées* or *lycées*, particularly captured the imagination of numerous Parisians. Incorporating a mixture of institutional styles, *musées* quickly entered into the late-eighteenth-century cultural milieu and won the approval of the public. In the years before the French Revolution, at least ten *musées* were established in Paris alone, all specifically formulated to provide their members an entrance into the Republic of Letters. In a description of the Musée de Monsieur, one observer claimed that it was "the idea of giving, in a way, to each mind a nourishment which is appropriate to it, through encouraging all preferences, and of obtaining an open worship of the sciences and the arts, that has given birth to the project of this *musée* dedicated to public utility." Usually organized by a single individual, the *musées* provided a concrete location for a variety of activities and, for a price, allowed members access to lectures, libraries, and laboratories. Courses, based on similar classes already offered throughout Paris, usually provided the main focus and gave subscribers the chance to watch and engage in Enlightenment undertakings rather than just read about them. . . .

Michael R. Lynn, "Enlightenment in the Public Sphere: The Musée de Monsieur and Scientific Culture in Late-Eighteenth-Century Paris," *Eighteenth-Century Studies* 32 (1999): 463–472. Copyright © American Society for Eighteenth-Century Studies. Reprinted with permission of The Johns Hopkins University Press.

I

The *musées* developed within the burgeoning public sphere of late eighteenth-century France. Jürgen Habermas's concept of a bourgeois public sphere has become the focus of many recent efforts to understand both the nature of politics and sociability in the decades before the French Revolution and the activities of groups and individuals in the creation and dissemination of public culture. The place of natural philosophy in the public sphere, however, has largely been ignored, despite the fact that the philosophes themselves assigned it such a key role in defining their efforts. Scientific activities also occupied a central place in the popular understanding of the Enlightenment and furnished the most spectacular and public demonstrations of the power of ideas. The impact of ballooning alone, first developed in 1783, gave the citizens of the French capital an extremely stunning and public view of the enormous potential of natural philosophy and the nearly miraculous results that stemmed from its pursuit. Balloons, however, were only the grand finale of a much longer love affair between the Parisian public and the sciences. . . . The importance of the *musées* derives in part from the work of their founders in repackaging and commodifying scientific knowledge, an effort that led to the formation of a popular scientific culture and contributed to the general commerce in Enlightenment ideas. . . .

The traffic in information and ideas attracted many people either seeking to learn something of value or, sometimes, just looking to occupy their leisure time in an entertaining but useful fashion. Located firmly in the public sphere, *musées* fulfilled just such a role by creating a center for the exchange of ideas. Culture, in the context of the late eighteenth century, had come to be something of a commodity. It was bought, sold, and traded in the form of popular periodicals, subscription fees, the cost of public lectures, the price of the cup of coffee you had to buy to join in the conversation or read the newspapers at your local café. Scientific cultural capital could take several forms, including the purchase of material objects, but could also, on the other hand, be a slightly more immaterial culture and come in the form of knowledge acquisition. The commercial trade in ideas held a significant place in eighteenth-century Paris as a familiarity with scientific language, methods, goals, and discoveries became a necessary and significant part of popular culture. In all of this, the *musées* performed an important function as purveyors of knowledge.

II

Musées gained notoriety by fusing together the best aspects of other eighteenth-century institutions. The first such club was the Salon de la Correspondance established in 1777 by Claude-Mammès Pahin de la Blancherie, an enterprising young man seeking to make his mark in the Republic of Letters. He designed his club to act as a place where individuals in Paris could get together to discuss new ideas and trends in the arts and sciences. La Blancherie also edited a journal, the *Nouvelles de la République des Lettres et des Arts*, that purported to relate all of the latest news from the Republic of Letters. The Salon de la Correspondance met on a weekly basis and its activities were reported in the journal. Generally, men gathered on Wednesday mornings in La Blancherie's main office to view and discuss objects contributed by artists and savants. The articles on display, frequently contributed by less well-known individuals and usually for sale, included such items as the following: a microscope created by the optician Dellebarre and approved by the Académie Royale des Sciences; an electrical machine constructed by Girardin, a manufacturer of scientific instruments; and a weather prediction device called the "Forecaster," developed by an unnamed savant but available for purchase at Jacques Bianchi's scientific instrument shop. Partially due to its attention to science, Pahin de la Blancherie's assembly earned an endorsement from the Académie Royale des Sciences. The format of this *musée* most closely resembled that of the salons. But, instead of *salonnières* guiding the ebb and flow of the conversation, individuals gathered around a specific object that provided the focus for the ensuing discussion. Participation required both some knowledge about science, or at least an ability to speak generally about things scientific, and an awareness of the rules for polite conversation. In fact, for some individuals, the Salon de la Correspondance operated too much like a salon since it tended to be dominated by rules of politeness and sociability and not necessarily by scientific skill or merit.

Another option appeared in 1780 when Antoine Court de Gébelin founded the Musée de Paris, a club that drew more inspiration from the academy model than from salons. He wanted a space below the academies but above the informal structure of public lecture courses. The Musée de Paris garnered some early praise, although its reputation suffered irreparably when an internal schism formed over its direction. Before the division, however, Court de Gébelin worked hard to create a forum where savants and amateurs could meet and share ideas. The hope was that the Musée de Paris, "by protecting itself from the epidemic of *bel esprit*, from scientific jargon, [and] the ranting and pompously soporific style" of other such clubs, would merit the approval of the nation and of the enlightened public. The usual format involved savants reading papers on a variety of subjects to a general audience. Court de Gébelin then published these memoirs in the annual *Mémoires du Musée de Paris*, in obvious imitation of the *Mémoires de l'Académie Royale des Sciences*. One issue of the memoirs included a poem praising Jean-François Pilâtre de Rozier for making the first voyage in a hot air balloon, an ode to electricity, and a lengthy treatise on the nature of fire.

Dissatisfaction with these early efforts led some later *musée* organizers to construct a space with a more specific audience or goal in mind. For example, the Lycée des Femmes opened its doors with the express hope of instructing women, who were frequently excluded from earlier *musées*, on the importance and usefulness of the sciences and the arts. The members of this *lycée* could attend, for example, a course in mathematics and experimental physics that met for two hours twice each week. Another alternative appeared when baroness Duplessy established the Musée des Dames in order to facilitate the dissemination of all the knowledge that she felt was suitable for ladies. The lectures there concerned many different topics with the sciences holding an important place. In particular, Duplessy thought that the members would profit from classes in experimental physics, a science well suited to amuse and instruct the members as long as the instructors avoided rehashing the ridiculous dispute between Newtonian attraction and Cartesian vortices.

In general, *musée* membership grew to encompass a large and varied audience drawn from a fairly broad spectrum of men and women ranging from the nobility to the lower middle classes. Membership usually required only the sponsorship of individuals who were already members and the payment of an annual fee that varied from as little as fifteen livres to as much as several hundred livres. Although complete lists are not available, the largest club, the Musée de Monsieur, at one time had more than seven hundred members while the Salon de la Correspondance boasted a membership of more than three hundred people and a subscription list for its journal of more than five hundred. Although membership figures for the Musée de Paris are unavailable, its seven-hundred-seat meeting hall suggests a substantial size. An overall membership for *musées* in late-eighteenth-century Paris probably reached as high as several thousand individuals, including men and, in some cases, women from a variety of social levels, economic circumstances, and educational backgrounds.

III

Both La Blancherie and Court de Gébelin had already established their societies when Jean-François Pilâtre de Rozier's Musée de Monsieur joined the fray. In the end, it proved to be the most popular such institution, especially for the dissemination of natural philosophy, thanks largely to Pilâtre de Rozier's ability to bring elite and amateur savants together with men and women from the noble and middling classes. Pilâtre de Rozier founded his *musée* in 1781 under the auspices of the count and countess of Provence, after whom he wisely named it. He led it under this name until his death in 1785; from 1785 to 1793 it was known simply as the Lycée and was operated by a consortium of rich individuals who had purchased the bulk of Pilâtre de Rozier's estate and donated it back to the club. . . .

Pilâtre de Rozier attempted to address several interrelated goals centered on the study of natural philosophy and a knowledge of the arts. In particular, he wanted the Musée de Monsieur to satisfy "the taste of the French people for the sciences." It was the nation, Pilâtre de Rozier claimed, that would receive the inestimable advantages of the Musée de Monsieur. Specifically, those advantages were threefold. First, the *musée* acted as an educational center for the dissemination of current scientific ideas. The intent, claimed the prospectus for 1788, was to instill a desire for self instruction. To this end, the Musée de Monsieur employed a wide variety of pedagogical methods designed to fit the individual needs of its members. Primarily, it offered a number of classes throughout the year. Courses in the sciences were available nearly every day and the total number of options increased almost yearly during the 1780s. The broad range of topics addressed by the professors provided a nearly encyclopedic coverage of the sciences and arts. In 1788, for example, a member could attend lectures on chemistry, natural history, and botany by Antoine François Fourcroy; mathematics and experimental physics by Antoine Deparcieux; theoretical physics by Gaspard Monge; anatomy and physiology by Jean-Joseph Süe; literature by Jean François de la Harpe; history by Jean-François Marmontel and Dominique-Joseph Garat; and other classes in English and Spanish. Many of these professors had offered versions of their courses to the general public in the years before the organization of the *musée*.

For members looking for more personalized instruction, other options were available. Two *cabinets de physique*, stocked with all of the latest machines and instruments, were set up so that individuals could perform or watch experiments. Members could duplicate the demonstrations they had witnessed or read about, an endeavor that helped create a sense of individual involvement in the Enlightenment enterprise. If they were not interested in performing experiments, members could always read about some other savant's scientific exploits in a library containing more than eleven hundred titles. Natural philosophy occupied a big place here, and works by both elite and midlevel savants could be found on the shelves. . . .

The second advantage of membership in the Musée de Monsieur centered on the practical value of that institution. Emphasis fell on the utility of knowledge and the desire to impart worthwhile information for savants, amateurs, and artisans. Pilâtre de Rozier hoped that in addition to instilling members with a taste for the sciences, his *musée* would concretely and specifically help individuals in the mechanical arts, sciences, and commerce. In theory, only the most interesting and most useful aspects of eighteenth-century thought were presented for the appropriation of the public. A course in mathematics, offered by Condorcet, provides a case in point. In his introductory remarks to the class he claimed that the object of the Musée de Monsieur was to allow people "the possibility of using the parts of the sciences which are of the most immediate utility to them, and to make them understand simple but certain principles which preserve them from the errors into which their own imagination or the prestige of charlatans might make them fall." Condorcet felt that the courses given at the Musée de Monsieur enabled individuals to understand the true fundamentals of the sciences, prevented them from proposing ridiculous ideas or mispronouncing scientific words, and allowed them to avoid being duped by fanciful systems composed of unintelligible and vague principles. Ultimately, claimed Condorcet, it was the utility of the knowledge available in the *musées* that made them such an invaluable resource for Parisians. This idea, that the Musée de Monsieur was devoted to public utility, echoed throughout most contemporary descriptions of its role in society and created a specific link between the work of the *musées* and the general goals of the Enlightenment.

The third advantage offered to members was an easy access to a vast array of amusing and entertaining demonstrations and displays. Not everybody who joined the *musée* sought to improve herself or himself or, more precisely, not all learning needed to be dry or dull. On the contrary, from what we know of the lectures given at the Musée de Monsieur, it would seem that several of the instructors drew heavily on the combination of utility and spectacle prominent in the pedagogical methodology of public lecture courses. Pilâtre de Rozier himself utilized overtly theatrical methods to attract and hold the attention of his audience. Perhaps most spectacular was his demonstration of the volatile nature of hydrogen by inhaling some and then blowing it out through a tube over a candle flame. The resulting fireball immediately captured the attention and the imagination of everybody in the room. . . .

This leads us to ask the question of who exactly was in the room? Who constituted this scientific public sphere? By combining scientific ideas with popular theatrics and by drawing on salons, academies, and public courses as models for his *musée*, Pilâtre de Rozier enabled his new institution to attract an extraordinarily diverse group of people. To begin with, Pilâtre de Rozier managed to entice many social and scientific elites to his club, some of whom counted among the most famous and important people of the late eighteenth century. The list of noble sponsors included Louis XVI and Marie-Antoinette, the count and countess of Provence, and the duke of Chartres. Members from among the scientific elite included academicians like Félix Vicq-d'Azyr, Süe, Fourcroy, and Condorcet, all of whom occasionally taught courses as well. Pilâtre de Rozier ensured that a large number of savants would join by allowing any member of a royal academy to enroll without having to go through the formal admission process. . . .

However, the Musée de Monsieur should not be considered an elite scientific institution. Instead, it had ample room for savants from every part of the scientific spectrum. Intermixed among the nobility and the elite philosophes, for example, were several scientific popularizers who had joined without any apparent objections raised concerning their social standing or academic credentials. These popularizers included such midlevel savants as François Bienvenu, an instrument maker and public lecturer who specialized in electricity and magnets;

the abbé Guyot, author of the *Nouvelles récréations physiques et mathématiques*, a book of physics experiments and games designed to educate and entertain amateurs; Monsieur Rouland, a popular demonstrator of experimental physics in the Paris colleges; the abbé Miollan, a public lecturer and aeronaut, later run out of Paris by an angry mob after a failed balloon launch; and Charles Deslon, the most prolific and vocal of Mesmer's disciples. The only thing required of prospective members, in addition to the annual fee, was the sponsorship of three current members. Under these conditions, the popularizers gained equal admittance along with the rest of the savants. In addition to opening its doors to science popularizers, the Musée de Monsieur also encouraged nonscientists from the middling level of society to join its growing membership. Advertisements claimed that people of any age and social status could spend their leisure time agreeably and usefully by joining the Musée de Monsieur. The official regulations concurred, stating that all honest persons could enter the *musée*. In reality, all social classes did not and could not enroll in the Musée de Monsieur. If nothing else, the annual fee, set at seventy-two livres for men and thirty-six livres for women, would have excluded most urban workers from even considering the possibility. The middling sorts, however, were well represented. Lawyers, secretaries, army officers, minor government officials, architects, teachers, a banker, a law clerk, a publisher, a grocer, and several shop owners all appear in the membership lists and several of them even sat on the governing council.

Significantly, Pilâtre de Rozier singled out women as important potential members of the Musée de Monsieur. The few available figures suggest a female membership ranging from ten to twenty percent. Since women had not been able to join La Blancherie's or Court de Gébelin's *musées* as equal members, they were understandably suspicious of Pilâtre de Rozier's offer of equivalent participation. They thought that their reduced membership dues, half that required of male members, would limit their access and force them into a position where they were only supporting masculine efforts without really being able to share actively in the advantages of the Musée de Monsieur. However, the reduced subscription fee for women was not uncommon for public lecture courses, on which Pilâtre de Rozier based the structure of his *musée*, and he was really just continuing a fairly typical practice among popularizers. To assuage the fears of women, Pilâtre de Rozier sent an open letter to the editors of the *Journal de Paris* claiming that women would share identical rights and privileges with the men. The degree of participation allowed to women in the Musée de Monsieur sets it apart from other mixed gender associations and, indeed, from other *musées*. But when seen in light of public lecture courses and women's frequent and active participation in those venues, their equal acceptance in the Musée de Monsieur was somewhat typical.

IV

The *musées* offered multiple educational and entertainment opportunities for men and women from the middling and upper classes. At the same time the *musées* contributed to the creation of scientific culture by establishing a concrete location where Parisians could gain access to the most recent discoveries and learn how to apply science to their lives. The mixture of elite and middling savants, upper and middle classes fostered an environment where they could meet on a relatively equal footing to discuss current scientific trends and ideas. Individuals joined the *musée* in order to acquire the kind of scientific cultural capital that had become particularly widespread at the end of the eighteenth century. Natural philosophy was not just an exclusive and elite activity practiced by nobles and philosophes: it had become an important part of urban culture. The *musées* also embodied and made more widely accessible much of the information and many of the ideals formulated and institutionalized by the *Encyclopedia*. By taking some of the different public lecture courses available around Paris and placing them in one location, the founders of the *musées* attempted to provide their members an easy and complete entrance to the Enlightenment project in one convenient location and for one annual fee. They formalized the system of popularization into a specific public space, thus giving their members access to the pedagogical revolution that had been sweeping Paris since Jean-Antoine Nollet first started teaching popular experimental physics classes in the 1730s. Never could so much Enlightenment be attained in one location and for such a low price.

Typically, when historians talk about the connections between commerce and the Enlightenment they are referring to the production and sale of books or periodicals. The function of institutions like the *musées*, however, offers a different perspective on the commercialization of eighteenth-century culture. In the *musées*, members purchased access to the material goods of Enlightenment, including books, scientific equipment, and machines, and were given the opportunity for a more general knowledge acquisition through lectures and discussion. Information was presented in such a way as to make learning entertaining as well as useful, a combination that allowed the *musées* to be more easily marketed to a Parisian audience that did have, after all, a number of other options if they were just looking to learn something. Thus, even as *musée* founders participated in the production and dissemination of Enlightenment ideas, they also worked as businessmen whose job was to sell Enlightenment as a commodity necessary for the culturally aware Parisian. . . .

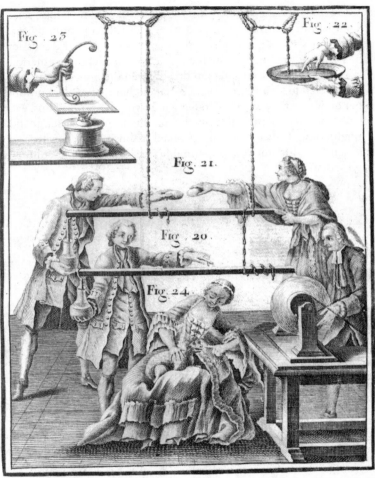

Lesson 21, plate 2, from Jean-Antoine Nollet, *Lessons in Experimental Physics*, vol. 6 (1784). The illustrations in this textbook aimed at a wide audience depict many different experiments that can be done to create electricity and demonstrate its effects. This plate shows how electrical charges can be passed from electrified metal wands through human beings or even eggs (figs. 20 and 21), and what kinds of equipment can be used to conduct electricity (figs. 22 and 23). Under especially favorable circumstances, the author notes, a woman, stroking the fur of a cat on her silk skirt, can produce an electrical spark when she touches its nose (fig. 24). Nollet's illustrated textbook encouraged readers to participate in the Enlightenment by conducting simple experiments such as these. (*University of Michigan Libraries*)

PART

IV Science and Enlightenment

According to your Cartesians, everything is done by means of an impulse that is practically incomprehensible; according to Mr. Newton it is by a kind of attraction, the reason for which is no better known.

Voltaire

While poorly instructed or badly intentioned adversaries made open war on it, philosophy sought refuge, so to speak, in the works of a few great men. *Jean le Rond d'Alembert*

We shall see that [social mathematics] is relevant to all our individual and public interests, that it can increase the precision of all our ideas and the certainty of all our knowledge, and that if it were more widespread and more widely cultivated, it would greatly enhance the welfare and progress of the human race.

Marquis de Condorcet

Against an older view that the "new science" . . . of the early and mid-eighteenth century was the underpinning of "the Enlightenment," we now have a developing perspective which points out the existence of a number of species of natural knowledge, and a number of opposed "Enlightenments." *Steven Shapin*

117

Mathematicians brought gendered connotations into the definition and legitimation of their practices, as they worked to purify enlightened mathematics from the taint of metaphysics and imprecise thinking.   *Mary Terrall*

Eighteenth-century medical thinkers sought to render their study truly scientific — or, in contemporary idiom, "philosophical" — in various ways. Observation and experiment became the watchwords of many.   *Roy Porter*

Enlightenment claims to authority were often grounded in scientific knowledge, and its expectations for progress were predicated on a new understanding of the sciences and the role of the scientist. As we have seen, Peter Gay argues that science was critical to the "recovery of nerve" that defined the Enlightenment, while Keith Baker shows that for d'Alembert, the scientist is a key figure in the reform of state and society. But if there was a reciprocal relationship between science and enlightenment—as most historians believe— what about eighteenth-century science was enlightened? What about the Enlightenment was scientific?

In the first three selections in this part, we explore the Enlightenment's own invocation of science as a fundamental and defining source of its new approach to knowledge and authority. In the selections that follow, historians weigh some of the concrete difficulties in determining the relationship between the sciences of the eighteenth century and the Enlightenment.

With their different approaches to discussing scientists, Voltaire and d'Alembert opened up a debate about the relationship between science and society that lives on today. Voltaire's whimsical accounts in *Philosophical Letters* (1734) of the lives and thought of the French philosopher René Descartes and the English scientist Isaac Newton were influential in shaping public perceptions about science and its exemplary practitioners. In the three letters included here, Voltaire contrasts the ascetic Descartes with the eccentric Newton. Just as important, he contrasts the France that Descartes was forced to flee with the open, intellectually hospitable environment of England. Voltaire's praise of Newton is thus simultaneously a critique of French society. Moreover, by disseminating popularized, simplified versions of Newton's important scientific ideas, Voltaire saw himself as providing a critical solvent against error and superstition. In his account, Newton represents the authority, reasonableness, and simplicity of science that can readily be used to undermine superstition, error, and credulity. At the same time, Voltaire subjects both science and scientists to his own corrosive wit: If the scientist is sometimes ridiculous, science, he suggests, is sometimes as much tied to fashion as to truth.

For d'Alembert, science also represents the power of reason against skepticism and superstition. D'Alembert, however, is less interested in the personalities of scientists and the social conditions of their work than in using their achievements to sketch out a historical narrative of human progress. In his "Preliminary Discourse" to the *Encyclopedia*, he proclaims the heroic character of scientists (here called "philosophers") for their contribution to the progress of human reason and society. His account reinforces the connections between philosophy, science, and truth. D'Alembert identifies a few "great men"—notably, the heroic triumvirate of Francis Bacon, Descartes, and Newton—as the foundation of a philosophy that will further the quest of the Enlightenment to make us "better or happier." The optimism so often associated with the scientific dimension of the Enlightenment lies partly in this narrative of progress. Because d'Alembert's story of progress based on advances in the sciences continues to define the narrative of the history of science to this day, a critical reading of this Enlightenment narrative provides a starting point for the formation of a more critical perspective on how we think about science and progress.

An important corollary to the narrative of progress in Enlightenment thought was the fervent hope that science could provide the means to understand not only nature, but also human beings and their society. In "A General Survey of Science" (1793), Condorcet compellingly asserts the value of applying science, and especially mathematics, to the investigation of society. The invention of the social sciences is often cited as a crucial legacy of the Enlightenment to the modern world, but Condorcet's text—written in the darkest days of the French Revolution—also raises the question of science's ability to solve social problems.

If proponents of Enlightenment were unambiguous in seeing science as both a crucial method and a guarantor of progress, the historical study of science in the Enlightenment has exposed a much muddier picture. Historians continue the debate suggested in Voltaire's and d'Alembert's different treatments of Newton: whether and to what degree scientists are best understood as remarkable individuals fully embedded in particular, concrete social contexts, as Voltaire portrayed them, or as great men central to the progress of a specific science, as d'Alembert did.

In "The Social Uses of Science," Steven Shapin surveys new research that places Newton and Newtonianism in an array of explicit social contexts so as to make a case for the fruitfulness of the "Voltairean" approach. Like Voltaire, Shapin looks to Newton—the scientist whom the philosophes almost uniformly claimed as their progenitor—for a case study of Enlightenment science in social context. Shapin cites the political and religious sources of some of Newton's fundamental theoretical positions. He also identifies English-Hanoverian foreign policy as an important source of Newton's conflict with his German rival, Gottfried Leibniz. In Shapin's account, not only was Newton's science shaped by the social issues of the day, but its positive reception was also affected by them: Newtonians and anti-Newtonians alike debated the merits of Newton's theories of matter with an eye toward what they saw as the social, political, and religious ramifications of these views. Shapin thus asks us to reconsider how scientific "progress" occurs, while also suggesting that the multiple *uses* of science define *different* Enlightenments.

If, as Shapin suggests, scientific theories and practices developed in a rich cultural context, their impact on society and culture sometimes had consequences that were—deliberately or unintentionally—at odds with other Enlightenment attitudes. Whereas Shapin notes the political and religious influences on Newton, Mary Terrall asks how gender functions in the Enlightenment construction of science. Terrall shows that arguments for a mathematical basis for science, derived from Newton and championed by such luminaries as d'Alembert and Condorcet, were also strategies for consolidating power in scientific academies. The success of this strategy, she argues, had several important consequences. First, it served to distinguish academic science from popular science. Second, it tied the Enlightenment to the state by making science useful and available to it. Third, it dissociated science from other institutions, such as the mixed-gender salon. Terrall concludes that the ascendancy of mathematics ultimately made progressive, utilitarian science masculine but left metaphysics—science in a theoretical and abstract form disparaged by the philosophes—feminine. As a result, women came to be considered less fit for science, less able to participate in the Enlightenment or to contribute to the narrative of scientific progress. Terrall thus asks us to consider the role of scientific academies as institutions of Enlightenment in relation to those we examined in "Institutions of Enlightenment," especially as they mediated between the Enlightenment and state power and promoted a gendered construction of scientific knowledge. She also anticipates the question of the relationship between women and Enlightenment, to be explored later in this volume.

If the physical sciences and mathematics provided the Enlightenment with a scientific method, medicine embodied for many the prospects for human improvement that scientific progress entailed—as it still does today. This assumed connection between medical science and Enlightenment progress leads Roy Porter to pose two fundamental questions: How did medicine, a particularly hidebound science rooted in many less than scientific practices, construe itself as both scientific and enlightened; and how did medicine contribute to the science of society, so vividly described by Condorcet? Porter documents medicine's attempts to identify with scientific progress and methods despite the problematic application of these ideals to the contested, and not notably edifying, arenas of medical practices and professional concerns. While eighteenth-century physicians applied their science to society with the optimism of Condorcet's exhortations, Porter notes that their appraisals of the diseased body did not always produce sanguine assessments of the likelihood of social improvement. If the tremendous advances of medical science in the twentieth century seem to validate the identification of medicine with science in the eighteenth century, Porter cautions us against viewing the Enlightenment through its own exaggerated claims.

Voltaire

Philosophical Letters

Letter Fourteen: On Descartes and Newton

A Frenchman arriving in London finds quite a change, in philosophy as in all else. Behind him he left the world full; here he finds it empty. In Paris one sees the universe composed of vortices of subtile matter; in London one sees nothing of the sort. With us, it's the pressure of the moon that causes the rising of the tide; with the English, it's the sea gravitating toward the moon; so that when you think the moon ought to give us high tide, these gentlemen think it ought to be low; none of which unfortunately can be verified, for in order to know the truth of it we should have had to examine the moon and the tides at the first moment of creation.

You will also notice that the sun, which in France has nothing to do with the business, over here contributes his twenty-five per cent or so. According to your Cartesians, everything is done by means of an impulse that is practically incomprehensible; according to Mr. Newton it is by a kind of attraction, the reason for which is no better known. In Paris you picture the earth as shaped like a melon; in London it is flattened on both sides. Light, for a Cartesian, exists in the air; for a Newtonian it comes here from the sun in six and a half minutes. All the operations of your chemistry are owing to acids, alkalis, and subtile matter; in England, the concept of attraction dominates even in this. . . .

This famous Newton, the destroyer of the Cartesian system, died in March of last year, 1727. In life he was honored by his countrymen, and he was buried like a king who had benefited his subjects. . . .

Descartes was born with a lively and strong imagination which made of him a man as extraordinary in his private life as in his thinking. That imagination could not be concealed even in his philosophical works, where at every moment one is struck by ingenious and sparkling comparisons. . . .

Voltaire, Letters 14, 15, and 16, in *Philosophical Letters*, trans. Ernest Dilworth (Indianapolis: Bobbs-Merrill, 1961), 60–78. Reprinted by permission of Pearson Education, Inc., Upper Saddle River, N.J.

He tried the profession of arms for a while, and afterward, having become a philosopher altogether, thought it not unworthy of himself to have a love affair. He had by his mistress a daughter named Francine, who died young, and whose loss he deeply mourned. And so he experienced all that belongs to the human lot. . . .

He left France because he followed after truth, which was persecuted there in those days by the miserable philosophy of scholasticism. . . .

The career of Sir Isaac Newton was altogether different. He lived for eighty-five years, always tranquil and happy, and held in honor in his own country. It was his great good fortune to have been born not only in a free country but in a time when, the irrelevancies of scholasticism being banished, reason alone was cultivated; and the world must needs be his pupil, not his enemy.

One curious difference between him and Descartes is that in the course of so long a life he was free from both passion and weakness. He never had intimacies with a woman; this was confirmed to me by the doctor and the surgeon in whose arms he died. One may admire Newton for it, but one should not blame Descartes.

According to public opinion in England, of these two philosophers the first was a dreamer and the other a sage.

Few people in London read Descartes, whose works, in effect, have lost their utility; hardly any read Newton either, for it takes considerable knowledge to understand him. Nevertheless, everybody talks about them, granting nothing to the Frenchman and everything to the Englishman. Some folk believe that if we are no longer satisfied with the abhorrence of vacuums, if we know that air has weight, if we use telescopes, we owe it all to Newton. Over here he is the Hercules of fable, to whom the ignorant attributed all the deeds of the other heroes. . . .

Letter Fifteen: On the System of Attraction

The discoveries of Sir Isaac Newton, which have brought him such universal fame, have to do with the system of the world, with light, with infinity in geometry, and last with chronology, which he played with for relaxation.

I will tell you (without verbiage, if I can) the little that I have been able to get hold of among all these sublime ideas.

As for the system of our world: there had long been dispute over what it is that causes all the planets to revolve, and what keeps them in their orbits, and also over what causes all bodies here below to come down to the surface of the earth.

. . . Having withdrawn in 1666 into the country near Cambridge, one day as he walked in his garden and noticed fruit falling from a tree he [Newton] drifted off into deep meditation on that problem of gravity, of which all the philosophers have so long vainly sought the cause, and in which the vulgar find nothing the slightest bit mysterious. He said to himself, "From whatever height in our hemisphere these bodies should fall, their descent would certainly be in the progression discovered by Galileo, and the distances covered by them would be as the squares of the times. This power that causes heavy bodies to go downward is the same, without any noticeable diminution, at whatever depth one may be within the earth and on the highest mountain. Why should this power not extend so far as the moon? And if it is true that it carries so far, is there not a great likelihood that this power holds it in its orbit and determines its movement? But if the moon does obey this power, whatever it may be, isn't it again very reasonable to suppose that the other planets are equally subject to it?

"If this power exists, it ought to increase (which has moreover been proved) inversely as the squares of the distances. All that remains is to compare the distance covered by a heavy body in falling to earth from a moderate height, with the distance covered in the same length of time by a body falling from the orbit of the moon. To learn what we wish to know, we only need the measurements of the earth and the distance to it from the moon."

That is how Mr. Newton reasoned it out. . . .

This force of gravitation is exerted in proportion to the quantity of matter a body contains—a truth that Mr. Newton proved by experiment. This new discovery has served to show that the sun, the center of all the planets, attracts them all in direct proportion to their mass, combined with their distance. From there, rising by degrees to a kind of knowledge that seemed not to have been made for the human mind, he boldly calculates how much matter the sun contains, and how much is to be found in each planet; and thus he shows that, according to the simple laws of mechanics, every celestial globe must necessarily be just where it is. His principle of the laws of gravitation alone explains all the apparent irregularities in the motion of the heavenly bodies. . . .

Letter Sixteen: On Newton's Optics

. . . Newton, with the help of nothing more than a prism, opened our eyes to the fact that light is an agglomeration of colored rays which, all together, produce the color white. . . .

What then is the cause of the colors we find in the world? Nothing other than the disposition of bodies to reflect rays of a certain sort and to absorb all the others. What is this hidden disposition? He shows that it is only the thickness of the little parts of which a body is composed. And how is this reflection done? It used to be thought that the rays rebounded, like a ball, from the surface of a solid body. Not at all. Newton taught the astonished philosophers that bodies are opaque only because their pores are large, that light is reflected to our eyes from the heart of those very pores; and that the smaller the pores of a body are, the more transparent is that body. Thus paper, which reflects light when it is dry, suffers it to pass through when it is oiled, because the oil, filling the pores, makes them much smaller.

. . . Having thus decomposed light, and in the brilliance of his discoveries having gone so far as to demonstrate the means of knowing a compound color by its primary colors, he shows that these primary rays, separated by the agency of the prism, are in their particular order because they are refracted in that order; and it is this property, unknown before him, of breaking in proportion, it is this unequal refraction of rays, this property of refracting red less than orange, and so on, that he names refrangibility.

. . .Wondrous as these discoveries are, they are only the beginning. He discovered how to observe the vibrations and agitations of light, which come and go endlessly, and which transmit light or reflect it according to the thickness of the parts they encounter. He ventured to calculate the thickness of the particles of air necessary between two object-glasses set one upon the other—one of them flat, and the other convex on one side—to produce such and such a transmission or reflection, and to make such and such a color. . . .

Jean le Rond d'Alembert

Preliminary Discourse to the *Encyclopedia*

... While poorly instructed or badly intentioned adversaries made open war on it, philosophy sought refuge, so to speak, in the works of a few great men. They had not the dangerous ambition of removing the blindfolds from their contemporaries' eyes; yet silently in the shadows they prepared from afar the light which gradually, by imperceptible degrees, would illuminate the world.

The immortal Chancellor of England, Francis Bacon [1561–1626], ought to be placed at the head of these illustrious personages. His works, so justly esteemed (and more esteemed, indeed, than they are known), merit our reading even more than our praises. One would be tempted to regard him as the greatest, the most universal, and the most eloquent of the philosophers, considering his sound and broad views, the multitude of objects to which his mind turned itself, and the boldness of his style, which everywhere joined the most sublime images with the most rigorous precision. Born in the depths of the most profound night, Bacon was aware that philosophy did not yet exist, although many men doubtless flattered themselves that they excelled in it (for the cruder a century is, the more it believes itself to be educated in all that can be known). Therefore, he began by considering generally the various objects of all the natural sciences. He divided these sciences into different branches, of which he made the most exact enumeration that was possible for him. He examined what was already known concerning each of these objects and made the immense catalogue of what remained to be discovered. This is the aim of his admirable book *The Advancement of Learning.* In his *Novum Organum,* he perfects the views that he had presented in the first book, carries them further, and makes known the necessity of experimental physics, of which no one was yet aware. Hostile to systems, he conceives of philosophy as being only that part of our

Jean le Rond d'Alembert, *Preliminary Discourse to the* Encyclopedia *of Diderot,* trans. Richard N. Schwab (Chicago: University of Chicago Press, 1995), 74–85. Reprinted with permission of The University of Chicago Press.

knowledge which should contribute to making us better or happier, thus apparently confining it within the limits of the science of useful things, and everywhere he recommends the study of Nature. His other writings were produced on the same pattern. Everything, even their titles, proclaims the man of genius, the mind that sees things in the large view. He collects facts, he compares experiments and points out a large number to be made; he invites scholars to study and perfect the arts, which he regards as the most exalted and most essential part of human science. . . .

Chancellor Bacon was followed by the illustrious Descartes [1596–1650]. That exceptional man, whose fortune has varied so much in less than a century, possessed all the qualities necessary for changing the face of philosophy: a strong imagination, a most logical mind, knowledge drawn from himself more than from books, great courage in battling the most generally accepted prejudices, and no form of dependence which forced him to spare them. Consequently, he experienced even in his own life what ordinarily happens to any man who has too marked an ascendancy over others. He had few enthusiasts and many enemies. Whether because he knew his country or only because he distrusted it, he took refuge in an entirely free land in order to meditate with less possibility of disturbance. . . .

One can view Descartes as a geometer or as a philosopher. Mathematics, which he seems to have considered lightly, nevertheless today constitutes the most solid and the least contested part of his glory. . . . But above all what immortalized the name of this great man is the application he was able to make of algebra to geometry, one of the grandest and most fortunate ideas that the human mind has ever had. It will always be the key to the most profound investigations, not only in sublime geometry, but also in all the physico-mathematical sciences.

As a philosopher he was perhaps equally great, but he was not so fortunate. Geometry, which by the nature of its object always gains without losing ground, could not fail to make a progress that was most sensible and apparent for everyone when plied by so great a genius. Philosophy found itself in quite a different state. There everything remained to be done, and what do not the first steps in any branch of knowledge cost? One is excused from making larger steps by the merit of taking any at all. If Descartes, who opened the way for us, did not progress as far along it as his sectaries believe, nevertheless the sciences are far more indebted to him than his adversaries will allow; his method alone would have sufficed to render him immortal. His *Dioptrics* is the greatest and the most excellent application that has yet been made of geometry to physics. In a word, we see his inventive genius shining forth everywhere, even in those works which are least read now. . . .

Descartes dared at least to show intelligent minds how to throw off the yoke of scholasticism, of opinion, of authority—in a word, of prejudices and barbarism. And by that revolt whose fruits we are reaping today, he rendered a service to philosophy perhaps more difficult to perform than all those contributed thereafter by his illustrious successors. He can be thought of as a leader of conspirators who, before anyone else, had the courage to arise against a despotic and arbitrary power and who, in preparing a resounding revolution, laid the foundations of a more just and happier government, which he himself was not able to see established. If he concluded by believing he could explain everything, he at least began by doubting everything, and the arms which we use to combat him belong to him no less because we turn them against him. . . .

Newton [1642–1727], whose way had been prepared by Huyghens, appeared at last, and gave philosophy a form which apparently it is to keep. That great genius saw that it was time to banish conjectures and vague hypotheses from physics, or at least to present them only for what they were worth, and that this science was uniquely susceptible to the experiments of geometry. It was perhaps with this aim that he began by inventing calculus and the method of series, whose applications are so extensive in geometry itself and still more so in explaining the complicated effects that one observes in Nature, where everything seems to take place by various kinds of infinite progressions. The experiments on weight and the observations of Kepler led the English philosopher to discover the force which holds the planets in their orbits. Simultaneously he showed how to distinguish the causes of their movements and how to calculate them with a precision such as one might reasonably expect only after several centuries of labor. Creator of an entirely new optics, he made the properties of light known to men by breaking it up into its constituent parts. Anything we could add to the praise of the great philosopher would fall far short of the universal testimonial that is given today to his almost innumerable discoveries and to his genius, which was at the same time far-reaching, exact, and profound. He has doubtless deserved all the recognition that has been given him for enriching philosophy with a large quantity of real assets. . . .

It appears that Newton had not entirely neglected metaphysics. He was too great a philosopher not to be aware that it constitutes the basis of our knowledge and that clear and exact notions about everything must be sought in metaphysics alone. Indeed, the works of this profound geometer make it apparent that he had succeeded in constructing such notions for himself concerning the principal objects that occupied him. However, he abstained almost totally from discussing his metaphysics in his best known writings, and we can hardly learn what he thought concerning the different objects of that discipline, except in the works of his followers. This may have been because he himself was somewhat dissatisfied with the progress he had made in metaphysics, or because he believed it difficult to give mankind sufficiently satisfactory and extensive enlightenment on a discipline too often uncertain and disputed. . . .

Locke [1632–1704] undertook and successfully carried through what Newton had not dared to do, or perhaps would have found impossible. It can be said that he created metaphysics, almost as Newton had created physics. He understood that the abstractions and ridiculous questions which had been debated up to that time and which had seemed to constitute the substance of philosophy were the very part most necessary to proscribe. He sought the principal causes of our errors in those abstractions and in the abuse of signs, and that is where he found them. In order to know our soul, its ideas, and its affections, he did not study books, because they would only have instructed him badly; he was content with probing deeply into himself, and after having contemplated himself, so to speak, for a long time, he did nothing more in his treatise, *Essay Concerning Human Understanding* [1690], than to present mankind with the mirror in which he had looked at himself. In a word, he reduced metaphysics to what it really ought to be: the experimental physics of the soul—a very different kind of physics from that of bodies, not only in its object, but in its way of viewing that object. In the latter study we can, and often do, discover unknown phenomena. In the former, facts as ancient as the world exist equally in all men; so much the worse for whoever believes he is seeing something new. Reasonable metaphysics can only consist, as does experimental physics, in the careful assembling of all these facts, in reducing them to a corpus of information, in explaining some by others, and in distinguishing those which ought to hold the first rank and serve as the foundation. In brief, the principles of metaphysics, which are as simple as axioms, are the same for the philosophers as for the general run of people. . . .

Jean-Antoine-Nicolas de Caritat, Marquis de Condorcet

A General Survey of Science—Concerning the Application of Calculus to the Political and Moral Sciences

When the sciences are in their infancy, an individual can study them all at once. But the fanciful *rapprochements* produced by some vivid imaginations are no more than scientific dreams, and the various sciences remain isolated. When, however, they progress so that the various branches of science must be divided up, lines of communication form between them, and the application of one science to another often becomes its most useful or striking function.

Two conditions must be met before one science can be applied to another: first, each of the sciences involved must have reached a certain stage of development, and second, there must be sufficient general familiarity with them to ensure the existence of men with a knowledge of both, who can pursue both faithfully and accurately.

Therefore, we could only begin to apply calculus to the moral and political sciences once mathematics had been successfully studied in nations where freedom was accompanied by peace and supported by enlightenment. . . .

My intention here is to present a general survey of this theory, which is now applied to so many different matters that it can be considered a science in its own right.

Since all its applications directly relate either to social interests or to the analysis of the operations of the human mind—that is, to a study

Jean-Antoine-Nicolas de Caritat, marquis de Condorcet, "A General Survey of Science—Concerning the Application of Calculus to the Political and Moral Sciences," in *Condorcet: Foundations of Social Choice and Political Theory*, ed. and trans. Iain McLean and Fiona Hewitt (Aldershot, Hants, UK, and Brookfield, VT: E. Elgar, 1994), 93–98. Reprinted with permission of Edward Elgar Publishing, Inc.

of man as perfected by society — I felt that it could best be christened the *social mathematic. . . .*

This account will demonstrate the many uses of this science. We shall see that it is relevant to all our individual and public interests, that it can increase the precision of all our ideas and the certainty of all our knowledge, and that if it were more widespread and more widely cultivated, it would greatly enhance the welfare and progress of the human race.

Two facts are sufficient to illustrate this. First, almost all the opinions and judgments which govern our conduct are based on some varying degree of probability which is always evaluated according to a vague, almost mechanical, feeling or to rough, uncertain ideas.

While it would of course be impossible to subject all these opinions and judgments to calculus, just as it would be impossible to calculate all the moves in a game of backgammon or piquet, we can still obtain the same advantages as a player who knows how to calculate his game gains over one whose moves are based only on instinct and routine.

Second, absolute truths, which subsist independently of all measurements or calculations, are often vague and inappropriate; for things which can be measured or combined in many different ways, they do not extend beyond first principles and are immediately inadequate. By limiting ourselves to reasoning without calculus, we risk making mistakes or even developing prejudices, either by unjustly generalizing certain maxims or else by deducing consequences which do not result from them when considered only insofar as we know them to be true. Finally, without the application of the rigorous methods of calculus and of the science of combinations, we would soon reach a stage where all progress became impossible; the progress of both the moral and political sciences and the physical sciences would thus soon come to a halt.

At the end of a revolution, this method of approaching the political sciences acquires a new kind and new degree of utility. Before the chaos which inevitably accompanies any large popular movement can return to order, and before the restoration of public prosperity, which alone can consolidate a new order against which so many different interests and prejudices conspire, stronger combinations and more precise methods are needed. These will be accepted only as a result of proofs which, like the results of calculus, silence insincerity and prejudice. We need to destroy the power that speech has usurped from reasoning, passion from truth, and active ignorance from enlightenment. Moreover, since all the principles of public economy have been shaken and all the truths accepted by enlightened men mixed up in a mass of uncertain and changing opinions, we need to bind men to reason by the precision of our ideas and the rigour of our proofs, and to protect our truths from attack by eloquence or self-interested sophisms. We need to accustom them to slow and peaceful discussion as protection against those who employ the evil technique, perfected in times of upheaval, of rousing their passions in order to lead them into error and crime.

Imagine the extent to which the rigour and precision which accompany all the operations to which calculus is applied would reinforce that of reason! Imagine its contribution to the progress of reason in this ravaged country, which, after profound upheaval, is still experiencing internal problems!

The social mathematic may study either man, or things, or both men and things at once.

It concerns men when it teaches us to work out the mortality rate in a particular area, or when it calculates the advantages or disadvantages of an election method. It concerns things when it assesses the advantages of a lottery or tries to determine the principles on which maritime insurance premiums should be based. And it concerns both men and things when it examines life annuities and life assurance.

It may study men as individuals whose lifespan and relationships are subject to the order of natural events, and it may also be applied to the operations of the human mind.

It studies men as individuals when it enables us to assess from the given facts the precise influence of climate, customs and profession on the length of a man's life, and it studies the operations of the mind when it weighs up our reasons for or against believing something, or when it calculates the probability of witnesses' reports or decisions. . . .

Whatever the subject of this science, it comprises three main parts: the determination of facts, the evaluation of these facts, including the theory of average values, and their results.

But after considering the facts, the average values or the results, we still need to determine their probability. The general theory of probability is therefore both a part of the science under examination and one of the foundation stones of all others. . . .

Science can progress only if it is studied by mathematicians who have a proper understanding of social science. But its practical applications can virtually become general knowledge for all who want to learn about the important subjects it embraces.

Science can be examined at a simple, basic level and made accessible to anyone who is familiar with fundamental mathematical theories and used to mathematical reasoning.

All the wisdom and genius of many great mathematicians was needed to produce a theory of lunar movements on which to base reliable tables. But the actual formation of these tables and their application for the determination of longitudes require only basic knowledge.

This is not an occult science whose secrets are shared by only a few devotees, but an ordinary, common science. Our discussion aims both to accelerate the progress of a theory on which the sciences most important for public welfare depend, and to shed light on several areas of these sciences and offer them general and practical assistance.

Steven Shapin

Social Uses of Science

. . . 'God said "Let Newton be," and all was light' is passable poetry, but lazy historiography.

In fact, it is in the area of Newtonianism and its career in the eighteenth century that . . . new notions of science and its uses display greatest promise. For, if the eighteenth century is seen (at least partly) as a period in which seventeenth-century scientific achievements were accredited and implemented, then a central question for historical research concerns the conditions in which Newtonian natural philosophy was received and institutionalized. Was the new philosophy (or antipathetic reactions to it) considered to be of social use? Of what relevance were such social uses to the production, evaluation and institutionalization of new science? Does sensitive consideration of the social uses of Newtonianism shed new light upon the career of natural philosophy in the period from *c.* 1680 to *c.* 1800? . . .

Steven Shapin, "Social Uses of Science," in *The Ferment of Knowledge: Studies in the Historiography of Eighteenth-Century Science*, ed. Roy Porter and G. S. Rousseau (Cambridge: Cambridge University Press, 1980), 95–97, 101–104, 111–112, 114–118. Reprinted with the permission of Cambridge University Press.

The Strategy of Newtonianism

It should not by now be surprising to historians of science that some of the bolder speculations about the links between natural knowledge and social developments often come from scholars not mainly concerned with science at all, and, therefore, not well-versed in the accepted categories of our discipline. Fifteen years ago E. P. Thompson, in a typically challenging aside, reckoned that 'the bourgeois and the scientific revolutions in England . . . were clearly a good deal more than just good friends.' We could do worse than to take this remark as our text, for much of the work on the social uses of science to be discussed here refines and expands the nature of this kinship.

. . . The priority disputes between Newton and Leibniz and, more generally, the evaluation and institutionalization of Newtonian philosophy in early eighteenth-century Britain, cannot be understood without examining the dynastic politics of the period from the 1680s to the 1710s. The controversy over the calculus, the suggestions of Leibniz's plagiarism, the episode of the *Commercium epistolicum*, and the depth of attachment of the Royal Society circle to Newton's natural philosophy, reflect, as Leibniz himself said, not 'a quarrel between Mr Newton and me, but between Germany and England.' Thackray reminds us of the political background of uncertainty concerning the Protestant succession to the crown following the Glorious Revolution of 1688, and of the probability (later, near-certainty) of the succession of the Elector of Hanover in the early years of the eighteenth century. As Newton was the 'autocrat' of English science, so Leibniz was the 'court philosopher' of Hanover. When it became likely that Leibniz would be 'translated,' along with the Hanoverian court, to London, Newton set in motion a sustained collective effort to discredit the worth, religious significance, and originality of the German's science. Differences in 'metaphysical style' and scientific worth are simply not adequate to understand the nature and course of the Newton–Leibniz disputes; the institutionalization of Newton's science as the '*Philosophica Britannica*' must be explained by making reference to a context of foreign politics and a contest for control of 'the business of experimental philosophy.' . . .

Present in the Civil War and Restoration materials are structural themes which appear again in treating Newtonianism and opposed natural philosophies later on. First, it is to be noted that philosophies of nature were routinely seen by the actors as imbued with social meaning.

This was not because of 'mere' metaphorical glossing, but because in these (and later) cultural contexts nature and society were deemed to be elements in one interacting network of significances. . . . Second, groups with conflicting social interests developed and sustained interestingly different natural philosophies; moreover, these philosophies were often produced explicitly to combat and refute those of rival groups. Third, the distribution of attributes between 'matter' and 'spirit' was an issue of intense concern in all these philosophies; the relations between the two entities seemed to be something upon which all cosmologies 'had to' decide, and the boundaries between 'matter' and 'spirit' were treated as having particularly strong social significance. . . .

Intellectualist historians of science have already documented in abundant detail how the technical problem-solving of the *Principia* and *Opticks* was founded upon Newton's ontologies of matter, force, space and time. Recent contextualist work proceeds to show how key features of Newtonian metaphysics were also deemed essential to solving the social problems confronting the groups which used the Boyle Lectures as the forum for creating and establishing the Newtonian world-view. How were such notions thought to serve social interests? If matter was self-sufficient and self-animating, then *external* spiritual agencies (and their delegates, 'active principles') were not required to produce regularity, order and motion. The Newtonians were explicit in their view that the implication of a 'hylozoist' (or 'pantheistic materialist') cosmology was atheism. 'Active principles' were deemed to be the manifestations of God's active powers in the world natural. They were apart from matter, and superior to it, in the same way that God was apart from and above nature, although working in it and through it. Such a God, and such a nature, was a crucial cultural resource for legitimating the moral authority of those groups who claimed to interpret God's ways to man, and to exercise their delegated right to sanction behaviour.

Intellectualist historians have already demonstrated that the role of providence in the Newtonian cosmology is properly to be integrated into the ontology of matter and force. Contextualist writings go on to show how a providentialist ontology was an important strategy in dealing with the social and political predicaments of groups which accepted and institutionalized the new science. Providence, according to the Newtonians, was manifest not only in nature's irregularities and catastrophes, but also in its regular, lawful operations. This was the role of providence in the world natural and the world politick which was required (and used) to legitimate the continuing moral authority of latitudinarian divines through the events of 1649, 1660, 1688 and 1707. Newton's God and Newton's ontology were evaluated according to their utility in constructing the apologetics of the new order. . . .

Strategies of Enlightenment Matter-Theory

If the new contextualism prompts methodological reassessments of the role of social uses of science generally, it also holds out the prospect of a highly challenging revision of a particular field of intellectual history. This section explores the potential of a number of recent contextualist studies for a new historical understanding of Enlightenment natural knowledge. What we begin to see in work of this kind is a sensitivity to the *variety* of conceptions of nature distributed among different social groups. We see how divergent bodies of natural knowledge were used to further social interests and were produced in processes of social conflict. Against an older view that the 'new science' (and especially the 'Newtonianism') of the early and mid-eighteenth century was the underpinning of 'the Enlightenment,' we now have a developing perspective which points out the existence of a number of species of natural knowledge, and a number of opposed 'Enlightenments.'

This approach is particularly apparent in studies of anti-Newtonian natural philosophies and the social groups which produced, sustained and used them. . . . 'Freethinking' groups continued and elaborated late-Renaissance and Civil War sectarian conceptions of matter which ascribed to it inherent animating principles. Their most celebrated spokesman, John Toland, followed Giordano Bruno in deploying a hylozoist cosmology in which 'outside, immaterial forces are unnecessary to move matter.' Properties of God and properties of matter were so intermingled that the hierarchical relations between the two, so insisted upon by corpuscularians and Newtonians, were erased. Nature was a self-sufficient system. Hylozoist 'freethinkers' and Newtonians formulated their philosophies in explicit opposition to each other.

Moreover, their opposed philosophies of matter and spirit were not merely expressions of differing metaphysical preferences, nor are they to be regarded as 'caused' by contrasting metaphysical 'influences.' Where the Newtonian cosmology of the Boyle Lectures was developed partly as a defence of the Protestant succession and the court which underpinned the moral and social authority of the latitudinarian Low Church, Toland's hylozoism was the voice of conflicting social tendencies. . . .

[John] Hutchinson and his followers were, like the Newtonians, concerned to construct a natural philosophy which would be the hand-maiden of correct religion. However, on a number of counts they maintained that the Newtonian philosophy failed to serve that function and, indeed, might serve to comfort and aid Dissenters and deists. . . . From Hutchinson's perspective, Newton's God was not transcendent *enough*; He was *too* immanent in the world; the material world was not *sufficiently* mechanical and self-contained. Hutchinsonianism, therefore, introduced into the cosmos 'the Names,' modifications of the aether and exceedingly fine matter, to replace Newtonian immaterial forces. It posited a plenum in place of Newton's void; contact action instead of action at a distance; a self-sufficient mechanical universe in the stead of one continually dependent upon God's tinkering; and a *totally* transcendent Deity as against a Deity who made periodic service-calls. . . .

The Hutchinsonian critique of Newtonianism shows the marks of the political processes of opposition which generated it. The anti-deistical Newtonians were said to be *insufficiently* anti-deistical; their God was associated with that of freethinkers and Socinians. The theistic Newtonian natural philosophy was said to involve God too much in the material world. Their epistemology was claimed to lay too little emphasis upon the tools of revelation and scriptural glossing. Thus the Hutchinsonian cosmos and epistemology maximized the competences of High Church clerics, while it impugned the theological purity of their enemies, the Low Church–Whig–Newtonians. . . .

British natural philosophers of the mid-to-late eighteenth century began increasingly to prefer explanations predicated upon divine causality manifested in active powers *immanent* in the natural order. Newton understood active principles to be both lawful *and* products of providence; he thus made the natural order to be utterly dependent upon external spiritual superintendence. Newton's aether, for example, was formulated as one such active principle subordinate to God's will. But by the 1740s, . . . British natural philosophers were tending to conceive of the aether as an active principle 'immanent in the fabric of nature' and were rejecting Newton's own theological rubric. . . .

Theology and matter-theory were once more inextricably intertwined. While discarding Newton's views on the nature of active principles, the eighteenth-century natural philosophers . . . also jettisoned Newton's conception of the nature of matter and the theological framework in which it was embedded. Matter was now seen as inherently animated and God's volition was no longer required to explain its activity. . . .

In fact, historians of science have not yet seriously begun to notice and to explain why it was that similar shifts in 'sensibility' seem to have occurred in several areas of inquiry during the eighteenth century. Not just natural philosophy and matter-theory, but also geology and physiology seem to have changed their preferences from 'Newtonian' theories which required external animating spiritual agencies to those which placed the principles of animation and pattern within the natural entities. The generality of this shift during the eighteenth century needs first to be acknowledged before an historical explanation can be attempted. But early impressions are that the pervasiveness of the change will make any explanation in terms of the 'immanent logic' of scientific inquiry very difficult to sustain. What is strongly suggested by these findings is that historians ought to look to the concrete contexts in which Newtonian accounts were rejected, and to the social, as well as the technical, bases for that rejection during the eighteenth century. . . .

Mary Terrall

Metaphysics, Mathematics, and the Gendering of Science in Eighteenth-Century France

When Condorcet was inducted into the Académie française in 1782, following a bitterly contested election, he took the opportunity to proclaim the triumph of reason over "ignorance and error": "The method of discovering truths has been reduced to an art, one could almost say to a set of formulae. Reason has finally recognized the route that it must

Mary Terrall, "Metaphysics, Mathematics, and the Gendering of Science in Eighteenth-Century France," in *The Sciences in Enlightened Europe*, ed. William Clark, Jan Golinski, and Simon Schaffer (Chicago: University of Chicago Press, 1999), 247–260, 267–269. Reprinted by permission of The University of Chicago Press and the author.

follow and seized the thread that will prevent it from going astray. . . . Every scientific discovery is a benefit for humanity." This optimistic assessment of the power of reason to save humanity from darkness rested on the conviction that nature endows every individual with the capability to recognize truth, and hence to become enlightened. In Condorcet's rhetoric, reason took on a life of its own, fighting the good fight by force of systematic method, strangely independent of individual philosophers. But in the elite world of the Académie française and the Académie des Sciences, reason and the analytic spirit belonged especially to the members of this meritocracy, which served the absolutist state as well as humanity in general. This double service is one root of the tension between exclusive privilege and universalism that underlies so many of the texts that make up the canon of the Enlightenment in France. In the abstract, all people—men and women, peasants and merchants—have access to reason and truth; in practice, the authorization of discoveries and their meanings was reserved for a small group of men.

The domain of the Académie des Sciences encompassed the tools and methods of science as well as its discoveries. As a privileged body with special ties to the crown, the academy worked to distinguish its expertise from the popular science of the marketplace and the enthusiasms of naive outsiders. This essay examines the role played by algebraic analysis as a language and an instrument of the academy's power to sanction certain forms of knowledge. In mathematical physics, "analysis" referred to the method of reducing problems to equations, which could then be solved using integral and differential calculus. Rational mechanics, which expressed idealized physical situations in systems of equations, was the prime field for the application of analysis in this sense.

. . . One feature of the academy's growing commitment to analytic methods in physics over the course of the eighteenth century was the erasure of teleological metaphysics from rational mechanics. This process of erasure contributed to the definition of analysis as the form of mathematics appropriate for understanding nature, and it also came to represent the exclusive right of its practitioners to demarcate truth from falsehood.

The term "metaphysics" appeared in quite a range of epistemological and theological contexts, in discussions of God, the human soul, space, time, force, and mind. . . . When used as a term of disparagement, as when d'Alembert described forces as "obscure and metaphysical," it became a generic buzzword for all that lay beyond the reach of human understanding and reliable scientific investigation. However, until the 1760s, such metaphysical principles still entered openly into some areas of rational mechanics, especially in debates about gravity, *vis viva*, and the principle of least action. By the 1780s, explicit claims about metaphysics had been written out of mechanics in the unadorned language of algebraic analysis. In these decades, the academy was also strengthening its ties to the government, and especially to officials intent on reforming traditional political practice. What was it about metaphysical principles that bothered mathematicians? How did they go about excising such principles from the domain of mathematics and physics? I will argue that the denigration of metaphysics . . . was elaborated by drawing parallels between the dangers of metaphysics and those of ignorance, imagination, delusion, and blind religious faith. In rejecting metaphysics, the mathematicians of the academy also set themselves up as the foes of superstition, imagination, and enthusiasm of all kinds, evils they construed as threats to social stability, as well as to their own authority.

Questions of intellectual authority and its links to political authority came into public view at a time when the very definition of publicity was in flux. At the same time, the cultural significance of science, as a royally sanctioned enterprise, was expanding and stabilizing. The academy presented science as something done by men with certain talents and skills to benefit a "public" made up of people without direct access to scientific knowledge. The crown could call on academic expertise to safeguard a vulnerable populace from the effects of ignorance, and the academy trumpeted the results of such consultations as evidence of its usefulness. But the academy's public face, visible in its journal and semiannual public meetings, was always backed up by the exchanges that took place in a more restricted space, behind closed doors. Analysis and rational mechanics occupied the most esoteric region of the academy's preserve.

Although the technical work of analysis was done only by a few "men of genius," the ideal of a powerful and universally applicable analysis was put forward by mathematicians as evidence for the utility and elite status of science. This ideal contributed to the enhancement of the cultural and political standing of science and of the academy. In the process, gender was insinuated into mathematical discourse in rather subtle ways. The meaning of gender differences was a central topic in Enlightenment debates, especially since claims and counterclaims about difference highlighted the tensions in discussions of universal human reason and the rejection of traditional hierarchies of authority. These debates about difference provided ideological resources for men trying to secure a stable and perhaps even a powerful place for science on shifting political ground. Mathematicians brought gendered connotations into the definition and legitimation of their practices, as they worked to purify enlightened mathematics from the taint of metaphysics and imprecise thinking.

Metaphysical Principles in Mechanics

Many of the technical disputes that embroiled mathematicians and fascinated readers of the periodical press in the Enlightenment entailed discussions of metaphysics as well as the question of what constituted proper scientific practice. Perhaps the most explicit use of metaphysics was in the principle of least action as propounded by Pierre-Louis Moreau de Maupertuis as part of a reformulation of the goals and methods of mechanics. In a paper on refraction read to the Paris Academy in 1744, he introduced the term "quantity of action" as the core of a new minimum principle governing the motion of light. He subsequently extended the notion of action to analysis of elastic and inelastic collisions, defining action as the product of mass, velocity, and distance traveled in a given time. . . . Maupertuis intended this principle to be both mathematically precise and metaphysically meaningful. Because it applied to optics, dynamics, and statics, he claimed to have brought diverse phenomena under the aegis of a universal principle that reflected the true economy of nature. . . . Nature had been designed so that every change required a minimal expenditure of "action," and God calculated that quantity continuously. In basing mechanics on an extremum principle, Maupertuis brought a mathematical version of final causation into physics, as all motions fulfill God's purpose in minimizing action and maximizing efficiency. . . .

Metaphysical considerations cannot be separated from the physical or the mathematical and hence cannot be ignored by the mathematician. "Action" is quantifiable, but not directly deducible from the concepts of matter and motion; Maupertuis took this as an indication of the critical importance of metaphysics for mechanics. . . .

Thus metaphysics is relevant to scientific knowledge as a system of reasons and practical rules, rather than abstract principles ambiguously connected to the empirical world. Other forms of abstraction are not so ambiguous; d'Alembert readily applied the abstractions of geometry to real-world problems. . . . The abstractions of metaphysics cannot serve the same function, in d'Alembert's view, because they cannot translate into unequivocal representations of phenomena.

In the context of evaluating scientific claims, d'Alembert represented metaphysics as an obfuscating cloud that interfered with the potential clarity of calculation and understanding. . . . D'Alembert likened the metaphysical formulation of problems in mechanics to confused perception, susceptible to error, as when a blind man interprets shapes by tapping with his stick. Mathematics brings problems into focus, and what's more, can do so perfectly well without the aid of metaphysics. . . .

Maupertuis saw metaphysics and mathematics as mutually reinforcing components of natural knowledge; d'Alembert undertook to clear away the metaphysical cobwebs that interfered with the clarity of mathematics. As a result, they drew the boundaries of their vocations as "philosophers" quite differently.

The Disappearance of Metaphysics

Maupertuis's teleological physics never gained the kind of prominence in France that he had initially anticipated. D'Alembert, in contrast, effectively laid the groundwork for the subsequent development of rational mechanics. By the 1780s, metaphysics no longer played an explicit role in mathematics or physics in the Académie des Sciences. . . .

The gradual disappearance of metaphysics coincided with the consolidation of the strength and status of the Académie des Sciences. The number of potential members grew decade by decade as more men acquired the technical prerequisites for making a career in science, so that elections became increasingly competitive and the institution ever more exclusive. . . .

In response to its rising fortunes, the academy stepped up the policing of its borders, asserting its jurisdiction over truth by formally disallowing claims made by certain categories of outsiders. In 1775, the academicians announced publicly that they would no longer waste their time considering claims having to do with squaring circles, trisecting angles, duplicating cubes, or designing perpetual motion machines. In relegating these "chimerical" solutions to the no-man's-land of fantasy, the academy claimed to be acting for the welfare of the "public" as well as reducing demands on its experts. . . . When the academy proclaimed certain problems insoluble, and hence out of bounds for serious mathematicians, it was exercising control over the line separating talent from false inspiration, truth from error.

Academicians augmented their authority by exercising what Condorcet called their "public function." This was most visible in the institution's responses to governmental requests for evaluations of a wide range of pressing industrial, economic, and social problems. The results of these inquiries went first to the ministers of the crown, but were also presented to the "public" in the pages of the academy's journal. The academy willingly made its expertise available to the state for the public good, but maintained its right to define the terms of its interactions with its various publics. . . .

The interchange between academy and state extended beyond the delivery of expert judgments in exchange for remuneration. . . . [R]eforming ministers dealing with a widening circle of crises invoked scientific rationality as an alternative to traditional formulations of authority. Administrators cast their attempts at making policy in terms of a social order grounded in the scientific principles familiar to readers of the academy's publications. . . . The scientific elite had worked hard to establish the superiority of the natural knowledge emanating from the academy; now that they had done so, they made it available to reforming ministers looking for new forms of legitimacy. . . .

Women, Gender, and Enlightened Rationality

Cultural historians have located another shift in the intellectual landscape at the end of the old regime, an undermining of the standing of elite women as facilitators and participants in the philosophical ferment in the decades before the revolution. . . . When the philosophic party got "stronger" in the 1780s, men found they could dispense with the "female governance" of the salons, and new institutions replaced the salons as the locus of enlightened sociability. . . .

As a corporation with an internal hierarchy of merit, the Académie des Sciences was the antithesis of the salons. Still, many academicians moved easily between the distinct but overlapping worlds of salon and academy, between the formal declamatory presentations of academic meetings and the modulated exchange of conversation. The institution maintained the inner sanctum of its own exclusively male space, but it also looked outward to a wider audience that included women. These women served as prestigious admirers and spectators whose attention validated the scientific enterprise, especially in the academy's early years. At just the time when the salons, characterized by polite conversation, were being displaced by men promoting less aristocratic forms of association, the academy was consolidating its role as arbiter of rationality and utility and relying less on its polite, and female, audience.

At the same time, the undifferentiated public that figured as the dupes of unsanctioned knowledge claims was commonly described in feminine terms. If the consolidation of the academy's position, with its attendant denial of the value of metaphysical principles, coincided both with a backlash against women's participation in the intellectual life of the Republic of Letters and with a feminizing of ignorant victims of charlatans, we might expect to find a link between metaphysics and femininity in the rhetoric of mathematics. In this context, feminizing metaphysics made sense as a way of excising it from scientific practice. The positive values assigned to calculation and precision measurement were subtly gendered as masculine, while metaphysics was castigated in feminine terms. . . .

The *Encyclopedia* also associated women with equivocality and dissimulation and stressed the mystery and inscrutability of women. The author of the article "Femme" bemoaned the difficulty of defining women at all: "In truth, everything speaks in them, but in an equivocal language." This cannot be the language of science, of course. Confessing himself helpless in the face of feminine tricks and seductions, the philosopher equates equivocation and femininity. The project of enlightenment, and the rational understanding of nature, must dispense with the temptations of feminine discourse and stick to the language of rationality and control. . . .

Conclusion

. . . The definition of rational thinking as a form of calculation, whereby ideas and sensory input are "compounded and decompounded," became commonplace in the Enlightenment. Mathematical equations, especially when they expressed general truths, were the most formal and visible expression of this analytic ideal. The value Lagrange placed on general formulations was rooted in the work of calculation. . . . In order to make analytical calculations, the mathematician manipulated symbols, but this was not a blindly mechanical process. . . . [I]t is the product of sustained attention and application by a specially endowed mind. As such, it is not suited to the flightiness often associated with female intelligence in the Enlightenment.

No one suggested that the implicitly feminine attributes of metaphysics marked it as something women could do well. Gender functioned rather to separate metaphysics from the real work of analysis, reinforcing the masculine value of this arcane and formal mathematics. Calculation was represented as a useful technology that maximized the human potential to understand the world. . . .

The dismissal of metaphysics from the realm of analysis elevated rigor, deductive mathematics, and formal precision over equivocation, arbitrariness, and imagination, all the latter being commonly linked to the feminine. The undisciplined and susceptible female imagination provided a model for representing pitfalls associated with metaphysics and its irrational and useless siblings, superstition and enthusiasm. These value-laden terms were called into play in the ongoing attempt to draw secure boundaries around academic expertise and mathematical practice. . . .

When they argued for the utility of their particular expertise for the effective working of the state and the well-being of the public, men of science used language that reflected and reinforced contemporary definitions of gender difference. One effect of this rhetoric was to bar the feminine, and hence women, from the world of the mathematician and the academy. But the gendered language of difference was available to academicians intent on marking the special value of their work partly because women were already securely outside the scientific enterprise. The qualities of female intelligence and imagination effectively confirmed the status of women as outsiders to the academy, and this confirmation also boosted the value of other attributes—generality, precision, focused attention, deductive reason, hard work—gendered masculine by contrast. Gender thus played a subtle and somewhat circular part in the complex process by which metaphysics was banished from analysis, and mathematicians asserted the value of their reductive program for natural knowledge.

Roy Porter

Medical Science and Human Science in the Enlightenment

. . . Medical luminaries drew on the triumphs of the "new philosophy" and the rhetoric of "the party of humanity" to create progressive profiles for medicine itself. For their part, the *philosophes* forged mythic histories of the arts and sciences, of morals and politics, chronicling battles down the centuries between the forces of good and evil, reform and reaction; paralleling these, medical authors too dramatized the former struggles of reason against superstition, open-mindedness against dogmatism, experience against blinkered book learning, to illustrate the adage that truth was great and would prevail. If the noble advances of the Hippocratics (supposedly the founding fathers of philosophical medicine) had been stifled throughout the Middle Ages by bigoted reverence for blind authority, the advent of printing, the genius of Leonardo, and the daring of Vesalius had rekindled the investigative spirit. William Harvey was the ideal icon: his connections with Padua, his friendships spanning the generation between Bacon and the founders of the Royal Society, his impeccable experimentalism—all bespoke the happy marriage of medicine and science, enshrined above all in the emblem of heart as a pump, perfect proof that knowledge advanced when medicine and the mechanical philosophy pulled together. Harvey's links with the Court told further exemplary tales of the place of patronage in the advancement of learning. . . .

Above all, Enlightenment historiography named for medicine a noble mission. . . . [P]hysic would be laid open to the people, health and humanity would march forward together. . . .

Eighteenth-century medical thinkers sought to render their study truly scientific — or, in contemporary idiom, "philosophical" — in various ways. Observation and experiment became the watchwords of many.

Roy Porter, "Medical Science and Human Science in the Enlightenment," in *Inventing Human Science: Eighteenth-Century Domains*, ed. Christopher Fox, Roy Porter, and Robert Wokler (Berkeley: University of California Press, 1995), 55–76. Reprinted by permission of The University of California Press.

. . . [I]t is clear that eighteenth-century biomedical theory had sub-
stantially taken on board the terms and tenets posited and popularized by
the new Newtonian natural philosophy. To some degree this shows the
weathercock of intellectual fashion at work. But weightier matters were
at stake. Confronted by the more bizarre, irrational manifestations of
human behavior—coma, convulsions, malformations, delirium, and the
like—traditional opinion had commonly looked beyond, seeking explanation in divine will or demoniacal possession, in astrological influences, or in imagination. Medical mechanists, by contrast, insisted
that such phenomena could and should be comprehensively accounted
for in terms of the internal organs and local operations of the body itself.
The mechanistic program thus promised to enlarge medicine's exclusive
explanatory authority. . . .

Medicine sought in other ways to subject the mysteries of the organism to
rational inquiry. Doctors participated in the wider quantifying quest. . . .
[T]he extension of the empire of science was furthered by the systematic
reduction to intelligibility of the marvelous, mysterious, and miraculous
through fact collection and processing, through *l'esprit géometrique*,
through application of the law of large numbers, and through the routine
digestion of data in tables, formulae, equations, and ratios. What could
be enumerated could be formulated as natural laws, albeit only laws
of probability. The empire of chance—so-called acts of God—could
thereby be tamed. . . .

Thus medical authors attempted to set their discipline upon more "scientific" footings. The advances of the "new philosophy" afforded many
attractions. But "scientific medicine" was also a highly contentious shib-
boleth, a pawn in intraprofessional rivalries, an ideological shuttlecock.
After all, the relations between medical reality and medical philosophy
were exceptionally problematic—large claims might be being staked for
medicine's potential, precisely because its actual state seemed the very reverse: an intellectual backwater, a sordid scandal. "Scientific medicine"
might thus be less a proud boast than a dream, even a compensatory wish
fulfillment. For what vexed many practitioners was that, in truth, medicine never had caught up with chemistry, or experimental physics, or
even botany: high time it did. To examine the politics of "scientific medicine," I wish briefly to discuss one such writer, whose decrial of medical
backwardness went hand-in-hand with an almost millennialist vision of
scientific medicine's potential: Thomas Beddoes.

Chemist, physician, researcher, educator, poet, political radical, Beddoes was a paladin of the late Enlightenment. . . .

Modern chemistry, Beddoes insisted, was a triumph; medicine, by contrast, a disgrace. . . . Clinical medicine was a swamp of ignorance, folly, and deception. Why? Society, judged the Enlightenment humanitarian, had its priorities all wrong. Pursuit of higher things had deflected the human race from the relief of suffering. . . .

But, worse, medicine itself was corrupt. Clinical practice—history taking, diagnosis, prognosis, therapeutics—ought to be scientific and objective. The reverse was the case. In Britain's booming commercial economy, medicine had been seduced from rational ends by the cash nexus: rich patients and grasping, servile doctors were equally to blame. . . .

So while chemistry was a freeway of scientific progress, medicine was a cul-de-sac of quackery. Radical change was imperative, but what was to be done? Beddoes pinned his faith on science. . . .

Beddoes's Promethean expectations of science's revolutionizing life were underpinned by an Enlightenment vision of *homo* as a creature of infinite possibility. Human attributes were not fixed, the mind not straitjacketed by original sin or innate ideas. A champion of Locke's philosophical empiricism, Hartley's physiological psychology, and the learn-by-doing educational theories of Rousseau and Richard Edgeworth, Beddoes set no limits to improvement under the stimulus of sense experience, and to progress through dynamic interaction with the environment, natural and social. Convinced that nature was truth, and lay open to the senses, Beddoes regarded education as necessarily, in the widest sense, experimental.

Thus experimental sciences such as chemistry were miniatures of the wider panorama of human progress. Chemistry had found its true locus: the laboratory, the scientific society. Medicine still lacked its own milieu and methods. . . .

Beddoes urged a mental revolution in the medical profession, accompanied by a measure of state aid. Trapped in the ethos of private practice, medicine was jealous and even secretive. Knowledge was rarely pooled, and often lost. Such "waste of facts" was shocking, for "the grand expedient for rendering physiology popular and medicine certain, is to enlarge our stock of observations on animal nature." Data must standardly enter the public domain.

Beddoes proposed two solutions. The first was personal: more energetic medical publication. . . .

The second was institutional: he urged agencies for systematic collection and storage of medical facts in some convenient archive. . . .

In short, Beddoes promoted the medical experimentalist as the analogue of the chemist. . . . Setting medicine thus on an experimental basis would change clinical relations. Under the benevolent care of experimentalists, patients should no longer meddle in doctors' decisions. But if the laity must not mess with medicine, they too, for their health's sake, should cultivate science. What better than to encourage every girl and boy to take up chemistry?—not merely as a schooling of the mind, but as a prophylactic against disease itself. "I should not be surprised," ventured the never-say-die *philosophe*, "if, in a few years, it should become as common for persons to go about to instruct private families in chemistry, mechanics, in tangible geometry and various sorts of manufactures, as it now is in music and drawing." . . .

As needs no emphasis, the moral and political thinkers of the Enlightenment, seeking to understand and change society, looked to science for their model. Science was a matchless engine of analysis: objective, critical, progressive. Natural order promised models of social order, in particular (for many *philosophes*) a vision of free individual activity in systems governed by natural law.

If humanists were looking to science, medical men were, as it were, returning the gaze, and looking out at society. The spirit of inquiry encouraged medicine away from individual cases in search of the laws of health and sickness in wider contexts, examining climate, environment, the rhythms of epidemics over the historical *longue durée*. . . . Certain eighteenth-century physicians developed an enlarged social awareness, confronting the interplay of medicine, sickness, and society. What determined the patterns and pathways of illness in the community? Why did sickness levels vary from group to group, society to society, region to region? Confronting such wider variables, many eighteenth-century physicians felt obliged to be more than bedside healers: they had to become anatomists, and doctors, of society.

. . . A central aim of the Enlightenment was to establish analysis of society on the same footing as that upon which the natural sciences had been emplaced in the previous century. It was a widespread ambition: it was not only Hume who sought to be the Newton of the moral sciences. The motives were manifold. A more secular age wanted to understand mankind in relation not merely to God and the scriptures but to nature, history, and society. An era of rapid sociohistorical change needed a philosophy of man that could embrace difference and relativism, yet simultaneously posit a framework of social laws governing difference and change. For some, a science of society offered legitimations for the present order. For most, social science would provide tools for criticism, reform, even revolution, and blueprints for the future. In any case, a science of man would serve the cause of emancipation from ignorance, would promote the mission of *sapere aude*, furthering man's escape from self-imposed tutelage, Montesquieu, Voltaire, Diderot, Rousseau, Condillac, Helvétius, Bentham, Cesare Beccaria, Turgot, Adam Smith, d'Holbach, Ferguson, Millar, Herder, Erasmus Darwin, Condorcet—the list could be extended *ad libitum*—no end of Enlightenment luminaries applied themselves to forging scientific accounts of man's mind, speech, imagination, emotions, psyche, gender relations, family structures, social organization, relations with nature, economic activities, legal systems, political development, and so forth, laying bare the hidden chains interlinking man and milieu, individual with group, and past, present, and future. . . .

Many prominent Enlightenment spokesmen were medics: Locke, Mandeville, David Hartley, J. O. de La Mettrie, the chevalier de Jaucourt, François Quesnay, Erasmus Darwin, and P. J. G. Cabanis, to mention a few. In the light of this fact, and of Gay's claims, discussed earlier, that medicine spurred the Enlightenment "recovery of nerve," surely medicine (or, more broadly, the biomedical sciences) played a crucial part in supplying the intellectual foundations, the images and idioms, of Enlightenment sciences of man? It is easy to find instances to substantiate this view.

Did not Montesquieu ground his theory of the determination of temperament by climate upon a physiological experiment?—showing, by putting ice on an animal's tongue, that cold produced sluggishness and diminution of sensations? Anatomy and physiology provided critical evidence (or, perhaps, ideological reinforcement) in other fields of human science. The new differentiation of gender roles widely touted in the eighteenth century was accompanied by shifts in biomedical teachings, accentuating the dimorphism between male and female skeletons, pointing to differential cranial capacity, and newly insisting upon radical differences in reproductive apparatus. . . . Women, it was further argued, had been proven by neurology to possess finer, that is to say, weaker, nervous organization. . . .

Acute observers of the affinities between knowledge and self-interest, *philosophes* would hardly have been surprised to find that various *médecin-philosophes* argued, as a matter of first principles, that there could be no scientific understanding of man without the firm foundation of a biomedical substrate. It was central to the program of the *idéologues*, that group of thinkers clustering in Auteuil in the salon of Mme. Helvétius, that a true knowledge of man demanded a *science* of ideas, which in turn presupposed analysis of the physiological basis of consciousness. The leading *idéologue*, Cabanis, himself prominent in medical circles, spent many years and much ink explicating the nervous roots of mind, above all in his *Rapports du Physique et du moral de l'homme* (1802): mind was not a separate, superadded principle but a function of higher nervous organization. So distasteful, so threatening, were such teachings, on account of their materialist overtones, that Napoleon responded in 1803 by closing down the section of the Institut devoted to the moral sciences.

In Britain, Cabanis's somewhat older contemporary, the Midlands practitioner Erasmus Darwin, evolved a rather comparable biomedical theory of the material basis of human powers and human progress, expounded within a bold philosophy of cosmic evolution. Drawing on both Hartley and Haller, Darwin delineated the gradual, progressive series of neurologically based phenomena (irritability, sensation, volition, and association) that marked the rise, simultaneously hierarchical and evolutionary, from the lowest molecule right up to mighty man. There were no sharp divides separating beings endowed with mere life from those possessing will and those finally blessed with consciousness. Nor was human nature fixed. Man, argued Darwin, possessed an unlimited capacity further to develop his faculties through learning, for acquired ideas and characteristics could be passed down to posterity through inheritance. Hence, as argued in his evolutionary poem, *The Temple of Nature*, medical materialism offered the grounds and the guarantee of the perfectibility — social, moral, intellectual, and scientific — of the human race. . . .

With Cabanis and Erasmus Darwin, the stipulation of a biomedical bedrock for a philosophy of social man, the assertion of the indissoluble and two-way association between the *physique* and the *morale*, was expressed with some subtlety and should not be viewed as a crude expression of professional prejudice or radical polemic. Rather more naked in his political program was La Mettrie. In his *L'Homme Machine* (1747), and, to a lesser degree, his *Histoire naturelle de l'âme* and his *Discours préliminaire*, this sometime student of Herman Boerhaave and long-practicing physician advanced an uncompromisingly reductionist vision of man as a predetermined being, whose consciousness was a function of his material-organic needs. La Mettrie's writings were militantly targeted against the tribe of metaphysicians—be they Sorbonne theologians or Cartesian metaphysicians—who postulated dualistic accounts of human nature, privileging Soul or Mind as separate from and superior to body. . . .

Less easy to place is Diderot. In a stream of provocative works—such as the *Lettre sur les aveugles* (1749), the *Rêve de d'Alembert* (written in 1769; it significantly uses the Montpellier vitalist, Théophile Bordeu, as fictive interlocutor), and the *Elémens de physiologie* (written around 1774); the last two works remained unpublished in the author's lifetime—Diderot posed and reposed, earnestly, teasingly, and certainly without resolution, the issues, already dealt with to his own satisfaction by La Mettrie ([doctors "have enlightened the labyrinth of man"]), of the relationship between man the material, and man the moral being. If man is a product of his biomedical makeup, does he have free will? Can he be held responsible for his actions? Is consciousness the captain of the soul? (Is there anything resembling a soul?) Or is consciousness just a by-product of the brain, as bile is a secretion of the liver? Is there, not least, any true difference between *homo rationalis* healthy and sick, sane and lunatic, man and beast? . . .

The Renaissance and neo-Classical Humanists had opted in favor of broadly Platonic, Stoic, and Christian propositions. Man was compounded of a dual nature; an immortal essence remained after one had shuffled off this mortal coil. . . . It was Descartes who had, most daringly and influentially, shored up dualism, by postulating a model of man as a corporeal mechanism presided over by a nonmaterial consciousness almost free—save for the pineal gland!—of any limiting connection with organic materiality.

Descartes had thereby mapped attractive intellectual territories with defensible metaphysical boundaries. There was a legitimate, if ultimately subordinate, role for a (natural) science of man as a physical being: there lay the charter of anatomy, physiology, medicine, and so forth. But, as commentators insisted, such studies could not be expected—for therein would lie an elementary category error—to offer significant accounts of mind, will, soul, inner states, behavior, values, morals, language, the achievements of art or intellect. These were the provinces of theology or philosophy, of the humanities, and, maybe, of the moral sciences. . . .

The role of Descartes's thought in the fabrication, and then the fall, of philosophical dualism is complex and much contested. It is, nevertheless, beyond dispute that, to a very large degree, Enlightenment endeavors to formulate sciences of man—"philosophical" or "natural" histories of man—operated overtly or tacitly within "Cartesian" guidelines. They engaged in analysis—often intentionally radical and subversive—of man as a social, moral, rational, historical being, not as a primarily material entity who happened to be endowed with a potential for psychological, social, and cultural developments. . . .

This point perhaps needs underlining with examples. Locke was, both by training and to some degree by practice, a physician. It might be expected, therefore, that he would have projected a fundamentally physiological account of man. Not so. The state of nature envisaged in his political writings is one in which the salient matters are man's duties under God and his rights vis-à-vis his fellow men. Locke's *Essay on Human Understanding* (1690), that cornerstone of Enlightenment empiricist epistemology, is essentially a philosophical inquiry into the coherence of consciousness. The physical basis or apparatus of perception is barely discussed: Locke's interest lies in mind, not brain. Locke celebratedly raises the possibility that matter might think, but far, say, from suggesting physiological experiments, translates the issue into theology (it would not be impossible for God to create thinking matter).

Post-Lockean empiricism and sensationalism drove still further Locke's repudiation of a priori ideas and other modes of innatism. Reason, will, and the passions were not "given"—innate, immutable, beyond analysis and alteration. They were the products of conditioning; they were amenable to change; they were open to investigation. . . .

Furthermore, it became axiomatic within Enlightenment thinking that some of the more intractable, bizarre, or irrational facets of human behavior could be understood—and, by extension, rectified—only by novel apprehension of their mental, or psychological, aspects. Take drunkenness. Late-eighteenth-century analyses contended that the phenomenon of habitual drinking could not be explained in terms of the material properties of liquor and the digestive system. Enslavement to the demon drink must be reinterpreted as a psychological disorder, a mental disease, or what would soon be called alcoholism. Similarly with sexual excess. Traditionally, excessive venery had been put down to exorbitant irritation of the genitals. Increasingly, nymphomania, satyriasis, and onanism were newly attributed to overstimulus of the imagination. In earlier traditions, malaises such as "hysteria" and "hypochondria" had been interpreted as essentially physical conditions; increasingly, they too were seen as mental aberrations.

In a parallel move, prominent penologists, including Beccaria and Bentham, argued that age-old corporal punishments for criminals—the wheel, lash, or gibbet—were ineffective. Efficient punishment must target not the body but the mind or spirit. Torture must be abolished, capital punishment minimized, for the only true corrective agent was the mental anguish of solitary confinement during protracted prison terms. In these and other respects, Enlightenment activists prided themselves that they were developing a more refined and more *humane* grasp of the subtleties of motivation and behavior, and so a more effective therapeutics. . . . Sociopolitical ills, and their remedies, seemed increasingly to lie in the realm of "mind": on the one hand, ignorance, prejudice, and propaganda; on the other, the remedies of education, enlightenment, and opinion. The Enlightenment began the march of mind.

. . . [D]espite Gay's emphasis upon the symbiosis between medicine and the *philosophe* movement, it is far from clear that Enlightenment intellectuals held the medical profession in specially high esteem or were bowled over by advances in medicine itself. *Philosophes* often castigated medicine, in the manner of Molière, for its oafishness, mercenariness, and precious pomposities; surgeons were seen as butchers, physicians as quacks. . . .

Medicine further suffered from the ambiguity of having for its object the sick body. It was a discipline oriented on defects, on pathology. In some respects, this epitomized the Enlightenment mission: dissection of the ills of society, a certain amount of bloodletting, discriminating social surgery. But the medical model also had pronounced limitations for progressives. Enlightenment propagandists needed eligible representations of a natural, harmonious, flourishing socioeconomic and political order, to serve to criticize, and then to reform, the ancien régime. Though one must avoid oversimplifying the *philosophes'* sociopolitical outlooks, it is clear that values such as individuality, freedom, and self-improvement were widely commended. These were often translated into visions of political liberalism and the free-market economy. It was expected that, thanks to the operation of the natural laws of supply and demand, and with a little help from the hidden hand, self-love and social would prove the same; allowed their free play, diverse interests would, in the end, prove identical. Did medicine provide useful analogies for such social blueprints? On the whole, not. Rather authors such as David Hume, Adam Smith, and Condorcet drew, time and time again, upon the authority of high-prestige Newtonian physics, with its image of matter perpetually in motion, governed by laws of force in a permanent system. The symbolism of the body had less to offer liberal individualists. . . .

Of course, models are multiple and metaphors are labile. There was at least a further potential attraction in medical models for the *philosophes*. The physician's vocation is to heal the sick, and ever since Plato, the doctor and the statesman have been doubles. Thus the image of the *médecin-philosophe*, doctor of a sick society, was ready to hand. And it was utilized, particularly in the programs of centralized public health. . . . Certain *philosophes* found attractions in enlightened absolutism, orchestrated by wise ministers: it opened a role for them as physicians to society, administering a new sociotherapeutics. . . .

Conclusion

I have been trying to plot the complex intertwining of medical men and biomedical ideas with the Enlightenment endeavor. The signs are that, insofar as capital was made of science to provide working models of natural order, physics came first (and, of course, as noted above, proved a serviceable model for medical thinking too). In their attempts to formulate fully naturalistic accounts of the human economy within a law-governed universe, radicals such as d'Holbach looked primarily to the physical sciences. The egalitarianism of atomism agreed with the liberal commitments of most *philosophes*. Condorcet conceived a social *mathematics*, a social *mechanics*.

Some social analysts found medical materialism valuable for dissecting metaphysics and idealism, but most prominent Enlightenment critiques of theology, corrupt mœurs, and political obscurantism drew on *philosophy* for the tasks of intellectual deconstruction and ideological demystification — reason, history, criticism, fiction. As an activist movement, the Enlightenment was principally interested in culture criticism, in formulating psychologies, learning theories, in the workings of publicity and propaganda.

Biomedical inputs had a role. Doctors could deal, literally or metaphorically, with individual sickness and psychopathology, and with specific, if in the end limited, fields of social pathology — witchcraft, religious enthusiasm, demagogy. And, of course, the biomedical sciences have had an enduring role within the Cartesian carving up of the human sciences, wherein, for instance, physical anthropology operates alongside cultural anthropology. Yet my argument has been that the medical model did not become hegemonic for the human sciences; it could equally be argued, that, for its part, "social medicine" made but slow inroads into the domain of "scientific medicine." . . .

"The Concert" (1774). Engraving by Antoine Jean Duclos after a drawing by Augustin de Saint-Aubin. This image of a private concert suggests how women and men mingled in the social and cultural spaces of the Enlightenment, but it leaves open the question of women's precise role, or the implications of the Enlightenment for women. (*Giraudon/Art Resource*, NY)

Did Women Have an Enlightenment?

Among a people in whom the spirit of society is carried so far, domestic life is no longer known. Thus all the sentiments of Nature that are born in retreat, and which grow in silence, are necessarily weakened. Women are less often wives and mothers.

Antoine-Léonard Thomas

One can thus conclude that courage is a gift of nature among women, just as it is among men, and, to carry this view farther, that it is of the essence of humanity in general to struggle against pain, difficulties, obstacles, etc.

Louise d'Epinay

Sophie ought to be a woman as Emile is a man—that is to say, she ought to have everything which suits the constitution of her species and her sex in order to fill her place in the physical and moral order.

Jean-Jacques Rousseau

Let woman share the rights, and she will emulate the virtues of man.

Mary Wollstonecraft

What is at stake here is not simply "woman" but the place of compassion in a society whose economic reproduction rested on the "war of all against all." The function of a moral authority, an

unfilled position in the masculine world of business, is fulfilled by
woman, who appears predestined for this role.

Lieselotte Steinbrügge

Within this tradition therefore women were anything but the passive
recipients of culture. Unlike the thesis which links woman to
nature, the one we have been examining does not leave women
hidden from history. Far from it. She makes it.

Sylvana Tomaselli

As in liberation movements since abolition, the cause of Enlightenment required the solidarity of both men and women. Women's
concerns, which in any event had not yet gained political legitimacy,
had to be subordinated to the "larger" philosophic battle.

Erica Harth

Graffigny's reception history suggests that Enlightenment critics were
ready to welcome a woman into the public forum of the Republic of
Letters on a par with men.   *Janet Gurkin Altman*

Women were a part of the Enlightenment, but what role did they
play in its institutions, and what contributions did they make to its
life and thought? Women were also a subject of Enlightenment
thought and critique, but was the discussion of women itself "enlightened"? Because the stated purpose of Enlightenment was to
spread itself to all through the written word, the question of women's
capacity for learning and their role in society was particularly
salient. The growing importance of science as a mode of knowledge
also had important ramifications. Feminist historians have argued
that the claims of science to truth were used to bolster established
power relations between women and men at least as much as to
call them into question.

This part presents feminist appraisals of the Enlightenment and
the efforts of historians of women to bring women into its history. It
also continues the debate about women that animated the Enlightenment itself. As these historians have brought a new appreciation
of the role of women of letters into conventional understandings of
Enlightenment culture, so they have also brought into focus the debates about the nature and appropriate roles for women that were
central concerns of both men and women of letters.

The first selections are drawn from the Enlightenment debate
on women. They present contrasting views of women's intellectual

ability, their appropriate roles in society, and their contribution to the social and intellectual world of the Enlightenment itself. By pairing the views of an Enlightenment man of letters with those of a female contemporary who challenged those views, we present examples of the kind of critical debate that characterized the Enlightenment at its best.

In 1772, the philosophe and academician Antoine-Léonard Thomas created considerable controversy with his *Essay on Women.* He praised women, but for reasons that betrayed his own prejudices about them. Thomas remarks on a new spirit pervading society, but claims that it is characterized by moral laxity and frivolity brought about by a "taste for the society of women." He distinguishes sharply between the serious, learned women of earlier ages and the frivolous women of the eighteenth century, for whom learning is simply an ornament to display. The essay ends with a call for a restoration of "nature and morals" in an ideal society that stands in stark contrast to that of the Enlightenment of the Paris salons Thomas himself frequented.

Thomas's essay provoked Louise d'Epinay to pen a biting critique in a letter to a friend, the Italian philosophe Ferdinando Galiani. Epinay, whose circle included Diderot and Rousseau, was also the author of a book on the education of girls. Her letter shows that female members of the Enlightenment Republic of Letters could perceive sexism as well as any twenty-first-century feminist. In particular, she challenges Thomas's claim that men and women are fundamentally different and suggests that the "science" underlying this view is simply prejudice. Epinay presents her own argument that men and women are by nature the same and forthrightly declares Thomas's essay unenlightened because it merely reiterates "received opinion."

The philosophe whose views on women were the most controversial and influential was Jean-Jacques Rousseau. In *Emile* (1762), he creates an ideal boy and shows the stages of his education. When Emile reaches manhood, Rousseau introduces the character of Sophie to be his ideal wife, companion, and mother of his children. Since Sophie's gender is her defining feature, Rousseau here articulates what he believes to be the essence of womanhood in contrast to what it means to be a man. Importantly, Rousseau views women only through the eyes of men and in relation to them. He values women, but only insofar as they contribute to the happiness of men. He thus elaborates a world in which men and women have complementary roles, strengths, and virtues, but are not equal. "Woman's empire," he notes, is purely moral and cannot encroach on the rights of the man to rule in his own household. Moreover, in Rousseau's view, the male head of household alone acts as the bridge from the family to society; it is he who represents the family members in the political life of the state. The relationship between Sophie and Emile, therefore, has political implications both within the household and in society at large. In defining a rigid, gendered chasm between the private sphere of women and the public sphere of men, Rousseau opened a debate that continues to shape feminist politics and theory to this day.

Emile provoked a sharp response from the Englishwoman who is considered to be the first modern feminist: Mary Wollstonecraft. Like many women of both her day and our own, Wollstonecraft was attracted to Rousseau's ideas about women, but also critical of them. In *Vindication of the Rights of Woman* (1792), she challenges his basic assumption that woman was "created for man" rather than, like man, for herself. She appreciates the way in which Rousseau gives women dignity and social significance as mothers, however, and she acknowledges that as mothers, wives, and daughters, women have particular duties to fulfill. But, Wollstonecraft argues, these are human duties and the equivalent of those of men. And just as all human beings have duties, so they all have rights. In the midst of the French Revolution, which declared the rights of man, Wollstonecraft responded to Rousseau by making a case not only for equal education for women, but also for their equal rights with men. As a woman of the Enlightenment, Wollstonecraft sees education as key to the development of independent women and men who are prepared for both citizenship and parenthood.

The Enlightenment debate on women and gender raised many questions that continue to animate historical scholarship today. Whereas some have simply asked whether the Enlightenment was "good" for women, and others have been satisfied to demonstrate that the Enlightenment included both male and female writers, the historians whose work is included here ask more difficult questions. In the introduction to her book *The Moral Sex,* Lieselotte Steinbrügge wrestles with the paradox that the emancipatory aim of

Enlightenment (articulated most powerfully by Kant in "What Is Enlightenment?" in this volume) could have been extended to women, but, in fact, was not. Why, she asks, was the tension between the economic need for women to be considered different, and the Enlightenment claim that all human beings are equally endowed with reason and the capacity for happiness and independence, resolved by declaring women incapable of emancipation? How, she asks, were Enlightenment principles used to justify the division of humanity into two unequal parts and thus to shape modern society? Rousseau's relegation of women to a moral sphere of the family even as men become political actors in the public sphere haunts Steinbrügge. She argues that in establishing this division, Rousseau represents not only the masculine perspective of the Enlightenment, but also that of later historians.

Sylvana Tomaselli approaches the Enlightenment's views on women in a very different way. In "The Enlightenment Debate on Women," she argues that the Enlightenment was unique in intellectual history because it associated women not with nature (as other feminist scholars argue philosophers always have), but with culture and civilization. A whole range of Enlightenment men of letters in Scotland and France, she shows, considered women to be a civilizing force that raised men above their animal nature and drove history forward. Women were thus key to the Enlightenment idea of progress. Whereas Steinbrügge argues that women were excluded from the emancipatory project of the Enlightenment, Tomaselli points to the association of female liberation with human progress that pervades Enlightenment thought. For Tomaselli, the role that women play in Enlightenment histories both represents their power within Enlightenment society and suggests a model for how history might be written today—a history that takes women seriously as political, social, and cultural agents.

In a sense, Erica Harth takes up Tomaselli's challenge by examining women's social and political roles in the cultural space of the Enlightenment salon. She argues that the "civilizing role" that women played in the salon was important for the Enlightenment but represented a setback for women. By contrasting the full participation of seventeenth-century women in salon discussions with the largely silent job of guiding discussion that women were assigned during the Enlightenment, she contests Tomaselli's claim that women's cultural status improved in the eighteenth century. More boldly, she argues that to "civilize" men, salon women were silenced and the concerns of women were excluded from the "serious" business of Enlightenment.

This part concludes with Janet Gurkin Altman's case for including the French novelist Françoise de Graffigny among the canon of Enlightenment writers. By tracing the history of the publication and reception of Graffigny's *Letters of a Peruvian Woman* from 1747 to the present, Altman shows how Graffigny's novel was first heralded as a contribution to the Enlightenment and only later dismissed because of the gender of its author. Through a discussion of the novel itself, Altman makes her own case for its importance as a literary expression of Enlightenment ideas and suggests that we might find in its heroine's quest for knowledge an affirmative answer to the question: Did women have an Enlightenment?

Antoine-Léonard Thomas

Essay on the Character, Morals and Mind of Women Across the Centuries

In the last years of Louis XIV's reign some terrible sort of seriousness and sadness had spread through the court and part of the nation. At heart, penchants were the same, but they were more repressed. A new court and new ideas changed everything. A bolder sensuality became fashionable. Audacity and impetuosity colored all desires, and a part of the veil which covered gallantry was torn away. The decency which had

Antoine-Léonard Thomas, *Essay on the Character, Morals and Mind of Women Across the Centuries*, trans. Dena Goodman and Katherine Ann Jensen, in *Lives and Voices: Sources in European Women's History*, ed. Lisa DiCaprio and Merry E. Wiesner (Boston: Houghton Mifflin, 2001), 243–246.

been respected as a duty, was no longer even maintained as a pleasure. Shame was dispensed with on both sides. Fickleness matched excess, and a corruption took shape that was at once profound and frivolous, that, blushing at nothing, laughed instead at everything.

The upsetting of fortunes precipitated this change. Extreme misery and extreme luxury followed from it; and we know what influence these have had. Rarely does a people receive such a quick jolt in regard to property without a prompt alteration in manners and morals. . . .

At the same time, and by the same general trend which carries everything along, the taste for the society of women grew. Seduction was made easier, the opportunities for it increased everywhere. Men lived together less; less timid women became accustomed to throwing off a constraint which honors them. The two sexes were denatured; one placed too much value on being agreeable, the other on independence.

Thus the weight of time, the desire to please, necessarily spread the spirit of society farther and farther; and the time had to come when this sociability pushed to excess, in mixing everything up, succeeded in spoiling everything; and this is perhaps where we are today.

Among a people in whom the spirit of society is carried so far, domestic life is no longer known. Thus all the sentiments of Nature that are born in retreat, and which grow in silence, are necessarily weakened. Women are less often wives and mothers. . . .

Put all of this together and a disturbing frivolity in the two sexes must arise, along with a serious and busy vanity. But what must above all characterize morals, is the fury of appearance, the art of putting everything on the surface, a great importance given to small duties, and a great value to small successes. One must speak gravely of petty things from last night and from the next morning. In the end the soul and the mind must be engaged in a cold activity, which spreads them over a thousand objects without interesting them in any, and which gives them movement without direction. . . .

As the general mass of enlightenment is greater, and as it is communicated through greater movement, women, without taking the least trouble, are necessarily better instructed; but faithful to their plan, they do not seek enlightenment, except as an ornament of the mind. In learning they wish to please rather than to know, and to amuse rather than to learn.

Moreover, in a state of society where there is a rapid movement and an eternal succession of works and ideas, women, occupied with following this panorama which flees and changes around them constantly, will better understand the idea of the moment in each genre, than eternal ones, and know the dominant ideas, rather than those which are forming. They will thus know the language of the arts better than their principles, and have more specific ideas than systems of thought.

It seems to me that in the sixteenth century women learned through enthusiasm for learning itself. There was in them a profound taste which derived from the spirit of the age and that was nourished even in solitude. In this century, it is less a real taste than a flirtation of the mind; and as with all objects, a luxury, [although] more represented than based on wealth. . . .

Today we see too much: and thanks to enlightenment, we see everything coldly. Vice itself ranks among our pretensions. The less we esteem women, the more we appear to know them. Each one prides himself on not believing in their virtues; and he who would like to be a fop and cannot succeed by speaking ill of them, prides himself on a satire that, as the height of ridiculousness, he has no right to make. Such is, with regard to women themselves, the influence of this general spirit of society which is their work, and which they do not cease to vaunt. They are like those Asian rulers who are never honored more than when they are seen less: by communicating too much to their subjects, they encourage them to revolt.

However, despite our morals and our eternal satires, despite our fury to be esteemed without merit, and our even greater fury never to find anything worthy of esteem, there are in our century, and in this capital itself, women who would do honor to another century than ours. Several bring together a strong soul and a truly cultivated reason, and bring forth by their virtues, feelings of courage and honor. There are some who could think with Montesquieu, and with whom Fénelon would love to be moved. There are some who, in opulence, and, surrounded by this luxury that today practically forces avarice to join with pomp and renders souls small, vain, and cruel, take from their property each year a portion for the unfortunate; they are familiar with shelters for the poor, and will learn to be sensitive in shedding their tears there. There are tender wives, who, young and beautiful, pride themselves on their duties, and in the sweetest of attachments offer a ravishing spectacle of innocence and love. Finally, there are mothers who dare to be mothers. In several houses beauty can be seen taking charge of the most tender cares of nature, and by turns pressing in her arms or to a breast the son whom she nourishes with her own milk, while in silence the husband divides his tender regards between son and mother.

Oh! if these examples could restore among us nature and morals! If we could learn how much superior are virtues to pleasures for happiness itself; how much a simple and calm life where nothing is affected, where one exists only for oneself, and not for the gaze of others, where one enjoys by turn friendship, nature, and oneself, is preferable to this anxious and turbulent life, in which one is forever running after a feeling that one does not find! Ah! then, women would regain their empire. It is then that beauty, embellished with morals, would command men, happy to be subjected, and great in their weakness. Then an honorable and pure sensuality seasoning every moment, would make of life an enchanted dream. Then troubles, not being poisoned by remorse, troubles softened by love and shared in friendship, would be a touching sadness rather than a torment. In this state society would doubtless be less active, but the interior of families would be sweeter. There would be less ostentation and more pleasure; less movement and more happiness. One would talk less to please, and one would please oneself more. The days would flow on pure and tranquil: and if in the evening one did not have the sad satisfaction of having during the course of the day played at having the most tender interest in thirty random people, one would have at least lived with the one whom one loves; one would have added for the morrow a new charm to the feelings of yesterday. Must such a sweet image be only an illusion? And in this burning and vain society, is there no refuge for simplicity and happiness?

Louise d'Epinay

Letter to Abbé Ferdinando Galiani

You haven't written me at all this week, my dear Abbé. I am not well: therefore, I don't have much to tell you. So. I am resolved to read in front of the fire Monsieur Thomas' book: *On the Character, Morals and Mind of Women*. This work just appeared a few days ago; and, if it gives rise to certain ideas, I will share them with you. I will tell you, as usual,

Louise d'Epinay, "Letter to Abbé Ferdinando Galiani," in *La Signora d'Epinay e l'abbate Galiani: Lettere inedite (1769–1772)*, ed. Fausto Nicolini (Bari: Laterza e figli, 1929), 151–152. Translated by Dena Goodman.

everything that comes into my head, provided that my views remain between you and me.

Well then! I've read it and to anyone but you I would be careful about saying what I think, or of taking so definite a tone in the world; but I confess that this [book] seems to me nothing but pompous chattering, very eloquent, a little pedantic, and very monotonous. One finds in it some little dressed-up sentences, the sort of sentences that, heard in a small circle, cause people to say of their author, that day and the next: "He has the wit of an angel! he is charming! he is charming!" But when I find them in a work that has the pretention to be serious, I have real difficulty being satisfied with them. This one doesn't add up to anything. One does not know, after one has read it, what the author thinks and if his opinion about women is anything but received opinion. He writes with great erudition the history of famous women in all fields. He discusses a bit dryly what they owe to nature, to the institution of society and to education; and then, in showing them as they are, he attributes endlessly to nature that which we obviously owe to education or to institutions, etc.

And then so many commonplaces! "Are they more sensitive? More devoted in friendship than men? Are they more this? Are they more that?" "Montaigne," he says, "decides the question clearly against women, perhaps like that judge who so feared to be partial that on principle he always lost cases in which his friends were involved." And then, in another place: "Nature," he says, "makes them like flowers in order to shine softly in the garden from which they rise. One ought thus perhaps to desire a man for a friend for the great occasions, and for everyday happiness, one ought to wish for the friendship of a woman." How petty, common, and unphilosophical these details are!

He claims that they are not able to transact business with as much continuity and constancy as men, nor with as much courage in their resolutions. This is, I think, a very false vision; there are a thousand examples of the contrary; there are even some very recent and rather remarkable ones. Moreover, constancy and courage in the pursuit of an object could be, it seems to me, calculated out of idleness, and this would be a strong argument in our favor. I don't have the time to work out this idea to the extent that I would like. But fortunately this is not necessary with you, and you will figure out the rest. "We have seen," says Monsieur Thomas "in [times of] great danger, examples of great courage among women; but this is always when a great passion or an idea that moves them strongly carries them beyond themselves," etc. But is courage anything else among men? Opinion or ambition is what moves them strongly. Were you to attach, in the institution and the education of women, the same prejudice to valor, you would find as many courageous women as men, since cowards are found among them, despite opinion, and the number of courageous women is as great as the number of cowardly men. Of the sum total of physical ailments spread over the face of the earth, women's share is more than two-thirds. It is quite constant also that they suffer them with infinitely more constancy and courage than do men. There is in this neither prejudice nor vanity for support: [woman's] physical constitution has, moreover, become weaker than man's as a result of education. One can thus conclude that courage is a gift of nature among women, just as it is among men, and, to carry this view farther, that it is of the essence of humanity in general to struggle against pain, difficulties, obstacles, etc. One could, to even greater advantage, make the same calculation regarding moral troubles.

In speaking of the minority of Louis XIV, he says: "All women of this era had this sort of restless agitation produced by partisan spirit: a spirit less far from their character than one would think." That's true, Monsieur Thomas. But, since you would like to be scientific, here was a case for examining whether this restless disposition, which they have by nature, is particular to them and is not found equally among men; whether men, deprived as they are, of serious occupations, excluded from business and strangers to all great causes, would not display this same restless disposition, which is, in your eyes, extinguished by the nourishment given them by the role they play in society. The proof of this is that [this restless disposition] is noticed nowhere as much as among monks and in religious houses. Your work is not at all philosophic, you examine nothing on a grand scale, and once again I do not find any point. . . .

He finishes his work by expressing a wish for a return to morality and to virtue. So be it, certainly! These last four pages are the most agreeable of his book because of the picture he paints of woman as she ought to be; but he sees it as a chimera.

It is well established that men and women have the same nature and the same constitution. The proof lies in that female savages are as robust, as agile as male savages: thus the weakness of our constitution and of our organs belongs definitely to our education, and is a consequence of the condition to which we have been assigned in society. Men and women, being of the same nature and the same constitution, are susceptible to the same faults, the same virtues, and the same vices. The virtues that have been ascribed to women in general are almost all virtues against nature, which only produce small artificial virtues and very real vices. It would no doubt take several generations to get us back to how nature made us. We could perhaps reach that point; but men would thereby lose too much. They are quite lucky that we are no worse than we are, after all that they have done to denature us through their lovely institutions, etc. This is so obvious that it is no more worth the trouble of saying than all that Monsieur Thomas has said.

It was difficult to say anything new on this subject, and, in general, as Monsieur Grimm was saying the other day, there are no longer any new subjects or new ideas: all that we need are new heads to get us to imagine things from different points of view. But where are we to find them? I know two of them, nonetheless: the abbé Galiani and the marquis de Croismare. The marquis is to society what you are to philosophy and administration.

Goodby, my abbé! I do not know if women are constant, brave, etc.; but I know at least that they are as chatty as philosophers. You will agree in reading this letter, but I hope nevertheless that you will not disdain to respond and to give me your views on this delicate question.

Jean-Jacques Rousseau

Emile

Sophie ought to be a woman as Emile is a man—that is to say, she ought to have everything which suits the constitution of her species and her sex in order to fill her place in the physical and moral order. Let us begin, then, by examining the similarities and the differences of her sex and ours.

In everything not connected with sex, woman is man. She has the same organs, the same needs, the same faculties. The machine is constructed in the same way; its parts are the same; the one functions as does the other; the form is similar; and in whatever respect one considers them, the difference between them is only one of more or less.

Jean-Jacques Rousseau, *Emile*, trans. Allan Bloom (New York: Basic Books, 1979), 357–358, 392–393, 407–409. Copyright © 1979 by Basic Books, Inc. Reprinted by permission of Basic Books, a member of Perseus Books, L.L.C., via the Copyright Clearance Center.

In everything connected with sex, woman and man are in every respect related and in every respect different. The difficulty of comparing them comes from the difficulty of determining what in their constitutions is due to sex and what is not. On the basis of comparative anatomy and even just by inspection, one finds general differences between them that do not appear connected with sex. They are, nevertheless, connected with sex, but by relations which we are not in a position to perceive. We do not know the extent of these relations. The only thing we know with certainty is that everything man and woman have in common belongs to the species, and that everything which distinguishes them belongs to the sex. From this double perspective, we find them related in so many ways and opposed in so many other ways that it is perhaps one of the marvels of nature to have been able to construct two such similar beings who are constituted so differently.

These relations and these differences must have a moral influence. This conclusion is evident to the senses; it is in agreement with our experience; and it shows how vain are the disputes as to whether one of the two sexes is superior or whether they are equal—as though each, in fulfilling nature's ends according to its own particular purpose, were thereby less perfect than if it resembled the other more! In what they have in common, they are equal. Where they differ, they are not comparable. A perfect woman and a perfect man ought not to resemble each other in mind any more than in looks, and perfection is not susceptible of more or less.

In the union of the sexes each contributes equally to the common aim, but not in the same way. From this diversity arises the first assignable difference in the moral relations of the two sexes. One ought to be active and strong, the other passive and weak. One must necessarily will and be able; it suffices that the other put up little resistance.

Once this principle is established, it follows that woman is made specially to please man. If man ought to please her in turn, it is due to a less direct necessity. His merit is in his power; he pleases by the sole fact of his strength. This is not the law of love, I agree. But it is that of nature, prior to love itself.

If woman is made to please and to be subjugated, she ought to make herself agreeable to man instead of arousing him. Her own violence is in her charms. It is by these that she ought to constrain him to find his strength and make use of it. The surest art for animating that strength is to make it necessary by resistance. Then *amour-propre* unites with desire, and the one triumphs in the victory that the other has made him win. From this there arises attack and defense, the audacity of one sex and the timidity of the other, and finally the modesty and the shame with which nature armed the weak in order to enslave the strong. . . .

Do you want, then, to inspire young girls with the love of good morals? Without constantly saying to them "Be pure," give them a great interest in being pure. Make them feel all the value of purity, and you will make them love it. It does not suffice to place this interest in the distant future. Show it to them in the present moment, in the relationships of their own age, in the character of their lovers. Depict for them the good man, the man of merit; teach them to recognize him, to love him, and to love him for themselves; prove to them that this man alone can make the women to whom he is attached—wives or beloveds—happy. Lead them to virtue by means of reason. Make them feel that the empire of their sex and all its advantages depend not only on the good conduct and the morals of women but also on those of men, that they have little hold over vile and base souls, and that a man will serve his mistress no better than he serves virtue. You can then be sure that in depicting to them the morals of our own days, you will inspire in them a sincere disgust. In showing them fashionable people, you will make them despise them; you will only be keeping them at a distance from their maxims and giving them an aversion for their sentiments and a disdain for their vain gallantry. You will cause a nobler ambition to be born in them—that of reigning over great and strong souls, the ambition of the women of Sparta, which was to command men. A bold brazen scheming woman who knows how to attract her lovers only by coquetry and to keep them only by favors makes them obey her like valets in servile and common things; however, in important and weighty things she is without authority over them. But the woman who is at once decent, lovable, and self-controlled, who forces those about her to respect her, who has reserve and modesty, who, in a word, sustains love by means of esteem, sends her lovers with a nod to the end of the world, to combat, to glory, to death, to anything she pleases. This seems to me to be a noble empire, and one well worth the price of its purchase. . . .

It also makes a great difference for the good order of the marriage whether the man makes an alliance above or below himself. The former case is entirely contrary to reason; the latter is more conformable to it. Since the family is connected with society only by its head, the position of the head determines that of the entire family. When he makes an alliance in a lower rank, he does not descend, he raises up his wife. On the other hand, by taking a woman above him, he lowers her without raising himself. Thus, in the first case there is good without bad, and in the second bad without good. Moreover, it is part of the order of nature that the woman obey the man. Therefore, when he takes her from a lower rank, the natural and the civil order agree, and everything goes well. The contrary is the case when the man allies himself with a woman above him and thereby faces the alternative of curbing either his rights or his gratitude and of being either ungrateful or despised. Then the woman, pretending to authority, acts as a tyrant toward the head of the house and the master becomes a slave and finds himself the most ridiculous and most miserable of creatures. Such are those unfortunate favorites whom the Asian kings honor and torment by marrying them to their daughters, and who are said to dare to approach only from the foot of the bed in order to sleep with their wives.

I expect that many readers, remembering that I ascribe to woman a natural talent for governing man, will accuse me of a contradiction here. They will, however, be mistaken. There is quite a difference between arrogating to oneself the right to command and governing him who commands. Woman's empire is an empire of gentleness, skill, and obligingness: her orders are caresses, her threats are tears. She ought to reign in the home as a minister does in a state—by getting herself commanded to do what she wants to do. In this sense, the best households are invariably those where the woman has the most authority. But when she fails to recognize the voice of the head of the house, when she wants to usurp his rights and be in command herself, the result of this disorder is never anything but misery, scandal, and dishonor.

There remains the choice between one's equals and one's inferiors: and I believe that some restriction must be placed upon the latter, for it is difficult to find among the dregs of the people a wife capable of making a gentleman happy. It is not that they are more vicious in the lowest rank than in the highest, but that they have few ideas of what is beautiful and decent, and that the injustice of the older estates makes the lowest see justice in its very vices.

By nature man hardly thinks. To think is an art he learns like all the others and with even more difficulty. In regard to relations between the two sexes, I know of only two classes which are separated by a real distinction—one composed of people who think, the other of people who do not think; and this difference comes almost entirely from education. A man from the first of these two classes ought not to make an alliance in the other, for the greatest charm of society is lacking to him when, despite having a wife, he is reduced to thinking alone. People who literally spend their whole lives working in order to live have no idea other than that of their work or their self-interest, and their whole mind seems to be at the end of their arms. This ignorance harms neither probity nor morals. Often it even serves them. Often one compromises in regard to one's duties by dint of reflecting on them and ends up replacing real things with abstract talk. Conscience is the most enlightened of philosophers. One does not need to know Cicero's *Offices* to be a good man, and the most decent woman in the world perhaps has the least knowledge of what decency is. But it is no less true that only a cultivated mind makes association agreeable, and it is a sad thing for a father of a family who enjoys himself in his home to be forced to close himself up and not be able to make himself understood by anyone.

Besides, how will a woman who has no habit of reflecting raise her children? How will she discern what suits them? How will she incline them toward virtues she does not know, toward merit of which she has no idea? She will know only how to flatter or threaten them, to make them insolent or fearful. She will make mannered monkeys or giddy rascals of them, never good minds or lovable children.

Therefore, it is not suitable for a man with education to take a wife who has none, or, consequently, to take a wife from a rank in which she could not have an education. But I would still like a simple and coarsely raised girl a hundred times better than a learned and brilliant one who would come to establish in my house a tribunal of literature over which she would preside. A brilliant wife is a plague to her husband, her children, her friends, her valets, everyone. From the sublime elevation of her fair genius she disdains all her woman's duties and always begins by making herself into a man after the fashion of Mademoiselle de l'Enclos. Outside her home she is always ridiculous and very justly criticized; this is the inevitable result as soon as one leaves one's station and is not fit for the station one wants to adopt. All these women of great talent never impress anyone but fools. It is always known who the artist or the friend is who holds the pen or the brush when they work. It is known who the discreet man of letters is who secretly dictates their oracles to them. All this charlatanry is unworthy of a decent woman. Even if she had some true talents, her pretensions would debase them. Her dignity consists in her being ignored. Her glory is in her husband's esteem. Her pleasures are in the happiness of her family. Readers, I leave it to you. Answer in good faith. What gives you a better opinion of a woman on entering her room, what makes you approach her with more respect—to see her occupied with the labors of her sex and the cares of her household encompassed by her children's things, or to find her at her dressing table writing verses, surrounded by all sorts of pamphlets and letters written on tinted paper? Every literary maiden would remain a maiden for her whole life if there were only sensible men in this world. . . .

After these considerations comes that of looks. It is the first consideration which strikes one and the last to which one ought to pay attention, but still it should count for something. Great beauty appears to me to be avoided rather than sought in marriage. Beauty promptly wears out in possession. After six weeks it is nothing more for the possessor, but its dangers last as long as it does. Unless a beautiful woman is an angel, her husband is the unhappiest of men; and even if she were an angel, how will she prevent his being ceaselessly surrounded by enemies? If extreme ugliness were not disgusting, I would prefer it to extreme beauty; for in a short time both are nothing for the husband and thus beauty becomes a drawback and ugliness an advantage. But ugliness which produces disgust is the greatest of misfortunes. This sentiment, far from fading away, increases constantly and turns into hatred. Such a marriage is a hell. It would be better to be dead than to be thus united. . . .

Mary Wollstonecraft

A Vindication of the Rights of Woman

. . . My own sex, I hope, will excuse me, if I treat them like rational creatures, instead of flattering their *fascinating* graces, and viewing them as if they were in a state of perpetual childhood, unable to stand alone. I earnestly wish to point out in what true dignity and human happiness consists. I wish to persuade women to endeavour to acquire strength,

Mary Wollstonecraft, *A Vindication of the Rights of Woman*, ed. Miriam Brody Kramnick (London: Penguin Books, 1992), 81–82, 86–87, 103, 108–109, 140–141, 271–272, 300–302, 327–328.

both of mind and body, and to convince them that the soft phrases, susceptibility of heart, delicacy of sentiment, and refinement of taste, are almost synonymous with epithets of weakness, and that those beings who are only the objects of pity, and that kind of love which has been termed its sister, will soon become objects of contempt.

Dismissing, then, those pretty feminine phrases, which the men condescendingly use to soften our slavish dependence, and despising that weak elegancy of mind, exquisite sensibility, and sweet docility of manners, supposed to be the sexual characteristics of the weaker vessel, I wish to show that elegance is inferior to virtue, that the first object of laudable ambition is to obtain a character as a human being, regardless of the distinction of sex, and that secondary views should be brought to this simple touchstone. . . .

Contending for the rights of woman, my main argument is built on this simple principle, that if she be not prepared by education to become the companion of man, she will stop the progress of knowledge and virtue: for truth must be common to all, or it will be inefficacious with respect to its influence on general practice. And how can woman be expected to co-operate unless she knows why she ought to be virtuous? unless freedom strengthens her reason till she comprehends her duty, and see in what manner it is connected with her real good. If children are to be educated to understand the true principle of patriotism, their mother must be a patriot; and the love of mankind, from which an orderly train of virtues spring, can only be produced by considering the moral and civil interest of mankind; but the education and situation of woman at present shuts her out from such investigations. . . .

Consequently, the most perfect education, in my opinion, is such an exercise of the understanding as is best calculated to strengthen the body and form the heart. Or, in other words, to enable the individual to attain such habits of virtue as will render it independent. In fact, it is a farce to call any being virtuous whose virtues do not result from the exercise of its own reason. This was Rousseau's opinion respecting men; I extend it to women, and confidently assert that they have been drawn out of their sphere by false refinement and not by an endeavour to acquire masculine qualities. . . .

Women are therefore to be considered either as moral beings, or so weak that they must be entirely subjected to the superior faculties of men.

Let us examine this question. Rousseau declares that a woman should never for a moment feel herself independent, that she should be governed by fear to exercise her *natural* cunning, and made a coquettish slave in order to render her a more alluring object of desire, a *sweeter* companion to man, whenever he chose to relax himself. He carries the arguments, which he pretends to draw from the indications of nature, still further, and insinuates that truth and fortitude, the corner-stones of all human virtue, should be cultivated with certain restrictions, because, with respect to the female character, obedience is the grand lesson which ought to be impressed with unrelenting rigour.

What nonsense! When will a great man arise with sufficient strength of mind to puff away the fumes which pride and sensuality have thus spread over the subject? If women are by nature inferior to men, their virtues must be the same in quality, if not in degree, or virtue is a relative idea; consequently their conduct should be founded on the same principles, and have the same aim.

Connected with man as daughters, wives, and mothers, their moral character may be estimated by their manner of fulfilling those simple duties; but the end, the grand end, of their exertions should be to unfold their own faculties, and acquire the dignity of conscious virtue. They may try to render their road pleasant; but ought never to forget, in common with man, that life yields not the felicity which can satisfy an immortal soul. I do not mean to insinuate that either sex should be so lost in abstract reflections or distant views as to forget the affections and duties that lie before them, and are, in truth, the means appointed to produce the fruit of life; on the contrary, I would warmly recommend them, even while I assert that they afford most satisfaction when they are considered in their true sober light.

Probably the prevailing opinion that woman was created for man, may have taken its rise from Moses' poetical story: yet as very few, it is presumed, who have bestowed any serious thought on the subject ever supposed that Eve was, literally speaking, one of Adam's ribs, the deduction must be allowed to fall to the ground, or only be so far admitted as it proves that man, from the remotest antiquity, found it convenient to exert his strength to subjugate his companion, and his invention to show that she ought to have her neck bent under the yoke, because the whole creation was only created for his convenience or pleasure. . . .

I wish to sum up what I have said in a few words, for I here throw down my gauntlet, and deny the existence of sexual virtues, not excepting modesty. For man and woman, truth if I understand the meaning of the word, must be the same; yet the fanciful female character, so prettily drawn by poets and novelists, demanding the sacrifice of truth and sincerity, virtue becomes a relative idea, having no other foundation than utility, and of that utility men pretend arbitrarily to judge, shaping it to their own convenience.

Women, I allow, may have different duties to fulfil; but they are *human* duties, and the principles that should regulate the discharge of them I sturdily maintain must be the same.

To become respectable, the exercise of their understanding is necessary, there is no other foundation for independence of character; I mean explicitly to say that they must only bow to the authority of reason, instead of being the *modest* slaves of opinion. . . .

As the care of children in their infancy is one of the grand duties annexed to the female character by nature, this duty would afford many forcible arguments for strengthening the female understanding, if it were properly considered.

The formation of the mind must be begun very early, and the temper, in particular, requires the most judicious attention—an attention which women cannot pay who only love their children because they are their children, and seek no further for the foundation of their duty, than in the feelings of the moment. It is this want of reason in their affections which makes women so often run into extremes, and either be the most fond or most careless and unnatural mothers.

To be a good mother, a woman must have sense, and that independence of mind which few women possess who are taught to depend entirely on their husbands. Meek wives are, in general, foolish mothers; wanting their children to love them best, and take their part, in secret, against the father, who is held up as a scarecrow. When chastisement is necessary, though they have offended the mother, the father must inflict the punishment; he must be the judge in all disputes; but I shall more fully discuss this subject when I treat of private education. I now only mean to insist, that unless the understanding of woman be enlarged, and her character rendered more firm, by being allowed to govern her own conduct, she will never have sufficient sense or command of temper to manage her children properly. . . .

To render mankind more virtuous, and happier of course, both sexes must act from the same principle; but how can that be expected when only one is allowed to see the reasonableness of it? To render also the social compact truly equitable, and in order to spread those enlightening principles, women must be allowed to found their virtue on knowledge, which is scarcely possible unless they be educated by the same pursuits as men. For they are now made so inferior by ignorance and low desires, as not to deserve to be ranked with them or, by the serpentine wrigglings of cunning, they mount the tree of knowledge, and only acquire sufficient to lead men astray.

It is plain from the history of all nations, that women cannot be confined to merely domestic pursuits, for they will not fulfil family duties unless their minds take a wider range, and whilst they are kept in ignorance they become in the same proportion the slaves of pleasure as they are the slaves of man. Nor can they be shut out of great enterprises, though the narrowness of their minds often make them mar, what they are unable to comprehend.

. . . [T]he sexual weakness that makes woman depend on man for a subsistence, produces a kind of cattish affection, which leads a wife to purr about her husband as she would about any man who fed and caressed her.

Men are, however, often gratified by this kind of fondness, which is confined in a beastly manner to themselves; but should they ever become more virtuous, they will wish to converse at their fireside with a friend after they cease to play with a mistress.

Besides, understanding is necessary to give variety and interest to sensual enjoyments, for low indeed in the intellectual scale is the mind that can continue to love when neither virtue nor sense give a human appearance to an animal appetite. But sense will always preponderate; and if women be not, in general, brought more on a level with men, some superior women like the Greek courtesans, will assemble the men of abilities around them, and draw from their families many citizens, who would have stayed at home had their wives had more sense, or the graces which result from the exercise of the understanding, and fancy, the legitimate parents of taste. A woman of talents, if she be not absolutely ugly, will always obtain great power—raised by the weakness of her sex; and in proportion as men acquire virtue and delicacy by the exertion of reason, they will look for both in women, but they can only acquire them in the same way that men do. . . .

Asserting the rights which women in common with men ought to contend for, I have not attempted to extenuate their faults; but to prove them to be the natural consequence of their education and station in society. If so, it is reasonable to suppose that they will change their character, and correct their vices and follies, when they are allowed to be free in a physical, moral, and civil sense.

Let woman share the rights, and she will emulate the virtues of man; for she must grow more perfect when emancipated, or justify the authority that chains such a weak being to her duty. If the latter, it will be expedient to open a fresh trade with Russia for whips: a present which a father should always make to his son-in-law on his wedding day, that a husband may keep his whole family in order by the same means; and without any violation of justice reign, wielding this sceptre, sole master of his house, because he is the only thing in it who has reason:—the divine, indefeasible earthly sovereignty breathed into man by the Master of the universe. Allowing this position, women have not any inherent rights to claim; and, by the same rule, their duties vanish, for rights and duties are inseparable.

Be just then, O ye men of understanding; and mark not more severely what women do amiss than the vicious tricks of the horse or the ass for whom ye provide provender—and allow her the privileges of ignorance, to whom ye deny the rights of reason, or ye will be worse than Egyptian task-masters, expecting virtue where Nature has not given understanding.

Lieselotte Steinbrügge

The Moral Sex

Legend has it that in France the eighteenth century was the century of women, and the facts would seem to substantiate this view. The intellectual elite met in salons led by women; the important thinkers of the age corresponded and discussed their ideas with women. A number of women took up writing themselves, producing scientific tracts, translations, novels, or pedagogical programs. Women such as Madame du Châtelet, Madame de Graffigny, Madame Riccoboni, Madame de Lambert, Julie de Lespinasse, and Madame de Genlis—to name only a few—represent this development. It was this integration of women into intellectual life which, a century later, moved the Goncourt brothers to devote a celebrated study to the women of the eighteenth century, in which they concluded that woman had been the governing principle of the age, a topos which has persisted virtually unbroken to this day.

The reasons for this persistence seem to me to lie not so much in the—at least initially convincing—power of facts but rather in the very logic of Enlightenment philosophy. Indeed, the philosophe's aspirations toward emancipation and education did not stop with women. The eighteenth century was an era of upheaval in which human nature, and with it the nature of men and women, was being rethought. The religious worldview was losing its validity, and with it the biblical curse which for centuries had allowed women to be conceived as subordinate to men. The bourgeois notion of natural human equality also facilitated a new anthropological definition of the female human being. "Woman in a state of nature, like man, is a free and powerful being," wrote Choderlos de Laclos in *Des femmes et de leur éducation* (On Women and Their Education), following Rousseau's postulate on the natural equality of all human beings.

This development, however, by no means culminated in the concept of the equality of the sexes. The eighteenth century is the period when the sex-specific character attributed to men and women developed and diverged; it is the epoch in which the ideological and institutional foundations were laid for women's exclusion from civil rights and higher education—in short, from public life. It is the age that saw the emergence of an image of female nature that allowed precisely these exclusions to be considered "natural."

Historians, particularly those studying the history of the family, have outlined the sociohistorical factors underpinning this development. The exigencies of the bourgeois system of production accorded the family a purely reproductive role. Women were relegated to work that, lying as it did outside the sphere of social production, did not allow them to participate in scientific-technological progress and thus demanded of them other qualities than those required there. At the same time, the physiocrats, for whom population growth represented the fundamental precondition for all economic progress, glorified the material virtues in a sort of large-scale advertising campaign aimed at reminding women of their demographic duties. Finally, the recognition of children as people in their own right also contributed to a new understanding of the maternal role.

All these factors belonging to the realm of social history and the history of mentalities are the premises upon which my analyses rest. I assume that the theories and literary representations of woman's nature I discuss cannot be explained without these actual historical factors. They do not, however, provide the ultimate explanation. Rather, they demarcate the tension between, on the one hand, the Enlightenment aspiration to emancipate a (female) sex maintained in ignorance and, on the other, the "objective necessities" of the bourgeois economic order, which required women to adopt the role of housewife and mother. What interests me is *how* this tension, within which the recasting of female identity occurred, could be resolved theoretically in order that the concept of a general female incapacity for human emancipation could become a universal anthropological truth.

This concept, which can still be encountered today, is by no means a product of the counter-Enlightenment. The division of humanity into two unequal parts was legitimated with genuinely Enlightenment principles—this in an age professing devotion to the equality of all human beings. The road there led past the very authority that allowed men to conceive of liberation from the shackles of tutelage: Nature. The feminist dialectic of Enlightenment shows that the idea of (human) nature, the paradigm of Enlightenment emancipation in general, when applied to women, comes to mean "subsumption" and "limitation." My task in what follows is to sketch the path this process took.

The question of woman's nature greatly exercized thinkers of the time. It was the object of medical, historiographic, anthropological, philosophical, and, not least, literary discourse. The *querelle des femmes*, that debate over the question of the equality of the sexes which had been raging at least since the *Roman de la rose*, had revived, particularly since the 1750s. This discussion was multifaceted, encompassing nearly all aspects of female existence, from woman's social role to her biological nature and sexuality. The aspect that particularly interests me here is the problem of women's intellectual capacity and the related ideal of the learned woman.

This aspect seems significant to me for two reasons. First, in an age in which the belief in progress was expressed as belief in the transformative power of reason, the way in which women's intellectual capacity was evaluated was a decisive determinant of their position within the culture. Second, it can be demonstrated that the alteration in the period's ideal of femininity occurred in express rejection of a female type primarily defined by active participation in intellectual life.

Poulain de la Barre's 1673 pamphlet *De l'égalité des deux sexes* (On the Equality of the Two Sexes), the first detailed examination of the theme of female intellect, broke ground for the Enlightenment *querelle*. Thus, it is no coincidence that virtually all of the polemics that were to follow addressed his arguments, either implicitly or explicitly. . . .

The form this discussion took can, I believe, only be understood against the background of the period's philosophical anthropology, . . . Research into the organic preconditions of human knowledge also set a precedent for the medical and philosophical discourse on women and was fundamental for the recasting of ideas of female nature. The reevaluation of the female body took on particular significance in this context. Argumentation in terms of sensory physiology at first facilitated the liberation of woman from the myths surrounding her corporeality, allowing for the emancipatory "mobilization" of nature against repressive superstition. On the other hand, it was precisely the great significance attributed to woman's physical nature that, in conjunction with physiocratic discourse, led to an unprecedented reduction of woman to the creatural. It was this final aspect that was to become ideologically dominant. . . . [T]exts from the *Encyclopedia* and by Thomas and Roussel . . . show that at the end of the age of Enlightenment, the woman who emerged from reflexions about female nature was not a full individual but a being viewed solely in terms of her sex. . . .

The Enlightenment debate was by no means limited to a dismantling of woman's human—particularly intellectual—capabilities, which at first made women appear as deficient men. Rather, this reduction was accompanied by a broadened anthropological definition of woman's sex-specific character, which was based precisely on woman's supposed closeness to nature. My central thesis here is that the accentuation of creatureliness, and thus also of emotionality, over enlightened rationality predestined women to adopt a particular role. The exclusion of women from public life and its complement, their relegation to private life, appeared to qualify women particularly for the realm of *morality*, conceived of in bourgeois society as a genuinely private morality, and one that could only be socially efficacious through the private sphere. And because this morality achieved an increasingly emotional basis in the age of Enlightenment, not least because of its private character, female nature could be proclaimed as particularly competent as emotional morality. With this, the definition of woman as "the sex" sealed women's destiny as the moral authority of a society that excluded certain direct human emotions from public interactions. Woman became *the moral sex.* Humane qualities survived (only) as a female principle.

. . . What is at stake here is not simply "woman" but the place of compassion in a society whose economic reproduction rested on the "war of all against all." The function of a moral authority, an unfilled position in the masculine world of business, is fulfilled by woman, who appears predestined for this role by virtue of biological propensities which place her closer than man to the sphere of compassion. . . .

Texts in many scholarly disciplines and literary genres took up the discussion of female nature. . . . Up until now, only Paul Hoffmann has devoted extensive and detailed consideration to the majority of these discourses. His book *La Femme dans la pensée des Lumières* (Woman in Enlightenment Thought) examines almost the entirety of eighteenth-century literature. The methodological approach of his monograph appears problematic, however. Hoffmann starts from the assumption that the discourse about woman cannot be analyzed rationally using either immanent logic or an examination of external reasons. "Neither logical nor sociological causality can explain the evolution of ideas about woman. The sum of the discourses which sketch its fleeting and eternal face at every period of history could never add up to a science." Thus Hoffmann denies the possibility that the discourses about woman might have the status of scholarly theories and, with it, the possibility of a scholarly analysis of the texts' contents. This denial also leads to a doubling of the discourse on woman. Here he influences his own interpretation. It is no accident that Hoffmann refers to Diderot's *Sur les femmes* (On Women) and adopts for his own study Diderot's generalization that one cannot discuss women objectively. According to Hoffmann, fantasies and "factual statements" about women's nature resist critical analysis, allowing instead for merely subjective evaluations: "We admit our partiality! But the object of our investigation forbade any objectivity. No one can speak of woman without becoming involved, without compromising himself."

This attitude is symptomatic of a (male-dominated) scholarly discourse on women which accepts uncritically the characteristics attributed to women, adopting them as the starting point for its investigations. Hoffmann's certainty that all discourses on woman are, of necessity, incoherent, changeable, vague, and subjective rests on the unspoken (because so widely shared) attitude that these are precisely some of the characteristics of women's nature.

Throughout his study, Hoffmann treats sex-specific character as a valid anthropological given. "At no moment does woman's freedom appear more problematic than when she is called, by her own nature, to bear a child and bring it into the world. At no moment is the body more sovereign, but there is also no more propitious occasion for reason to demonstrate her duties and capabilities." This approach appears methodologically questionable because Hoffmann takes as his starting point ideas which were the *result* of developments during the eighteenth century. Whether it was a woman's duty to bear children, and whether this duty restricted her freedom, was precisely one of the issues at stake in the *querelle*. Hoffmann's own assumptions preclude his grasping this evolution. . . .

Sylvana Tomaselli

The Enlightenment Debate on Women

. . . The present essay . . . seeks to put women back in their place in history by examining a forgotten tradition which linked women, not, as is all too swiftly done, to nature, but to culture and the process of its historical development. . . .

Our purpose is to offer a re-interpretation of what eighteenth-century thinkers argued the positions of women to be. It is also to challenge the

Sylvana Tomaselli, "The Enlightenment Debate on Women," *History Workshop Journal* 20 (Autumn 1985): 101–124. Reprinted by permission of The Oxford University Press.

facile alignment of the conceptual opposition of woman to man under the perennial nature–culture dichotomy. . . .

One would have thought the conception of woman as civilising a commonplace, indeed, an unassailable assumption within Western culture. Yet judging by some recent currents in feminism, in radical science and other forms of culture critique, including ecology, to think of woman within the register of civilisation and culture or, inversely, of civilisation and culture as pertaining in an essential way to the realm of the feminine is to commit nothing short of a confusion at the most fundamental philosophical level, a category mistake. . . .

Except at the cost of dismissing a good deal of feminist literature, of writings by ecologists and a growing number of histories of science and culture which attempt to be sensitive to issues raised by feminism, this view of the relation between man and culture and woman and nature cannot be readily ignored. Nor is this simply a recent and ephemeral trend. The assumption that Western civilisation simply *does* regard woman as part of nature, not culture, and that this belief can essentially be taken for granted runs through much of the literature on women. . . .

The primacy of the category of nature within feminine discourse can be traced back, however, at least as far as Mary Wollstonecraft's *Vindication of the Rights of Woman*. Outside of feminism, woman and nature have been bound together since early Christian readings of Genesis. . . .

In fact, the view that woman civilises, that she cultivates, refines, perhaps even adulterates and corrupts is as recurrent as the view that she is nature's most dutiful and untouched daughter, or to put it less palatably, a being closer to animals, one link, at least, lower than man in the Great Chain of Beings. Were the connection between woman and nature as unproblematic as some writers seem to think it is within our culture, there simply would be no language in which to articulate the questions which make up feminist discourse. We do indeed think of gender relations and differences in terms of other bipolarities just as we do conceptualise the dynamic between nature and culture in masculine and feminine terms, but our symbolic universe is far richer and more complex, perhaps also confused, than many critics of the relations between man and woman, man and nature, seem to suspect. Moreover, and this is perhaps what is really overlooked, such has always been the case. . . .

Our purpose here is not to devise yet another language, nor to proffer an entirely novel way out of this predicament. What we will question instead is whether the woman-nature thesis really does reign supreme.

For once the issue is pressed and investigated a little more deeply, it is at once clear that the woman-culture view, the notion that she civilises, can be articulated in terms of the relation between woman and the family, the family and civil society and, finally, in terms of the sexual division of labour. . . .

Few periods gave as much consideration to the issue of the merit and demerit of the growth of society, of culture and civilisation as the eighteenth century. The categories of nature and culture were absolutely pivotal to nearly every aspect of the Enlightenment. It produced perhaps the greatest reassessment of the value of society by contrasting it with a hypothetical state of nature out of which social life emerged in distinctive and progressive stages. It is often assumed that when writing the history of Man and society, eighteenth century thinkers were subsuming woman within the notion of man—yet one more example of the sexist categories of male political thought. But this was not always the case. . . .

Woman's life in the state of nature or in primitive societies was not only confined to securing the means of subsistence, but it was marked in addition by their subjugation to the unremitting and universal tyranny of men. As long as commentators focused on women, the history of the species was unquestionably one of progress towards liberty. The issue of the condition of women present or past could be passed over in silence of course, but once raised, the question of the comparative freedom, and indeed happiness, of the savage and civilised woman seems to have afforded only one answer. . . .

Reviewing Antoine-Léonard Thomas's (1732–85) *Essai sur le Charactère, les Moeurs et l'Esprit des Femmes dans les différents Siècles* (Essay on the Character, Manners and Spirit of Women throughout the Ages), Diderot did have a lot of abuse to vent. Thomas, or so the review seems to indicate, had essentially wasted a brilliant chance to treat a subject of great interest and importance. On a topic such as this, Diderot thought, there was no excuse for being as excruciatingly dull as Thomas. But however boring Thomas might have been, Diderot did not dispute his thesis. In fact, he accepted the claim that:

> *In nearly every land the cruelty of positive laws has united with the cruelty of nature against women. They have been treated as imbecile children. There is no manner of vexation which man cannot with impunity exercise against woman amongst civilised people; the only retribution which she can exert leads to domestic trouble and contempt the extent of which*

varies with the level of civility the nation has reached. There is no manner of vexation which the savage doesn't exert against his woman; the unhappy woman in the cities is far unhappier still in the midst of the forests. Listen to the speech of an Indian woman from the banks of the Orenoco, and listen to it, if you can, without being moved by it.

. . . There was scarcely any discussion of women in the eighteenth century which did not find much to criticise and in the age of Enlightenment, education was the most frequent target of such criticisms. Even if the ideal curriculum for women was a subject on which there was considerable disagreement, no one in the period seems to have been pleased with what education they did receive. . . .

The realisation that the law was man-made found many an expression in the century, not least in the *Encyclopedia* where, for instance, the product of enlightened despotism, the 'Code Frédéric,' was treated with dismay by the *Encyclopedia*'s most prolific contributor, M. le Chevalier de Jaucourt. Nothing in his view justified its claim of the authority of the husband over his wife and household, least of all natural law, which it wholly contradicted.

The point then of such histories of women was not to promote self-congratulation. What they revealed and highlighted instead was the fact that, however bad conditions were for women in civilised nations, they had been a great deal worse in primitive societies. As Diderot saw it,

> *if women are subjugated in civilised nations, they are under complete oppression in savage nations and in all barbarous regions. Entirely occupied with meeting his needs, the savage has time only for his safety and his subsistence.*

. . . Nor was this theory peculiar to the French Enlightenment. In Scotland, . . . John Millar (1735–1801), in *The Origins of the Distinction of Ranks*, argued that

> *we may form an idea of the state and condition of the women in the ages most remote from improvement. Having little attention paid them, either upon account of those pleasures to which they are subservient, or of those occupations which they are qualified to exercise, they are degraded below the other sex, and reduced under that authority which the strong acquire over the weak: an authority, which, in early periods, is subject to no limitation from the government, and is therefore exerted with a degree of harshness and severity suited to the dispositions of the people.*

Millar was the only author who tried to resist judging the nature of the relations between men and women in early societies by contemporary standards. . . . Millar, however, did not dissent from the view generally held within this debate, that the coming of the pastoral age was a blessing for women. As life became less precarious, as mankind no longer needed to spend all its waking hours hunting and gathering, more effort and time could be diverted away from these tasks towards those of making living conditions more agreeable. . . .

This point can be found in French and Scottish authors alike. Women are less unhappy amongst pastoral peoples. . . .

Nor did women benefit any the less from the growth of commercial society. Turning to Diderot again we find him arguing that women acquire a new importance with the advent of the arts and of commerce as men grow increasingly dependent on women in the daily running of their business—an activity at which women excel. Not even luxury, in Diderot's view, puts an end to the progress of women, for when labour is scorned and wealth increases, mankind has only one obsessive concern: 'In such times, women are eagerly sought after, both on account of the attributes which they owe to nature and of those they acquire by education.'

Each step towards the full development of commercial society could thus be happily undertaken by women. Now, this is by no means as obvious as it might first appear. In order to come to appreciate that this argument about the absolute gain which women made out of the growth of civilisation isn't simply a special case within a wider brief for the rise of commercial society, we must first turn back to the descriptions given within this discourse of the beginnings of society. We must in particular note the extent to which something like a master–slave dialectic is pervasive in such accounts of the early stages of the natural history. . . . This conceptualisation of the condition of women as one of slavery is so frequent as to be almost a commonplace in the Enlightenment. Condorcet's (1734–94) *Esquisse d'un Tableau Historique des Progrès de L'Esprit Humain* (Sketch of a Historical Table of the Progress of the Human Mind) told of the slow development from a state in which 'women were condemned to a kind of slavery.' Much earlier in the century, even Rousseau (1712–78), in his collaboration with Mme Dupin (as their secretary, Rousseau collaborated with both Mme and M. Dupin, during the period from 1745–49) on her projected history of women, urged us to conceive of the matter in these very terms. Men had first deprived women of their liberty, according to him. Masters of all things they had grounded their tyranny in a theory of natural right which had no foundation other than their superior might. Had it not been for this original enslavement women would have surpassed men in every act of virtue and courage. . . .

Eighteenth century histories of women thus began with their loss of liberty. They continued with an account of how and to what extent the master–slave or tyrant–slave relation was redressed, if not reversed. Power and freedom were the central categories through which the relation between the sexes were analysed. The history of women therefore was the history of their conflict with men, of the conflict between the sexes, to borrow a phrase.

Montesquieu's (1689–1755) *L'Esprit des Lois* (The Spirit of the Laws) (1748) provides the classical statement of this vision of the relation between men and women. The concept of liberty and its appendant register of captivity, servitude and enslavement lie at the heart of his treatment of what he calls 'le gouvernement domestique' (domestic rule), no less than they do that of his analysis of any other form of government. In his view, in fact, the two, political and domestic, were indissolubly intertwined. . . . The language of liberty and servitude, the interconnection between the status of women and the spirit prevailing in a nation was not restricted to these two forms of government, despotism and monarchy. Montesquieu's description of republics exhibited no less of an awareness of the consequences which the near equality of citizens had on the condition of women—it provided a check to the tyranny of men. Free under the law, women in republics were restrained by its mores: as luxury was banned, corruption could not find its nest. The conflict between men and women was therefore neutralised. The laws protected women against the tyranny of men, while men were themselves assured that they would not fall prey to the ensnarement of women through what we might call commodity fetishism. The condition then of all citizens was therefore genuinely equal and free, though men and women retained their gender differences, a fact reflected in the very nature of the laws which governed them.

But Montesquieu did not stop there in his use of the tyrant–slave dialectic. He applied his description of the nature of the slavery of women, domestic slavery, to help conceptualise what he called 'real slavery'—productive labour. True degradation resided in the addition of domestic slavery to the burden of real slavery—such had been the condition of the Helots in Spartan society. The status of women therefore informed Montesquieu's theory at all levels. . . . [T]he idea that women were the barometers on which every aspect of society, its morals, its laws, its customs, its government, was registered had gained much ground since the publication of Montesquieu's *De L'Esprit des Lois* in the middle of the century. The nature and extent of their subjection or liberty said everything.

If such was the conceptual grid used to discuss the relation between men and women, if, that is, the language of liberty and slavery provided the terms in which the relation between the sexes was spoken of, then the notion that their respective judgement of the merit and demerit of the growth of civilisation might not necessarily coincide seems a great deal more plausible. . . .

With such concerns in mind, there was only one unequivocal answer to Diderot's original question: 'Ask civilised man whether he is happy. Ask the savage whether he is unhappy. If both reply 'No,' the dispute is settled.'

To have asked a woman the same set of questions would have yielded, judging by Diderot's own account, both a 'no' and a 'yes.' And this because the laws, the masters, the prejudices and the fashions marked not only, as they did for man, her loss of freedom; they also gave her a taste of liberty. For she discovered in some of these constraints the means of her liberation. . . .

[I]t is essential to note that Diderot was not blind to the mechanisms by which civilization proceeded, nor of the genuine gains, in human and material terms, it brought in its wake. It was both his genius and his predicament to see all aspects of an issue of debate at once. . . .

The coming of the pastoral age, we recall, was a positive turn of events in the history of women. The increased security in the means of subsistence and the resulting diminution in the time and effort required to ensure survival meant greater comfort and leisure. What leisure allowed was the cultivation of beauty. It enabled the savage to develop taste, his own taste. The more particularised the desire, the more unique the love object, the less women were open to male abuse. What the improvements in the condition of women required in the first instance was a shift away from the randomness of male libido, from their liking of women in general to their liking only very specific ones, if not just one single woman. What was necessary in effect was the beginnings of romantic or chivalric love, if these be apt labels, for it entailed an acute desire in men themselves to be singled out, specifically desired, loved. To be loved, desired, men had to become loveable, desireable. Brutality was unlikely to be attractive in the eyes of women, of *the* woman they wanted. They had to become civilised.

. . . All parties were thus agreed. In the state of nature or in primitive societies mankind did not discern each other as individuals. There was no basis for such discernment. For those who wrote the history of women, the beginnings of this selective gaze were wholly welcomed. Rousseau, on the other hand, had begun the body of his *Discourse* with, 'C'est de l'homme que j'ai à parler,' 'Man is my concern.' In his writings 'Sur Les Femmes' (On Women) he had urged his would-be readers to think of the relation between men and women in terms of men's tyranny over women. In view of the sharp contrast between those reflections and the *Discourse*, there seems to be some good reason to take his opening statement literally.

The relation between man and woman was one of power for Rousseau. His work was partly devoted to tracing the history and nature of this power relation. With some exceptions, as when he wrote fragments of Mme Dupin's history of women, Rousseau essentially wrote with men in mind. What he described to them was the impact of the growing ascendancy of a feminine culture. What he told them was to resist it. . . .

Within this tradition therefore women were anything but the passive recipients of culture. Unlike the thesis which links woman to nature, the one we have been examining does not leave women hidden from history. Far from it. She makes it. There is hence a history of women to be written. That history may well be the history of civilisation and manners. To pursue this theme would lead us to examine the essential place she occupies within discourses about the nature and consequence of luxury, about the origins of language and development of literature, about religion, ritual and medicine. . . .

At the level of the real, there have been many exceedingly valuable contributions to the history of women in the last few decades. But the history of the family or of individual great women which such histories have tended to consist in does not exhaust the history of woman's role in making the world we live in. In the histories we have been considering societies and stages of society were characterised in terms of the degree to which women were subjected to or free from the tyranny of men. But the degree to which they were recognised as enslaved or possessed of liberty was always measured by the extent to which they took part in the political, social and cultural life of their communities. To deny them such agency and responsibility was true slavery. Let us not do so posthumously. . . .

Erica Harth

The Salon Woman Goes Public . . . or Does She?

It is hardly possible to evoke the cultural and intellectual life of early modern France without mentioning the special role played by salon women. Here consensus ends. Alternately reviled and praised in her own day, the salon woman continues to befuddle us. In the wake of Jürgen Habermas's *Structural Transformation of the Public Sphere,* questions have been raised as to the public versus the private character of the salon. On this issue hinges the role of its host: the more public her part, one would think, the greater her effect on social, political, cultural, and literary history. Meanwhile, scholars are far from agreement on the demarcation of public from private, or even on the meaning of these terms. Nevertheless, one cannot ignore the significance of the current debates for the reassessment of the salon woman's place in literature and publishing and of the place of the salon woman's literary activities in women's history.

Just what might "going public" have meant for the salon woman of the seventeenth and eighteenth centuries? How public was her social role, and what impact did she make on publishing? Although the public nature of the salon expanded from the seventeenth to the eighteenth century, and although women throughout the period were crucial to the salon's publicity and to publishing, the public functions of the *salonnière* herself had actually diminished by the time of the French Revolution.

The mixed-sex social gatherings identified by historians of France as salons date from the sixteenth century, and their prehistory reaches even farther back. The salon's golden age, however, extends from the early seventeenth century to the Revolution. With the death of Louis XIV in 1715, the rules of *bienséance,* or decorum, were somewhat relaxed, and topics of conversation in the salon began to swing from belles lettres, natural philosophy, and questions of love to matters of current political

Erica Harth, "The Salon Woman Goes Public . . . or Does She?" in *Going Public: Women and Publishing in Early Modern France,* ed. Elizabeth C. Goldsmith and Dena Goodman (Ithaca: Cornell University Press, 1995), 179–193. Copyright © 1995 by Cornell University. Used by permission of the publisher, Cornell University Press.

and economic concern. The philosophic salon of the 1760s is a far cry from Madame de Rambouillet's *chambre bleue* of the 1630s. Nevertheless, the eighteenth-century salon never shed the mantle of tradition it inherited from its predecessor. Regulated conversation led by a female host continued to be its hallmark. What did change were the social and gender composition of the guests and the *salonnière's* relation to them, as well as the substance of the conversations. These changes had profound implications for the salon woman's location in or out of the public sphere and for her relation to writing and publishing.

. . . The primary function of the eighteenth-century *salonnière* . . . was a kind of *mission civilisatrice*, a task of keeping the discourse between potentially warring philosophes civil enough for enlightenment to proceed. This was hardly a trivial job. Yet its effect on the status of women is open to question. Beyond providing the social glue that held the philosophes together, what did the *salonnière* do? How were salons different from all-male gatherings, such as Baron d'Holbach's coterie or the official academies? . . .

The Seventeenth-Century Salon: Women's Secret Publishing

Some light can be shed on these matters by returning to the seventeenth century and a consideration of the "secret" and the public sides of the salons. . . . To the extent that the seventeenth-century salon offered its habitués—male and female—a space for speaking *and* writing, it was a public space. Writing nonetheless seems to have been the more "public" form of publishing. . . .

In the seventeenth-century lexicon the "secret" may be contrasted to the "public," but it should not be conflated with the domestic. . . . In the salon the "public" and the domestic were, if anything, conjoined. . . .

The salon was the place to "publish" conversation that marked the guests as members of a social elite. Whether the conversations were written or spoken matters little in this understanding of the "public." In fact, much of the literature that emanated from the salons or that was related to salon culture . . . bears the stamp of its conversational origin.

The salon's "exclusive conversations" . . . were generally directed by a woman, and so the *salonnière* came to play the part of power broker or protector, perhaps her chief public role to endure through the vicissitudes of French history. . . .

If in her public capacity as host of a social gathering the *salonnière* gained some acceptance among her contemporaries, as author of a printed work she found herself tied to a certain conventional secrecy. Among those seventeenth-century women novelists who hid behind anonymity or a pseudonym were the redoubtable leaders of the genre, Madeleine de Scudéry and Madame de Lafayette. . . .

By 1690, the publication date of Furetière's *Dictionnaire universel,* an "author," as Furetière specifies under this entry, had become associated with a printed book. Since most men had readier access to printed publication than did most women, print culture left many "published" women to fall by the wayside of literary renown. . . .

The Seventeenth-Century Legacy

From at least the sixteenth century . . . the salon was a literary place, home to readings, disputes, theoretical discussions, structured debate, composition, and improvisation. By the seventeenth century the literary activities of a salon were often the source of its fame—or its notoriety. The *salonnière*'s "published" judgment of a given writer or work—which continued to be a sore point with detractors of the salon from Boileau to Rousseau—could make or break a reputation or a guest. . . .

It was partly in the literary-critical function of the seventeenth-century salon that its "seriousness" resided. . . .

In the seventeenth century, before the full realization of the oppositional discursive space that Habermas terms an authentic public sphere, "serious" salon conversation was no less so for not challenging the established political order. . . . The subversive stuff of salon conversation had to do with a radical reexamination of love and marriage that positioned the *salonnières* and their male guests on what we would now term the feminist side of the *querelle des femmes.*

From the seventeenth to the eighteenth century, the form and content of the salon's seriousness changed. . . .

Whereas the seventeenth-century salon was still very much linked to the court in style, the eighteenth-century variety was stylistically closer to the circles of the *libertins érudits,* those freethinking scholars whose activities in the seventeenth century were of necessity conducted in a "secret" underground. The philosophic salon was in fact a kind of freethinking circle "gone public." Especially by the 1760s, when philosophes began to enter the official academies in statistically meaningful numbers, the distinguished eighteenth-century salons can be convincingly cited as a major formative factor in Habermas's bourgeois public sphere. We may well wonder why the mixed-sex social and intellectual gatherings in women's homes persisted into the eighteenth century and were not displaced by all-male gatherings such as Baron d'Holbach's, or why the philosophes did not dispense with a host altogether and simply congregate in Parisian cafés such as the celebrated Procope.

The gatherings of Anne-Thérèse de Marguenat de Courcelles, marquise de Lambert, which she instituted at the age of sixty-three in 1710, indicate that by tradition women were uniquely positioned to host the philosophic salon. Scholars since Sainte-Beuve have become accustomed to viewing Lambert's salon at the Hôtel de Nevers as a transition between the older *précieux* style of sociability and the eighteenth-century philosophic kind. Lambert divided her circle into two: the "Tuesday people" (the *mardistes*), who were intellectuals, artists, and literati; and the Wednesday crowd (the *mercredistes*), who were society people (*gens du monde*). . . . In giving the literati their day, Lambert accorded them a formal distinction which a somewhat altered personnel would later enjoy in the philosophic salons. It is as if the lady of the Hôtel de Nevers were redrawing the map of sociability.

In this geography the Hôtel de Nevers was in effect the center of a new "seriousness." Despite the *mercredistes* and the *précieux* residue, Lambert's passion was for ideas. Her salon was likened to a *"conference académique"* (academic lecture series). Philosophy, science, and literature dominated the discussion. As the subjects widened, the nature of the salon became less "secret" and less feminocentric in its concerns. Even the physical setting of Lambert's salon announced a new era. Although she did sometimes entertain from a bed, her gatherings typically took place in a reception room or a dining room. Most eighteenth-century salons were organized around a *dîner* or *souper*, as the intimate *ruelle* gave way to larger, more public rooms—*salles* and *salons*—in which one could take a meal and then enjoy leisurely postprandial conversation in comfort. . . . An invitation to join this circle was much coveted. Moreover, Lambert's influence was formidable. According to the marquis d'Argenson, half the academicians owed their seats to her. She was instrumental in securing Montesquieu's election to the Académie Française in 1727.

The gatherings at the Hôtel de Nevers renewed a seventeenth-century tradition of sociability in which a respected female host lent distinction to talent from various ranks and brokered her guests' relationships with powerful people in good society. Informal men's academies were not so well suited to these purposes, in part because of the greater range of subjects broached there. The *libertin* underground had been a haven for discussion of officially taboo matters. . . . But censorship went hand in hand with decorum, and it was the very propriety of the salons that facilitated the philosophes' entrée to positions of power.

It was by no means the case that opportunities for what we would now call networking were unavailable to philosophes in the men's circles, especially by the 1760s. . . . It was rather that, since at least the seventeenth century, female-led salons (with the possible exception of Lambert's) had provided an established place for intellectuals, artists, and literati to rub elbows with one another as well as with the great and the powerful. For the philosophes to have closed off this avenue to privilege would have been self-defeating.

The great salons from Madame de Lambert's day to the French Revolution benefited from a centuries-old legacy of divertissement combined with seriousness. . . . In the age of the philosophes, the salon became weighted toward the kind of seriousness that had been confined mainly to "secret" or unofficial academic venues under Louis XIV. Women had not traditionally been party to the wholesale questioning of authority that marked "enlightened" talk. They paid a price, however, for their directorial role in such discussions. . . . Only by subtly orchestrating a conversation serious enough to attract the philosophes and yet censored enough to meet the standards of decorum could the *salonnière* remain the adjunct to Enlightenment that she turned out to be.

What happened to women's publishing and salon writing under these circumstances? Poetry and the novel, the preeminent genres of salon writing, . . . were not noticeably associated with the philosophic salons. Love, marriage, and the controversies of the *querelle des femmes*, the stuff of so many seventeenth-century novels, no longer dominated polite conversation. Instead, subjects discussed included some that had been part of the masculine discursive tradition: politics, economics, even religion. So long as Old Regime patriarchy, in effect, was put in question, women's concerns were central to the salon. By the eighteenth century the *querelle des femmes* had quieted down, despite the work of Madame de Lambert and faint echoes in the writings on women by Antoine-Léonard Thomas and Denis Diderot. Female guests no longer held sway in the salon. . . . Although salon women continued to write, they rarely "published" in their own voices in the salon, nor were they associated with a distinctive genre of printed literature.

We can only speculate as to why subversion of the patriarchy, the major chink in the seventeenth-century *salonnière's* armor of propriety, ceased for all practical purposes to play a significant part in Enlightenment salon culture. As in liberation movements since abolition, the cause of Enlightenment required the solidarity of both men and women. Women's concerns, which in any event had not yet gained political legitimacy, had to be subordinated to the "larger" philosophic battle. The fate of the feminist revolutionary Olympe de Gouges, guillotined in 1793, and of the Revolutionary women's clubs, shut down in the same year, speaks eloquently to the dangers of invoking sexism in a political movement led by men. Once the salon was annexed to the struggle against all forms of arbitrary authority, its concerns were primarily masculine. As the salon became more public, then, in the Habermasian sense of providing an institutional base for the critical debate of public issues, salon women became less so. Or perhaps we should say that in this sense salon women had, almost without exception, never been "public" at all.

Janet Gurkin Altman

A Woman's Place in the Enlightenment Sun

When Françoise de Graffigny published the *Lettres d'une Péruvienne* [Letters from a Peruvian Woman] in 1747, the abbé Raynal wrote to the subscribers of his *Nouvelles littéraires*, ["it has been a long time since we have been given anything as pleasant as the *Lettres d'une Péruvienne.*"] Graffigny's novel was immediately hailed by the major literary journals as a new kind of novel, departing radically from its predecessors by the way that it invested its sentimental heroine with intellectual curiosity

Janet Gurkin Altman, "A Woman's Place in the Enlightenment Sun: The Case of F. de Graffigny," *Romance Quarterly* 38 (August 1991): 261–269. Reprinted with permission of the Helen Dwight Reid Educational Foundation. Published by Heldref Publications, 1319 Eighteenth St., NW, Washington, DC 20036–1802. Copyright © 1991.

and an ingenious mind. Reviewers of the first edition prophesied that this novel was destined for numerous reprintings. For sixty years after Graffigny died in 1758, literary critics repeatedly referred to the novel as a work that would guarantee Graffigny's immortality. . . . Enlightenment critics perceived Graffigny not only as the originator of the French epistolary novel tradition but more importantly as an unparalleled innovator in the area of the philosophic novel.

Graffigny's novel burst upon the Parisian scene of the late 1740s and early 1750s at a time when the ideas of the *philosophes* were being vehicled primarily through essays, dialogues, and encyclopedic writing (including world history with Voltaire, natural history with Buffon). After the flowering of the novel in the 1730s — under Lesage, Marivaux, Tencin, Crébillion, and Prévost, among others — creative minds in France seemed to have abandoned the novel as a form of public art, indulging in it only as a clandestine libertine recreation, like Diderot in his *Bijoux indiscrets* (1748), published anonymously in Holland around the same time as Graffigny's novel. The *Lettres d'une Péruvienne*, therefore, took Paris somewhat by surprise. Though its author was a member of the intellectual circles surrounding Caylus and Helvétius, and a *salonnière* in her own right, she was by proclivity a private person and was relatively unknown. Little publicity preceded the publication of the novel, and critics reviewed it in many instances simply because everyone was reading it. Gradually, as critics had time to reflect upon the popularity and originality of the novel, they began to change their attitude toward the novelistic genre itself. Fascinated by Graffigny's ability to meld cultural criticism with subtle descriptions of sensation, critics of the 1750s who had previously regarded the novel as a frivolous form of literature began to see it as a legitimate form for addressing subtle philosophic questions. For Turgot and other readers of the 1750s, Graffigny's novel eclipsed the *Lettres persanes* by conflating novel and philosophy more successfully than Montesquieu [had].

While Enlightenment critics were acclaiming Graffigny's artistic accomplishments, readers were busy making her novel a best seller. The *Lettres d'une Péruvienne* quickly became one of the most widely read French novels throughout Enlightenment Europe, enjoying a critical prestige and sustained popularity that would be rivaled only by *La Nouvelle Héloïse* and *Candide*. Over 130 editions, reissues, and translations kept it available in France, Italy, Spain, and England between 1747 and 1835.

Between 1835 and 1966, however, there were almost no new editions and very few citations of Graffigny's novel. . . .

Today, thanks to a paperback edition that appeared in 1983, many of us have discovered the considerable interest of Graffigny's novel, not just for women's studies, but also for expanding our understanding of the way the French Enlightenment was represented in literature. For while the heroine of Graffigny's novel corresponds in some respects to the new type of sentimental heroine popularized by Marivaux and Richardson, she is also an intellectual heroine. . . . Zilia's quest for knowledge drives the novel, and she articulates this desire early on, in letter 9: ["I had resolved not to think anymore, but how is one to slow the movement of a soul deprived of all communication . . . that is spurred to reflection by such strong interests? . . . I seek enlightenment with an urgency that consumes me, yet I continually find myself in the deepest darkness."] Indeed, Zilia's itinerary as novel heroine offers a complex literary set of answers to a question that we might raise, pastiching Joan Kelly-Gadol, "Did women have an Enlightenment?"

Graffigny positions her protagonist complexly in relation to the French Enlightenment: Zilia is a writer, a woman, a Peruvian, and an Inca princess educated to govern her country. At the beginning of the novel, she has already participated in a Peruvian Enlightenment in her home country, as an heir of Inca civilization. Graffigny imagines Zilia as having received the same Inca education as her fiancé Aza, who wants her to share responsibility for ruling Peru coequally with him. When the Spanish conquest interferes, and she is shipped off as a captive to Europe, Zilia recovers from her initial despair by pursuing knowledge of her new milieu. The novel traces her slow turning away from the Peruvian Sun toward the brilliance of the French Enlightenment.

Not a passive sunflower, however, Zilia describes her own turning with ambiguity and complexity, and her talent for articulating that complexity is one of the interests of the novel. Zilia experiences her assimilation to the culture of France and her acquisition of a European language as identity-altering processes. Each letter of this highly condensed epistolary novel richly describes her acculturation process. Unlike Montesquieu's Persians, who speak from the very beginning like Frenchmen in a Persian costume, Zilia apprehends European culture from a coherently Peruvian perspective, speaking always from the locus of a Peruvian body of knowledge and retaining her mother tongue, even while successfully acquiring a second language. Thus even though Zilia actively pursues European knowledge and technology, she questions the uses to which that knowledge has been put by Europeans who are more interested in exercising mastery than in disseminating the benefits of knowledge. The cultural outsider that Graffigny imagines as her heroine is uncannily close to protagonists we now find in the postcolonial immigration novel.

At this juncture we know relatively little about how ordinary readers responded to Graffigny's novel in the eighteenth century. . . . . What we do have, however, is a rather remarkable spectrum of responses by literary critics. . . .

When the abbé Raynal and Pierre Clément penned the first brief reviews within a few months after the novel appeared in 1747, they identified Graffigny as author of a work that had captured public attention. . . . Raynal and Clément remain gender blind for the bulk of their reviews, which stress the originality of the novel within the stream of current production. Both Raynal and Clément locate the strengths of the novel in the highly original way it paints sentiments, particularly love, but both find it incongruous for a heroine who is in love to employ philosophical language and engage in cultural criticism. They articulate these reservations, however, as afterthoughts and footnotes. Clément, who is a far more subtle reader than Raynal in this instance, distinguishes between representation and reality; he points out that he is not disputing Graffigny's very real talent as author but is simply questioning the way the fictional Zilia breaks the conventions for sentimental heroines. Raynal, by contrast, indulges in an overt *ad feminam* jibe at the end of his review, asserting that Graffigny herself has overstepped the bounds of her sex, that she has engaged in intellectual activity because she lacks beauty. . . . Raynal's comment is worth citing only because it is an anomaly in the history of the critical reception Graffigny will receive throughout the eighteenth century. Raynal's effort to ridicule Graffigny as a woman writer will not find much support among other Enlightenment critics.

Elie Fréron, one of the best-known journalists of this period, announced early in 1748 that he was writing a review of the *Lettres d'une Péruvienne*. . . . Fréron's article seems in fact to have developed as a rebuttal to Raynal and Clément, for he begins by alluding to critics who cannot accept intellectual activity in women. Paraphrasing Zilia's own critique of women's limited education in Peru and in France, Fréron argues that such restrictions deprive men and women of the pleasure of intellectual exchange with each other, and he asserts that women's poor education can only come from men's fear: ["we have feared that they would no longer have any superiority over us in enlightenment and talents."] In this essay, occasioned by a woman's novel that dared to make its heroine an intellectual, Fréron outlines a position that is more radical than most other Enlightenment thinkers on the issue of women's education. He proposes that women's education be strictly equal to men's, at least for aristocrats, who do not have to assume a trade or domestic responsibilities. Women, says Fréron, should study history, geography, philosophy, the best works of literature, and most importantly Latin, for it is the key to all of the sciences.

. . . Fréron emphasizes that Graffigny has contributed not just to ["the glory of her sex"] but to the glory of her nation as well. Fréron grasps the significance of the work as a philosophical novel, citing it as an ingenious blending of satire, philosophy, and portrayal of love. . . .

Graffigny received another long response to her novel before completing her definitive edition, this time from the political economist Turgot. . . .

After praising Graffigny's novel and belittling his own qualifications as literary critic, Turgot proceeds to offer precisely what he says Graffigny had requested: criticism, not praise. The thrust of Turgot's letter is a request for additions to the philosophical component of the novel. Turgot is greatly attracted to Zilia's potential to serve as cultural critic, and he outlines a set of changes that would make her the mouthpiece for his own program of reforms. . . . Turgot wants Zilia (1) to weigh the advantages of nature and culture, (2) to elaborate a plan for children's education, and (3) to "preach the need for marriage, good marriages." . . . Turgot is effectively asking for the kind of ["moral novel"] that Rousseau and others would soon provide. Where Zilia had simply raised questions, Turgot wants didactically exposed answers. Turgot says he feels a particular affinity with Graffigny, whom he describes as ["so zealous for the happiness of humanity."] He tells her that she is in the best possible position to "disseminate the maxims" that he has outlined, because she has invented such a powerful formula for the novel. . . .

Graffigny solicited Turgot's advice, but she did not take it. And I think that this was not only because she fundamentally disagreed with him on matters of content, such as the need to defend marriage and the class system. Turgot found Zilia's critique of the class system dangerous and attributed it to Zilia's ignorance. A more enlightened Zilia, or a more "French Zilia," as he put it, would understand and defend the need for maintaining inequality. Graffigny not only retained her critique of the class system but reinforced it in her 1752 edition. Graffigny diverged from Turgot on much more than matters of content, however. Her overarching style and discursive strategies simply were not Turgot's. Graffigny's heroine raises questions and speculates on answers, but she resists closure of debate, just as she resists the traditional closure of the novel through marriage or death for the heroine. Zilia seeks Enlightenment, but not a final Truth, for she remains aware of the limits of knowledge. . . .

The next substantive response to Graffigny is the lengthy review that Joseph de La Porte devoted to Graffigny's definitive edition, when it appeared in 1752. For La Porte, as for Turgot, the compelling originality of the novel lies in the way it uses the foreign observer simultaneously as sentimental heroine and cultural critic. For La Porte, however, the overriding alchemy that makes gold out of every sentence in the novel is Graffigny's ingenious style. Her Peruvian heroine describes the whole realm of experience, sensations, sentiments, and customs in a brand new way, defamiliarizing and reconceptualizing them in ways we have not imagined. . . . La Porte is the first critic to emphasize Zilia's role as political heroine: he would like to see Zilia fight even harder for the sovereignty of her Inca throne. Furthermore, La Porte considers it absurd to assert, as Clément did, that Zilia has too much intelligence for a Peruvian woman. To that silliness, La Porte flippantly replies that ["as a goldmine has just been discovered in France, one might just as well have found an intelligent woman in Peru."] La Porte is thus the first critic to perceive Zilia as representing the value of not only a woman's but also a Peruvian intellect. . . .

What is most striking in Graffigny's critical reception in the eighteenth century is its relative blindness to gender. Graffigny is acclaimed as a writer, not as a woman writer. Critics position her within generic traditions, not gendered traditions, citing her as the peer of Montesquieu for the philosophic novel and of Richardson for the sentimental novel. Many consider Graffigny more original than either of her predecessors, because of her ability to create an entirely new genre: condensed figurative narrative that welds probing cultural critique with engaging sentimental interest. The brevity of the novel and its quotable phrases moved Enlightenment critics with classical as well as modern tastes to laud Graffigny's wit as ingenious.

Such will not be the case in the nineteenth century. Coincidentally, Graffigny's novel went out of print in 1835, during the decade when France embarked upon the conquest of Algeria. . . . [W]hen a handful of literary critics chose to discuss Graffigny's novel after it went out of print in the nineteenth century, they systematically resurrected her novel in order to bury it, and they did so for patently political reasons.

Sainte-Beuve in 1850 was the first, and he consciously played Marc Anthony, announcing in the essay he devoted to Mme de Graffigny that he had come not to praise Graffigny but to bury her. . . . According to Sainte-Beuve, the only merit of the novel was that it inspired Turgot's wise reflections on the need to uphold social inequality and promote good marriages. Sainte-Beuve . . . recommends that his audience read Turgot, not Graffigny.

Sainte-Beuve wrote in 1850, after the failure of the 1848 Revolution. His influential *Causeries du lundi* set the canon for Second Empire readers interested in restoring order and hierarchy. In 1871, shortly after the Paris Commune, another critical essay on Graffigny appeared. Louis Etienne brandished Graffigny's novel as ["A socialist novel of old."] Etienne announced that he had selected this novel for review because it is the best and "most curious woman's novel of the [eighteenth] century." He has reread the *Lettres d'une Péruvienne* simply in order to reassure his audience that they should not read it. After all, Etienne argues, no one could be interested in a novel that deprives a man of his voice by limiting itself to the point of view of a woman who "does not understand French during half of the story." Etienne describes the novel as an absurd "dream" about "a certain republican vision" of France, whose "human rights legislation" is a "disease" that has destroyed patriarchal monarchy. Like the 1848 and 1870 revolutionaries, Graffigny foolishly represents France as a nurturing mother rather than as a father whom one must obey unquestioningly, even if his orders are tyrannical. Etienne roundly condemns Graffigny for having engaged in "communist cookery." . . .

If the nineteenth-century critics' accusations seem a little silly, especially since Graffigny's socialist ideas are muted in the novel, we should nonetheless remember that Sainte-Beuve [and] Etienne . . . were taken seriously as literary critics. Their essays constituted the only sustained attention paid to Graffigny's novel in the nineteenth century, and their evaluations went unchallenged. The twentieth century inherited the nineteenth-century devaluation of Graffigny, without realizing the highly politicized contexts in which her work had been reread and repressed by critics writing between 1850 and 1913.

For both the eighteenth- and nineteenth-century literary critics, Graffigny was a charged symbol. For the Enlightenment critics who reviewed her work, she was an outstanding European writer, destined . . . for a pantheon of the outstanding persons of the century. In 1770, when Gautier d'Agoty published a luxurious folio volume of eleven portraits designed to memorialize the French eighteenth century, he chose ten men and one woman. Graffigny is the only writer chosen. . . . D'Agoty's portrait gallery, . . . was one of the early efforts of the French Enlightenment to represent itself to posterity, and it emphasizes the cosmopolitan, "Enlightened" accomplishments of the persons selected. For D'Agoty in 1770, Graffigny was the deceased writer most capable of representing Enlightenment ideals.

. . . One hundred years after D'Agoty enshrined her in his 1770 Pantheon, however, critics following Sainte-Beuve resurrected Graffigny for their own symbolic purposes. For the conservative literary establishment of the prewar Third Republic, Graffigny was a convenient target for venting anti-Republican, xenophobic, and misogynist venom. . . .

The history of Graffigny criticism suggests that far from being a "minor" work, the *Lettres d'une Péruvienne* was a work of great impact, a charged symbol through which the French Enlightenment represented itself and was subsequently attacked. Indeed, by demonstrating that philosophic fictions could reach a wide audience, Graffigny's innovative work carved a path for Diderot, Voltaire, and Rousseau — who turned toward philosophical novels and drama after Graffigny had illustrated the potential of these genres to vehicle the *philosophes'* ideals. In this instance, a woman's myth of Enlightenment, so brutally extinguished in the colonial era, is being rekindled, and we may each determine for ourselves what should be Graffigny's place in the Enlightenment sun.

"Europe Supported by Africa and America." Engraved by William Blake for John Gabriel Stedman, *Narrative of a five years expedition, against the Revolted Negroes of Surinam, in Guiana, on the Wild Coast of South America; from the Year 1772 to 1777 . . .* (London, 1796). The eighteenth-century abolitionist Blake presents a visual critique of Europe's enslavement of Africans and colonization of America in this image of the continents as three beauties bound together. The necklace that adorns Europe contrasts with the gold bands of slavery that encircle the arms of the other two women. (*The Bridgeman Art Library International*)

PART

VI Critiques of the Enlightenment

In this enlightened age I am bold enough to confess, that we are generally men of untaught feelings; that instead of casting away all our old prejudices, we cherish them to a very considerable degree, and, to take more shame to ourselves, we cherish them because they are prejudices; and the longer they have lasted, and the more generally they have prevailed, the more we cherish them.

Edmund Burke

It is impossible to attack for long the awe of gods and demons and yet maintain reverence for the categories and principles of universal morality. This, however, is precisely the path which the philosophical founders of modern society . . . tried to follow.

Max Horkheimer

Feminist analysis will alter our understandings of the meanings of modernity/modernisation. Hence, these perspectives must be included within our stories about them. Further elaboration of feminist perspectives is necessary before we can render judgments about the emancipatory character and potential of modernity/modernisation.

Jane Flax

Enlightenment philosophy was instrumental in codifying and institutionalizing both the scientific and popular European perceptions of the human race. The numerous writings on race by Hume, Kant, and Hegel played a strong role in articulating Europe's sense not only of its cultural but also *racial* superiority.

Emmanuel Chukwudi Eze

The language of development, here coming into being as an Enlightenment theory of history, is still very much with us, allowing our one world to be read through a metaphor of maturation in which some are—when not "children"—always junior to the European standard.

Peter Hulme

The polemical use of history is common. . . . The legacy of the Enlightenment, in particular, has always been contested because so many enduring religious, political, and philosophical issues were engaged in the historic episode that bears its name. But during the last quarter-century, the Enlightenment has been an extreme case of this dynamic in the United States.   *—David A. Hollinger*

We should not be surprised that the Enlightenment has always been the subject of intense criticism and debate. As a social practice that reflected the gender relations in its society even as it developed and promoted the tools to criticize those relations, the Enlightenment inevitably stimulated the debate about women and gender explored in the previous part, "Did Women Have an Enlightenment?" As a critical practice that challenged the very basis of belief and tradition, however, the Enlightenment was also bound to provoke a conservative reaction. Perhaps equally predictably, the success of that challenge has attracted criticism from those who attribute to the Enlightenment many of the problems of the modern world. In this final part we turn from the gender debates internal to the Enlightenment to the ongoing critique of the Enlightenment's legacy. From the point of view of both traditionalists and "postmodernists," the Enlightenment represents modernity, and modernity is profoundly flawed. And yet, as Michel Foucault noted in the first part of this volume, the greatest legacy of the Enlightenment is its critical perspective, and all those who challenge it are, in this sense, its heirs. The debates that characterized Enlightenment thought and practice continue today in debates about the meaning and value of the Enlightenment and the modern world it has come to represent.

Throughout the eighteenth century, doomsayers predicted that God's wrath would fall upon the society that, in embracing the new philosophy, rejected His truth and the church and state that embodied it. When the French Revolutionaries declared the universal rights of man as part of their new constitution in 1789, and the confiscation of Church lands a year later, critics knew where to look for the culprit. The Englishman Edmund Burke was one of the first critics to interpret the French Revolution as a product of the dangerous ideas of the Enlightenment. In *Reflections on the Revolution in France* (1790), he associates the "literary men" of the Enlightenment with the politicians of the Revolution and attributes to both parties a common aim to destroy "all establishments." For Burke, the French Revolution was the political and violent result of a French Enlightenment that aimed to destroy traditional society, institutions, and culture. Addressing himself to a French friend, Burke associates Enlightenment values with French culture and character, and contrasts them with his notions of English values. Burke thus raises the question not only of the relationship between the Enlightenment and the French Revolution, but between the Enlightenment, French culture, and the nationalism that would emerge as a powerful force in the nineteenth century.

Just as the French Revolution provoked Burke to indict the Enlightenment as the cause of modern society's ills, so the Holocaust would drive Max Horkheimer to make a similar claim. Writing in the 1950s, when memories of Nazi atrocities were still fresh, Horkheimer holds the Enlightenment responsible for creating a modern world in which morality is subordinate to scientific rationality and the individual is powerless before a rational-bureaucratic state. He points to the contradiction that, in elevating reason above all else, the Enlightenment undermines its own ideals of the importance of the individual and human happiness. Like Burke, Horkheimer associates the Enlightenment with reason and scientific—especially technological—progress, but he rejects Burkean nostalgia and urges the reader to push forward with reason "even in the face of its most paradoxical consequences," to complete the emancipation heralded by Kant—now as an emancipation from reason's own "fear of despair."

In 1784 Kant defined the Enlightenment as an emancipation of human beings from "self-incurred tutelage." Two hundred years later, the feminist critic Jane Flax challenges the story of human emancipation told and foretold by Kant by pointing to the gendered assumptions that underlie it. Flax shows how Kant's rational man implies and depends upon an embodied woman, arguing that the public sphere of rational discourse depends upon a private sphere of home and family in which women remain. The universality of reason, she declares, depends on "naming women as different in relation to the true measure of humanity." If Enlightenment is emancipatory, she asks, whom does it emancipate and at whose expense? If emancipation is to remain our goal, how can we go beyond the gender distinctions that underlie Enlightenment to achieve it for women and men alike?

The philosopher Emmanuel Chukwudi Eze draws inspiration from the feminist critique of Enlightenment to argue for taking a more critical look at the writings of key Enlightenment figures from the perspective of race. Eze asks why "the concept of race gained such currency" in Enlightenment thought, when previous philosophical traditions had been able to explain cultural difference without recourse to theories of race. Just as Flax connects reason and gender in her critique of Enlightenment, so he argues that for Enlightenment thinkers both reason and civilization were attributes of whiteness. Calling attention to the whitewashing of canonical Enlightenment texts, Eze calls upon modern readers to pay attention to the philosophes' ideas about race rather than simply dismissing them as irrelevant to the critical project of Enlightenment. If we do so, he suggests, we will find disturbing connections between Enlightenment science and modern racism.

For postcolonial scholar Peter Hulme, the English philosopher John Locke represents an Enlightenment that underpins a modern world defined by European expansion and power over others. Through a reading of Locke's *Second Treatise on Government*, Hulme, like Eze, locates the origins of a scientific racism that would become one of the Enlightenment's most powerful legacies, as "universal" reason came to be seen as differentially distributed among the peoples of the earth. In portraying Native Americans as living "naturally" off the bounty of the land and contrasting them with rational and industrious Europeans who improved it, Hulme argues, Locke not only adopted the language of the first colonizers of America, but also legitimized their usurpation by denying that the people they displaced were rational and thus human. In this way,

Hulme challenges us to consider the implications of Enlightenment for non-Europeans by asking how the Enlightenment is implicated in the colonialism and imperialism that define the modern world.

We bring this part on critiques of the Enlightenment's legacy to a close with a reflection on them by historian David Hollinger. Hollinger's aim is not to refute the critiques or even to defend the Enlightenment against them. Rather, he shows how both the Enlightenment and its critiques are embedded in the cultural history of the United States and suggests the impossibility of dispensing with either. In an important sense, he concludes, it is not the Enlightenment that defines modernity, but the struggle over it. As we bring this volume to a close, we hope that students who have read it will find themselves prepared to engage in that struggle in an informed way.

Edmund Burke

Reflections on the Revolution in France

. . . Thanks to our sullen resistance to innovation, thanks to the cold sluggishness of our national character, we still bear the stamp of our forefathers. We have not (as I conceive) lost the generosity and dignity of thinking of the fourteenth century; nor as yet have we subtilized ourselves into savages. We are not the converts of Rousseau; we are not the disciples of Voltaire; Helvetius has made no progress amongst us. Atheists are not our preachers; madmen are not our lawgivers. We know that *we* have made no discoveries; and we think that no discoveries are to be made, in morality; nor many in the great principles of government, nor in the ideas of liberty, which were understood long before we were born, altogether as well as they will be after the grave has heaped its mould upon our presumption, and the silent tomb shall have imposed its law on our pert

Edmund Burke, *Reflections on the Revolution in France* (Oxford: Oxford University Press, 1993), 86–91.

loquacity. In England we have not yet been completely embowelled of our natural entrails; we still feel within us, and we cherish and cultivate, those inbred sentiments which are the faithful guardians, the active monitors of our duty, the true supporters of all liberal and manly morals. We have not been drawn and trussed, in order that we may be filled, like stuffed birds in a museum, with chaff and rags, and paltry, blurred shreds of paper about the rights of man. We preserve the whole of our feelings still native and entire, unsophisticated by pedantry and infidelity. We have real hearts of flesh and blood beating in our bosoms. We fear God; we look up with awe to kings; with affection to parliaments; with duty to magistrates; with reverence to priests; and with respect to nobility. Why? Because when such ideas are brought before our minds, it is *natural* to be so affected; because all other feelings are false and spurious, and tend to corrupt our minds, to vitiate our primary morals, to render us unfit for rational liberty; and by teaching us a servile, licentious, and abandoned insolence, to be our low sport for a few holidays, to make us perfectly fit for, and justly deserving of slavery, through the whole course of our lives.

You see, Sir, that in this enlightened age I am bold enough to confess, that we are generally men of untaught feelings; that instead of casting away all our old prejudices, we cherish them to a very considerable degree, and, to take more shame to ourselves, we cherish them because they are prejudices; and the longer they have lasted, and the more generally they have prevailed, the more we cherish them. We are afraid to put men to live and trade each on his own private stock of reason; because we suspect that this stock in each man is small, and that the individuals would be better to avail themselves of the general bank and capital of nations, and of ages. Many of our men of speculation, instead of exploding general prejudices, employ their sagacity to discover the latent wisdom which prevails in them. If they find what they seek, and they seldom fail, they think it more wise to continue the prejudice, with the reason involved, than to cast away the coat of prejudice, and to leave nothing but the naked reason; because prejudice, with its reason, has a motive to give action to that reason, and an affection which will give it permanence. Prejudice is of ready application in the emergency; it previously engages the mind in a steady course of wisdom and virtue, and does not leave the man hesitating in the moment of decision, skeptical, puzzled, and unresolved. Prejudice renders a man's virtue his habit; and not a series of unconnected acts. Through just prejudice, his duty becomes a part of his nature.

Your literary men, and your politicians, and so do the whole clan of the enlightened among us, essentially differ in these points. They have no respect for the wisdom of others; but they pay it off by a very full measure of confidence in their own. With them it is a sufficient motive to destroy an old scheme of things, because it is an old one. As to the new, they are in no sort of fear with regard to the duration of a building run up in haste; because duration is no object to those who think little or nothing has been done before their time, and who place all their hopes in discovery. They conceive, very systematically, that all things which give perpetuity are mischievous, and therefore they are at inexpiable war with all establishments. . . .

We know, and what is better we feel inwardly, that religion is the basis of civil society, and the source of all good and of all comfort. In England we are so convinced of this, that there is no rust of superstition, with which the accumulated absurdity of the human mind might have crusted it over in the course of ages, that ninety-nine in an hundred of the people of England would not prefer to impiety. We shall never be such fools as to call in an enemy to the substance of any system to remove its corruptions, to supply its defects, or to perfect its construction. If our religious tenets should ever want a further elucidation, we shall not call on atheism to explain them. We shall not light up our temple from that unhallowed fire. It will be illuminated with other lights. It will be perfumed with other incense, than the infectious stuff which is imported by the smugglers of adulterated metaphysics. If our ecclesiastical establishment should want a revision, it is not avarice or rapacity, public or private, that we shall employ for the audit, or receipt, or application of its consecrated revenue. — Violently condemning neither the Greek nor the Armenian, nor, since heats are subsided, the Roman system of religion, we prefer the Protestant; not because we think it has less of the Christian religion in it, but because, in our judgment, it has more. We are protestants, not from indifference but from zeal.

We know, and it is our pride to know, that man is by his constitution a religious animal; that atheism is against, not only our reason but our instincts; and that it cannot prevail long. But if, in the moment of riot, and in a drunken delirium from the hot spirit drawn out of the alembick of hell, which in France is now so furiously boiling, we should uncover our nakedness by throwing off the Christian religion which has hitherto been our boast and comfort, and one great source of civilization amongst us, and among many other nations, we are apprehensive (being well aware that the mind will not endure a void) that some uncouth, pernicious, and degrading superstition, might take place of it. . . .

Max Horkheimer

Reason Against Itself: Some Remarks on Enlightenment

The collapse of a large part of the intellectual foundation of our civilization is to a certain extent the result of technical and scientific progress. Yet this progress is itself an outcome of the fight for the principles which are now in jeopardy, for instance, those of the individual and his happiness. Progress has a tendency to destroy the very ideas it is supposed to realize and unfold. Endangered by the process of technical civilization is the ability of independent thinking itself.

Reason today seems to suffer from a kind of disease. This is true in the life of the individual as well as of society. The individual pays for the tremendous achievements of modern industry, for his increased technical skill and access to goods and services, with a deepening impotence against the concentrated power of the society which he is supposed to control. He is ever engaged in modeling his whole existence, down to the minutest impulse, after prefabricated patterns of behavior and feeling. . . .

One specific development in the history of philosophy will exemplify the self-destructive tendency of Reason. The eighteenth century in France has been called the era of Enlightenment. The school of thought to which this term refers includes some of the greatest names of

Max Horkheimer, "Reason Against Itself: Some Remarks on Enlightenment," in *What Is Enlightenment? Eighteenth-Century Answers and Twentieth-Century Questions*, ed. James Schmidt (Berkeley: University of California Press, 1996), 359–367. Reprinted by permission of The University of California Press.

human history. The movement was not limited to a small elite but had a broad base in the French middle class. However, it was in the philosophical works of the *encyclopédistes* that the idea of enlightenment received its classical formulation. We might characterize this movement by two quotations from Voltaire: "Oh, philosopher," he exclaims, "the experiences of physics well observed, professions and industry, there you have the true philosophy." The second quotation, taken from the same work, is: "Superstition sets the whole world in flames; philosophy extinguishes them." The movement of Enlightenment, so typical of Western civilization, expresses the belief that the progress of science will finally do away with idolatry. Indeed, there are good reasons for this prediction.

. . . Science gives to man the power over that which earlier seemed completely under the control of uncanny forces. The awe of nature as an overwhelming unpredictable Being has been replaced by confidence in abstract formulae. . . .

As far as the French Enlightenment is concerned, it tried to attack mythology in all its forms, even when incorporated in the most powerful institutions of the day. However, there were certain points at which they wittingly or unwittingly compromised. Among these were the body of principles believed essential to the functioning of the commonwealth, i.e., ethical and sometimes religious truths. These basic moral laws, according to the great enlighteners, were engraved on the mind of man. As Voltaire said,

> It is proven that nature alone instills in us useful ideas which precede all our reflections. . . . It is the same in morals. . . . God has given us a principle of universal Reason as he has given feathers to the birds or a fur to the bears; and this principle is so persevering that it subsists despite the passions which combat it, despite the tyrants who want to submerge it in blood, despite the imposters who want to destroy it through superstition.

This principle of Reason expressed itself in the sentiments of justice and pity, which were, according to Voltaire, the basis of society.

Voltaire is not aware of the inconsistency between this doctrine and his other philosophical teachings. . . . It is impossible to attack for long the awe of gods and demons and yet maintain reverence for the categories and principles of universal morality. This, however, is precisely the path which the philosophical founders of modern society, including Locke himself, tried to follow. Clearly it runs counter to the inner logic of enlightened thought itself. Scientific Reason . . . is not in harmony with the doctrine of "native ideas" or any natural law or principle demanding respect as an eternal truth. . . .

Since the sixteenth and seventeenth centuries metaphysics has been the attempt of representative thinkers to derive from Reason what in earlier days had come from revelation: the meaning and eternal maxims of human life. They tried to integrate theory and practice through intuition or dialectical insight. The more philosophical rationalism later on lost out to a nominalistic and empiricist epistemology, the more apparent became the weakness of the transition from the first to the second concept of philosophy, from the epistemological part of the respective system to the basic concepts of society. As far as Religion was concerned, the Epigoni of Enlightenment made a truce with it. The need for Faith was too imperative. Industrialist society put religion and science in two different drawers of its chromium filing cabinet. Metaphysics, however, during this rearrangement of the office, was thrown into the closet.

This process was not just intellectual. What we have outlined so far is merely one aspect of the economic and social development of this era: the streamlining of social life for the ruthless struggle for power over nature and man. In this fashion we may describe humanity's transition into the epoch of industrialism and mass culture. The consequences can hardly be exaggerated. By no means does industrial progress as expressed in intellectual enlightenment affect only such concepts as man, soul, freedom, justice, and humanity, which have a direct impact on moral and practical problems. It also concerns the meaning of the basic concepts of all philosophy, primarily the notions of concept, idea, judgment, and reason. . . . But there is no doctrine which would be in line with the modern development in technics and industry, and at the same time be able to supply these culturally decisive concepts with any adequate philosophical foundation or with any of the qualities that could inspire the reverence that was once given them. The respect which these principles today receive in speeches and treatises, and even in the hearts of people, should not lead us to overestimate their impregnability. They are undermined not only in scientific thought but in the public mind as well. Whereas Voltaire thought metaphysics was only for the *honnêtes gens* and too good for shoemakers and housemaids, for whom he wanted to preserve religion, we now see religion preserved for society in but a neutralized form, and metaphysical reason in disrepute even with what he called the "*canaille.*"

The dwindling away of the philosophical substance, as it were, of all the decisive ideas in the face of the seemingly victorious Enlightenment, is one of the instances of the self-destructive trends of Reason. It is useless to differentiate here between individual Reason and Reason in social life, since the effects are felt in both of them and are brought about through a continuous and very delicate interaction of the various historical forces. As soon as our culture is put to a crucial test, we shall realize the extent of the destructive process which has taken place.

The concept of the individual, which in the history of Christian society results from the secularization of the idea of the eternal soul, shares the fate of all metaphysical categories. The entities to which these categories once referred lead a shadowy existence in the minds of men who still respond to their names if not to their meaning. However, such categories appear as completely irrational when confronted with the conceptual framework of modern science. The reverence which the modern scientist may exhibit with regard to them when they are used in a context other than that of his specific studies does not change the fact that the inner logic of science itself tends toward the idea of one truth which is completely opposed to the recognition of such entities as the soul and the individual.

The positivistic attempt to take refuge in a new kind of pluralism in order to maintain, in the face of scientific enlightenment, the moral and religious principles so necessary to the functioning of society, betrays the crisis in which society finds itself. Pluralism is the streamlined revival of the doctrine of "double truth" which, from the Averroists to Francis Bacon (that is, during the transition from the religious to the bourgeois idea of the individual), has played such a great role and now, at the decline of bourgeois individualism, is tried out again. Originally, double truth was invoked in order to permit science to emancipate the individual from dogmatic ideologies. Today, philosophy tries to keep science from emancipating society too energetically from even the secularized forms of such dogmas as the absolute value of the individual soul. But in the eager assurance of prominent representatives of science that it does not even so much as touch the conceptual framework of individualism, secular or theological, we notice a sign of bad conscience and despair. The times in which old and intelligent nations could shed their high humanistic culture overnight, as though it had been a dead skin, while science itself was worshiped and applied down to the last details of the murder factories, are still too fresh in our memories. Pluralism is a veil behind which the beliefs of the Western world, separated from the idea of binding truth, are fading away. . . .

One might ask whether our thesis of the self-liquidation of reason in recent Western history is not one-sided. Are there not many philosophical and other public currents which are in contradiction to the general development to which we referred? Although there are naturally some important countertendencies, attempting to bolster the collapsing categories, most of the philosophical and religious attempts at artificial respiration of old metaphysical doctrines contribute, against their will, to the pragmatization and dissolution of the concepts they hope to revive. The direct or naïve contact with any supposed eternal entities or principles, whether they belong to a pagan or an orthodox philosophy, has been disrupted by technological development. Through being used for the purpose of modern mass manipulation the antiquated dogmas lose, as it were, the last spark of genuine life. There is no intellectual way back. The more strongly the masses feel that the concepts which are to be revitalized have no real basis in today's social reality, the more can they be led to accept these concepts only by mass hypnosis and, once accepted, the more will they adhere to them with fanaticism and not with reason. Mythologies which at one time represented the level of development reached by humanity are now left behind by the social process. Yet these same mythologies are often used by political factions which want to turn back the course of history. If these factions are victorious the masses must embrace their respective ideologies despite their incongruence with man's experience and skill in his industrial existence. The masses must force themselves into believing them. Truth is thus replaced by purpose and naïve faith by boisterous allegiance. This is what we have witnessed so often in history and recently in Germany and other Fascist states.

The situation is similar when, instead of antiquated philosophies, new synthetic beliefs are to be instilled in the public mind. As long as they are not enforced by the state, they play the role of "mind cures" and fashions. However, as part of the manipulating machinery of any authoritarian government, they become commands, even more dehumanizing than those requiring abject outward behavior, for they dispossess man of his own conscience and make of him a mere agent of modern social trends. Each change in these synthetic beliefs, as decreed by the small group in power, however trifling in content, is accompanied by purges, by the destruction of human beings, intellectual potentialities, and works of art.

But if neither the revival of old nor the invention of new mythologies can check the course of Enlightenment, are we not thrown into a pessimistic attitude, a state of despair and nihilism? The answer to this critical objection is very simple but so seldom heard nowadays that the Sartrean version of existentialism appears to be quite revolutionary because it has assumed this attitude. The absence of a predetermined way out is certainly no argument against a line of thought. The resolution to follow the intrinsic logic of a subject regardless of the comforting or discomforting outcome is the prime condition of true theoretical thinking. As far as our situation today is concerned, there seems to be a kind of mortgage on any thinking, a self-imposed obligation to arrive at a cheerful conclusion. The compulsive effort to meet this obligation is one of the reasons why a positive conclusion is impossible. To free Reason from the fear of being called nihilistic might be one of the steps in its recovery. This secret fear might be at the bottom of Voltaire's inability to recognize the antagonism between the two concepts of philosophy, an inability contrary to the idea of Enlightenment itself. One might define the self-destructive tendency of Reason in its own conceptual realm as the positivistic dissolution of metaphysical concepts up to the concept of Reason itself. The philosophical task then is to insist on carrying the intellectual effort up to the full realization of the contradictions, resulting from this dissolution, between the various branches of culture and between culture and social reality, rather than to attempt to patch up the cracks in the edifice of our civilization by any falsely optimistic or harmonistic doctrine. Far from engaging in romanticism, as have so many eminent critics of Enlightenment, we should encourage Enlightenment to move forward even in the face of its most paradoxical consequences. Otherwise the intellectual decay of society's most cherished ideals will take place confusedly in the undercurrents of the public mind. The course of history will be hazily experienced as inescapable fate. This experience will provide a new and dangerous myth to lurk behind the external assurances of official ideology. The hope of Reason lies in the emancipation from its own fear of despair.

Jane Flax

Is Enlightenment Emancipatory? A Feminist Reading of "What Is Enlightenment?"

. . . Nowhere is a gendered subtext more necessary and constitutive than in one of the foundational articulations of modernity: Kant's essay, 'What Is Enlightenment?' (1748). In this essay, Kant develops a gendered geography and defence of modernity which recur and are further developed by later, equally immanent theorists such as Sigmund Freud and Max Weber. Read with a feminist eye, then, this essay reveals much about the gendered qualities of modernity/modernisation and the modern constitution of gender.

Feminist analysis will alter our understandings of the meanings of modernity/modernisation. Hence, these perspectives must be included within our stories about them. Further elaboration of feminist perspectives is necessary before we can render judgements about the emancipatory character and potential of modernity/modernisation. . . .

Critique of Enlightenment

. . . Feminists have begun to question whose differentiations, whose renunciations, and whose emancipation modernisation both effects and requires. Is justice possible within the gendered spheres and practices of modernisation? Is the modern subject/subjectivity emancipated, and at what (and whose) cost? Is modernisation and its promise of enlightenment as articulated by Kant and others desirable or possible; and what happens when women and feminist commitments are inserted into it?

Jane Flax, "Is Enlightenment Emancipatory? A Feminist Reading of 'What Is Enlightenment?'" in *Postmodernism and the Re-Reading of Modernity*, ed. Francis Barker, Peter Hulme, and Margaret Iversen (Manchester: Manchester University Press, 1992), 232–233, 239–248. Reprinted with permission from the author.

First we can consider the promise of enlightenment; what is to be gained as it progresses? The answer to this question appears to be well known: rationalisation. Society is to be ordered such that reason can be fully developed. Public reason will be given its autonomous sphere, guarded and anchored as long as necessary by countervailing institutions such as the family and the state. In turn, as reason develops it will produce knowledge that is useful and beneficial. This knowledge will be utilised in the public sphere of the state, in the private sphere of work and within the subject himself. Eventually as the subject becomes more rational, he will be able to manage freedom better; hence like a child who becomes an adult, his need for countervailing (constraining) institutions will diminish. As general enlightenment occurs and the great mass of humans becomes rational, it will be able to order its self and its practices according to the ever-expanding knowledge that an unconstrained reason can produce.

In the public world of the state, humans will be able to be self-determining, to live by the dictates of reason and without irrational constraint. Hence the public world of the state will approximate the public world of reason; both will become spheres in which autonomous, equal individuals can engage in argument, rule by a rationally attained consensus and enjoy freedom.

However, these rational individuals will also be able to recognise when reason cannot rule. In such cases, we must renounce our demands for freedom and self-determination. The family is one such case, since it is a relationship among dependent unequals whose purpose is to guard those (women and children) who are unable to utilise their own reason. Institutions such as bureaucracies and the army are other instances. They cannot always serve the ends for which they are intended if their mechanical parts engage in a rational critique of these purposes or their authority.

What this promise assumes is that reason can operate autonomously . . . and that ordering our selves and our practices according to its dictates is emancipatory. Why should we accept the validity of either of these claims? These assumptions rest upon a prior set of beliefs about the constitution of the subject and the structure of the external world which have been called into question by feminists, psychoanalysts and postmodernists. All three kinds of theorists question whether reason can operate autonomously and whether even if it could do so, the resulting knowledges and practices would be universally emancipatory.

1. The Constitution of Subjectivity

The plausibility and coherence of Kant's story depend upon the assumptions that an innate, homogeneous form of reason exists with all (male?) humans and that this reason is not determined or affected by other (heterogenous) factors such as desire, patterns of childrearing, or other historical experience and social relations. The subject must be irrevocably split internally so that the rational kernel can unfold unaffected by its bodily and social experiences. All such experiences are merely contingent and are in principle separable from pure reason. As contingent beings we are all different, but as bearers of reason we are all the same. . . .

Psychoanalysts, feminists and postmodernists all deny that a pure transparent reason is possible. While the capacity to reason may or may not be innate, it can only develop in relation to the other parts of the child's inner world and social relations. . . .

Since the ego is first of all a 'bodily ego,' reason may be pervaded by desire. . . . The boundaries between psyche and soma, between desire, embodiment and thought are never impermeable or fixed. . . . Since unconscious processes operate outside of and by different rules from rational thought, their affects and hence rational processes can never be transparent or fully controlled.

If we can offer good reasons to believe that reason cannot have the character which the Enlightenment story both posits and depends upon, why do people remain committed to this belief? Feminist theorists, with their emphasis on gender, can pursue this question in ways that psychoanalysts alone cannot. The split between mind and body reflects a division of labour in which some people only or primarily engage in abstract thought and others take care of the necessities that arise out of embodied existence—the reproduction of daily life including childbearing and rearing. As Kant's (and Freud's) story tells us, modernisation alters but reincorporates previously existing divisions between household/private and public/rational/political worlds. The household remains the locus of passion, tutelage, feeling, the concrete and particular, the subjective, the mortal, the familial and kinship. It represents the childhood of every adult and of the species. These qualities are posited as existing in opposition and inferior to reason. . . .

Traditionally philosophers have argued, as Kant does, that engagement in such activities disqualifies one from the life of reason. No true knowledge can arise out of such activities and indeed involvement in them impedes or clouds 'true' thought. They produce biases that must be 'controlled for.' . . .

The relevance of gender to this view of reason is apparent when another facet of modern social life is considered: the sexual division of labour. Necessary labour is divided along gender as well as race and class lines. Women have primary responsibility for the reproduction of daily life, including the care of small children. Since children develop in and through the context of relations with others, both men and women will first begin to develop a self in interactions with a woman — a mother and/or other female relations. To some extent, male identity is built out of oppositional moves. He must become not-female, and in a culture where gender is an exclusionary and unequal pair of opposites, he must guard against the return of the repressed — his identification with his mother and those 'female' qualities within him. This provides a powerful unconscious motive for identifying with and overhauling the abstract and the non-relational and for reinforcing gender segregation, including within intellectual work, to ensure that women will never again have power over men.

The very appearance of neutrality or universality of reason depends upon an interdependent and simultaneous set of moves: naming women as different in relation to the true measure of humanity; men, devaluing difference, and suppressing men's dependence on and complicity in this difference. Our understanding of reason depends on what it is not, on its difference from and superiority to other faculties such as the passions. Associating women with the body and the particular are two of the necessary conditions for the possibility of conceptualising a disembodied and universal faculty (e.g., the Cartesian ego or Kant's pure reason). Woman = the body; therefore men are not possessed/determined by it. The effects of male embodiment and social experiences on reason and its products are defined out of existence. With the contaminating effects of difference suppressed or denied, reason can take on its unitary and universal appearance. By locating men as well as women within gender relations, this purity/privilege is removed and both reason and knowledge production are resocialised. Rather than engaging in the enlightenment move of insisting that women's reason can be as 'pure' as men's, a more promising path may be to question the claim that such reason is possible for anyone and that no valuable or truthful knowledge can arise from the activities traditionally associated with women or the passions.

2. The Metaphysics of Enlightenment

Just as the Enlightenment story rests on untenable assumptions about the nature of subjectivity and reason, so too it depends upon problematic beliefs about the nature of the external world and the possible fit between reason, knowledge and practice. Part of the appeal of Kant's story is its promise to solve a problem that has plagued political theorists and philosophers at least since Plato: how to reconcile knowledge and power. Many philosophers and political theorists have wished to solve this problem in a way that could maintain the innocence of knowledge, power and themselves. For example, Kant claims that there is a particular kind of truth 'out there' which reason can grasp. This truth is simultaneously universal and benign so that governing according to its principles will result in the best for all and the domination of none. The philosopher/intellectual has a unique ability to investigate and establish the conditions of knowledge and to adjudicate truth claims. This epistemological skill/privilege grounds and warrants their position as guardian and benign representative of humanity's emancipatory interests.

Knowledge in this scheme has a curious double character. The Enlightenment hope is that utilizing truthful knowledge in the service of legitimate power will assure both freedom and progress. If knowledge is grounded in and warranted by a universal reason, not particular 'interests,' it can be both 'neutral' and positive, e.g., socially beneficial (powerful). The accumulation of more knowledge (the getting of more truth) results simultaneously in an increase in objectivity (neutrality) and in progress. To the extent that power/authority is grounded in this expanding knowledge it too is progressive, e.g., it becomes more rational and expands the freedom and self-actualisation of its subjects who naturally conform their reason to its (and their) laws. . . .

Obviously this set of beliefs rests on a number of wishes which are impossible to fulfil. We must assume that the social as well as the physical universe is governed by a uniform, benign and ultimately unconflictual set of laws. Conforming our behaviour to non-unitary or malevolent laws would generate conflicts and difference that could not themselves be lawfully resolved. No neutral 'decision procedure' would exist that could determine how conflict could be resolved without privileging one position rather than another. Power loses innocence without its protective grounding in a universal, neutral good for all. Order would have to be (at least to some extent) imposed rather than discovered. Knowledge would be seen as useful for some (persons and effects) and oppressive to others. . . .

3. Is Enlightenment Emancipatory?

Feminists answer this question in at least two contradictory ways. Some argue there is nothing intrinsically gender biased about the process of modernisation. The fact that the process has generated sexual divisions of labour (in the family and in the economy) and the exclusion of women from the public worlds of work and knowledge production is merely contingent. Women must be integrated into the differentiated spheres of the public and private/economic and men must assume more responsibilities in the private/domestic one. Then the Enlightenment promises of equality, justice and rationality will be redeemed.

Others argue that the exclusion of women from most of modern culture is not contingent. The splits and differentiation that mark this culture reflect and constitute a distinctively masculine subjectivity. Women can integrate into this culture only at the expense of our femininity; we must be willing to reject or annihilate everything that is 'different' about us. In adopting the modern ('universal') practices of reason and citizenship as regulative ideals, feminists will in fact be complying with and reinforcing a regime of domination in which differences of many kinds become the basis for asymmetrical relations of power. Hence integration is a delusory and self-destructive strategy: the male/universal remains unchallenged as the norm and difference remains the 'other' of its superior 'same.'

The second position is more compelling. None of the spheres of modern life appear clearly differentiated once we begin to track the organisation and effects of gender relations. The claim of differentiation reflects the experience of and benefits (at best) a few privileged (white) men, and it is often asserted to preserve relations of power and privilege. For example, the private/family actually extends into the private/work sphere in many ways. Sexual harassment, predominantly of women by men, is prevalent at work and is in part motivated by a wish to resituate women within familial relations even in a work context. Yet, differentiation is invoked when women attempt to reconcile the contradictory demands of private/family and private/work by questioning the standard of a good worker as one who is almost always available to the employer and is willing to place organisation demands above all others. It is evident that no clear line of demarcation between public/state and private/family exists. The modern state regulates aspects of family life such as marriage, child custody and support and divorce. However, 'separate spheres' is invoked when male privilege is threatened in case of wife battering or marital rape. Children become private obligations/possessions of their

parents when questions of childcare or the redistribution of resources to
the poor are raised. . . .

4. The Poverty of the Public Sphere

Models of democracy based on the characteristics of the ideal speech
situation provide impoverished visions of public life. Political life remains
impoverished in its absence of ritual, sensuality, spectacle, community,
moral education and aesthetics. Habermas claims that a fully realised
and autonomous public sphere is necessary to fulfil Enlightenment
promises of emancipation. . . .

The privileging of speech and rational argument over other qualities such as nurturance and caretaking (traditionally female activities)
or a commitment to beauty or pleasure remains unquestioned within
these theories. All individuals are to value a certain kind of rationality as
the superordinate public virtue. One may not speak out or make public
demands on the basis of desire or aesthetic commitments. Consensus is
privileged over conflict; yet the productive uses of conflict in developing and maintaining civic virtue are never explored. The importance of
spectacle, drama, rhetoric, painting, sculpture or music in constructing a
rich public life (as for example in the classic Greek polis or the French
revolution) are nowhere acknowledged or incorporated.

These theorists do not question the biases that are built into their view
of the model person who is to engage in argument. The family/public
split is replicated. As in classical liberal theory, adults simply spring up
in the public sphere like mushrooms. Enquiry into how persons capable
of demanding and sustaining a rich public life come to be is absent. Apparently all relevant parties in the processes of justice are equal, autonomous, rational, individual adults who can speak for themselves. This
assumption is problematic because in some policy debates the interests of
the speechless (children, animals, the environment) may be very much at
stake. Even discourse might be very different if we conceptualised ourselves in the variety of positions most people do find themselves in eventually as children, as dependent on the care of others, as physically or
mental incapacitated. Public discourse will remain impoverished as long
as we assume someone else (mostly women in private/families) will tend
to these Others.

The conflating of discourse and reason is also quite problematic because it excludes many other qualities which are often necessary to a full

public life or speech about it—loyalty, empathy, fantasy, courage, a sense of righteous rage, for example. Since subjectivity is partially constituted in and through public life, qualities necessary to the full development of public actors will be lacking. . . .

We cannot have a rich public life if questions of the visions of the good to which we are committed are excluded. Politics . . . always involves assumptions and questions about what kinds of people we want to be, what kinds of practices and obligations people believe are right or necessary and what resources (family, economic, political, knowledge, emotional, etc.) are required to make such practices and people exist. These questions have public and private dimensions and cannot be neatly mapped on to one or the other domain.

My dissatisfactions with these visions of the public sphere do not arise out of a longing for an organic (premodern) totality which in any case, as feminists are quite aware, never existed. Rather they speak to and from a preference for further differentiation—for the play of differences within a single domain rather than a distribution across different domains. . . . Our institutions are already interdependent and mutually constituting. Modern, instrumental rationality could not survive without its interconnected 'opposites'—the worlds of nurturance (family) and 'free' subjectivity/expressivity (including 'high art'). . . .

It has become increasingly clear that no institution can thrive if we pretend it is the unique locus of or has the sole responsibility for any of these capacities. For example, Kant and others are correct to argue that families cannot withstand the corrosive effect of public reason and that the demands of work do estrange people from the capacities necessary to be good parents and lovers. This does not mean that the private/family should be exempt from rational criticism or that efforts should be made to constitute it as a 'haven' from a 'heartless' world. Rather, we need to find modes of justice appropriate to family life and modes of nurturance appropriate to work so that the world is less heartless and both genders in many forms of relations can move more easily between and within domains. This does not require the collapsing of the public and private but rather the transformation of both so that the variety of needs and motives already at play will no longer be distributed by and through the differentiated disciplining of men and women and the replication of gender-based relations of domination. . . .

Emmanuel Chukwudi Eze

Race and the Enlightenment

. . . The philosophical reception of the Enlightenment in our times has largely ignored the writings on race by the major Enlightenment thinkers. Despite the rapid growth of interest in the interconnectedness of race and culture in the fields of cultural and black studies in recent years, there still exists to date no volume that brings together the most important and influential writings on race that the Enlightenment produced. Quite often, teachers and students of the history of modern science and the history of modern philosophy pay little or no attention to the enormous amount of research and writings on race and cross-cultural anthropology that was undertaken and accomplished by the philosophical luminaries of the eighteenth century, in the Age of Reason. For example, in nearly all standard programs of study of Immanuel Kant, rarely is it noted that Kant devoted the largest period of his career to research in, and teaching of, anthropology and cultural geography. Before, during, and after he wrote the better-known critical works, Kant researched, developed, and regularly taught what he called the "twin" sciences of anthropology and physical geography. Kant was the first to introduce geography into the curriculum of study at the University of Königsberg, in 1756. When he started teaching anthropology at the same university in the winter of 1772–3, it was the first such program of study in any German university. J. A. May (1970) has calculated that at the University of Königsberg where he spent his entire career, Kant offered as many as 72 courses in anthropology or geography, compared to only 54 in logic, 49 in metaphysics, 28 in moral philosophy, and 20 in theoretical physics. Given these statistics, and the fact that the questions of race and of the biological, geographical, and cultural distribution of humans on earth occupied a central place both in Kant's science of geography and in anthropology, it can hardly be said that his interest in the "race question" was marginal to other aspects of his career.

Emmanuel Chukwudi Eze, Introduction to *Race and the Enlightenment: A Reader* (London: Blackwell, 1997), 2–5, 8. Reprinted with permission of Blackwell Publishing, Ltd.

When writings on race by the major Enlightenment figures have been noted in traditional philosophical scholarship, it is often to dismiss them as journalistic, or as having little that would be of serious philosophical interest. While some of the works are dismissed as popular, or recreational, others resilient to such conventional dismissal are interpreted away as "cast in ironical tone." Such were the opinions expressed by Willibald Klinke and Hannah Arendt on Kant's "non-critical" work, and Robert Palter on Hume's racial remarks in "Of national characters." Among those in the long list of philosophers who have studied the philosophical anthropology of Kant are Max Schiller, Martin Heidegger, Ernst Cassirer, Michel Foucault, van de Pitte; none of them discusses Kant's theories on race or his work in cross-cultural anthropology. More glaring, however, is the condition of a recent Kant publication, Howard Caygill's otherwise excellent reference work, *A Kant Dictionary*, which contains absolutely no entry headed "race." Yet, throughout his career, Kant published voluminously in the subject area: at least five long, self-standing essays . . . and two books, one edited by Kant (*Anthropology from a Pragmatic Point of View*), and the other edited posthumously (*Physical Geography*). Kant's theories on race abound in these essays and the books. . . . It seems to me that in order to appreciate Kant not only as the author of critical philosophy but also as a cultural thinker, we need to explore seriously his "non-critical" writings, and seek to establish in a developed manner possible thematic and theoretical relations that might exist between his anthropological or geographical interests and the critical projects. . . .

From a historical perspective, if we compare the European Enlightenment to Greek antiquity, we notice that in both the realms of philosophy and politics, the major thinkers of Greek antiquity articulated social and human geographical differences on the basis of the opposition between the "cultured" and the "barbaric." Aristotle, for example, defined the human being as a rational animal, and supposed that the cultured people (such as the male, aristocratic Greeks) were capable of living in a reasonable way and organized their society accordingly (democratically), while the "barbarians," the non-Greeks, incapable of culture and lacking the superior rational capacity for the Athenian-style democratic social organization, lived brutishly and under despotism. European Enlightenment thinkers retained the Greek ideal of reason, as well as this reason's categorical function of discriminating between the cultured (now called the "civilized") and the "barbarian" (the "savage" or the "primitive"). It can be argued, in fact, that the Enlightenment's declaration of itself as "the Age of Reason" was predicated upon precisely the assumption that reason could historically only come to maturity in modern Europe, while the inhabitants of areas outside Europe, who were considered to be of non-European racial and cultural origins, were consistently described and theorized as rationally inferior and savage.

Why had the concept of race gained such currency in European Enlightenment scientific and socio-political discourse? Although in the area of philosophy of history, for example, the rise of science (*Wissenschaft*) in the Enlightenment period had overthrown the biblical story of creation and replaced the authority of religion with that of reason, nature was still conceptualized as a hierarchical system (the Great Chain of Being), in which every being, from humans down to fauna and flora, had a "naturally" assigned position and status. Influential natural historians, such as Carl von Linné and Georges-Louis Leclerc, Comte de Buffon embarked upon the classification of the human races (and indeed all objects of existence) according to this "naturally" ordered hierarchy. At the top of the human chain in this general schema was positioned the European, while non-Europeans were positioned at lower points on the scale of a supposed human, rational and moral, evolutionary capacity.

In addition to the above quasi-religious scientific classification of humans in the eighteenth century, the classical century of the Enlightenment also saw—especially from the European's perspective—a period of growth in the scope of the natural world to be classified. During the two centuries prior to the European Enlightenment, an enormous amount of exploration and voyages around the world had produced numerous published accounts of distant lands and peoples as well as the great expansion of European wealth. These popular travel writings contributed significantly to the perception of Europe as familiar and "civilized," living in the Age of Light, while the peoples of other lands (Asia, Africa, America) were of "strange" habits and mores. Savagery could then be physically located outside Europe, outside of light, so that Africa, for example, was considered the Dark Continent, and a *terra nulla.*

Enlightenment philosophy was instrumental in codifying and institutionalizing both the scientific and popular European perceptions of the human race. The numerous writings on race by Hume, Kant, and Hegel played a strong role in articulating Europe's sense not only of its cultural but also *racial* superiority. In their writings, . . . "reason" and "civilization" became almost synonymous with "white" people and northern

Europe, while unreason and savagery were conveniently located among the non-whites, the "black," the "red," the "yellow," outside Europe. . . .
. . . Whereas feminist critics have extensively examined the gender-inflected nature of eighteenth-century science and philosophy, a similar critical engagement is lacking in the area of race. I am therefore interested in what, if anything, might be uncovered of the possible relation between philosophy and anthropology and race theories in the Enlightenment, especially among the writings of prominent philosophers such as Hume, Kant, and Hegel.

Peter Hulme

The Spontaneous Hand of Nature: Savagery, Colonialism, and the Enlightenment

from college days I had learnt that one can imagine nothing so strange and incredible but has been said by some philosopher; and since then, while traveling, I have realized that those whose opinions are quite opposed to ours are not, for all that, without exception barbarians and savages; many of them enjoy as good a share of reason as we do, or better. Again, I considered how a given man with a given mind develops otherwise among Frenchmen or Germans than he would if he had always lived among Chinese or Cannibals; how, again, even in the fashion of dress, the very thing that we liked ten years ago . . . seems to us at present extravagant and ridiculous. Thus it is by custom and example that we are persuaded, much more than by any certain knowledge; at the same time, a majority of votes is worthless as a proof, in regard to truths that are even

Peter Hulme, "The Spontaneous Hand of Nature: Savagery, Colonialism, and the Enlightenment," in *The Enlightenment and Its Shadows*, ed. Peter Hulme and Ludmilla Jordanova (London: Routledge, 1990), 18–34. Reprinted with permission of Thomson Publishing Services.

a little difficult of discovery; for it is much more likely that one man should
have hit upon them for himself than that a whole nation should. Accord-
ingly I could choose nobody whose opinions I thought preferable to other
men's; and I was as it were forced to become my own guide.

(*Descartes*)

A phenomenon as complex as the Enlightenment could have no single beginning but, if the matter were pressed, a claim might be staked for these words of Descartes, published in 1637: they certainly manifest that selfless commitment to truth which has always been such an important part of the self-image of the Enlightenment and they mark, in dramatic fashion, the emergence of an individual and uncompromised project from the plethora of mere example and custom. Descartes forced to become his own guide is a graphic image of temporary loss, assuaged by the knowledge that the authorial subject has emerged from the dark forest of intellectual confusion and is dramatizing in retrospect the quest in which he is inscribed as solitary hero.

The cultural geography of the passage obviously owes much to the 'age of discovery' in which France was just beginning to participate: Descartes' mental universe contains Chinese and Cannibals as well as Frenchmen and Germans. The mapping here is straightforward enough: Frenchmen and Germans constitute the European centre with the Chinese and Cannibals at the eastern and western extremes of the periphery. For Europe China had represented an ideal of oriental civilization ever since the time of Marco Polo. The West Indian Cannibals — whose name was given to the area they inhabited as 'Caribbean' — had, from the earliest reports of the New World, occupied the opposite end of that spectrum, their purported anthropophagy so fitting them for the role of archetypal savages that 'cannibalism' soon came to displace the classical word. Yet if a cultural spectrum is implicit, the Cannibals remain, for Descartes, within the pale. They are a nation, Cannibals rather than cannibals; and so the 'given man,' the universal subject of Descartes' sentence, can be as easily imagined developing his 'given mind' among the Cannibals as amongst the Germans. The presumption of a common humanity underlies differences of custom and opinion, however severe.

From a philosophical point of view, Descartes is usually considered to have been writing within a tradition of skeptical humanism associated with the essayist Michel de Montaigne. . . . But culturally he also draws on Montaigne . . . with a paraphrase of Montaigne's own famous axiom that . . . 'men call that barbarism which is not common to them,' made in the course of his remarkable essay 'Of the Caniballes.' Yet the general thrust of Descartes' paragraph eventually breaks away from such relativism. A different language begins to emerge, in which 'truths' are 'discovered' like new lands, in which the model for the scientist is that of the new explorer sailing beyond the boundaries of the old world of tired shibboleths, across 'strange seas of Thought, alone' (in Wordsworth's later words about Newton) towards the brave world of new knowledges. . . .

A geographical revolution had indeed preceded and in many ways provided a language for the revolution in thought that constituted the Enlightenment. At around the time that Descartes began his European travels, Francis Bacon published the first outline of his *Great Instauration* (1620), the most confident statement of the new science. Like Descartes after him, Bacon begins by rejecting what he calls the 'enchantments of antiquity and authority' which have 'so bound up men's powers that they have been made impotent (like persons bewitched) to accompany with the nature of things.' The book, traditional symbol of knowledge and authority, is denigrated for its 'endless repetitions.' The spell of the library is to be broken through the example of the voyagers. . . . For this new challenge the existing guides are puzzled and worthless. The ancients were, after all, limited to coasting the shores of the old continent or crossing inland seas like the Mediterranean. Just as the mariner's needle provided a new guide across the ocean, so a new scientific method will lead out of the 'woods of experience' into 'the open ground of axioms'. . . .

Some of the earliest accounts of the inhabitants of America had been written from within that same humanist tradition that Descartes was to subvert. . . . This vision of the simplicity and innocence of the Golden Age drew its essential elements from the opening book of Ovid's *Metamorphoses*, not accidentally the very first book translated into English in America, by George Sandys, treasurer of the Virginia Company at the time of the Jamestown settlement in the early seventeenth century:

> *The Golden Age was first; which uncompeld,*
> *And without rule, in Faith and Truth exceld.*
> *As then, there was no punishment, nor feare;*
> *Nor threatning Laws in brasse prescribed were;*
> *Nor suppliant crouching pris'ners shooke to see*
> *Their angry Iudge: but all was safe and free. . . .*

But this humanist ideal of a Golden Age uncorrupted by old world vices was applied to America only from the libraries of Europe: it was a perspective whose soft tones required the distancing provided as readily by the Atlantic as by the centuries separating Europe from its pre-history. . . . But this utopian vision did not long survive the complexities of American topography: colonists' demands for land grew more extensive and more violent, exhausting native hospitality and eventually provoking reprisals. . . .

The turning-point for English commentators on this matter was undoubtedly March 1622 when a concerted effort by the Powhatan confederacy under the leadership of the formidable Opechancanough narrowly failed to extirpate the English colony at Jamestown. After this event the attitudes and practices of the settlers themselves remained necessarily pragmatic with regard to contact with the native population; but the 'massacre'—as it was called in England—provided a different and in some ways more powerful impulse to the colonizing process. The dangers could no longer be elided but, since the natives were seen by their action to have relinquished any conceivable natural rights they might have had to the land, the potential rewards for colonial enterprise were now much greater, or at least the difficulties in justifying the rewards less considerable.

Samuel Purchas, chief ideologist of the Virginia Company, drew out the consequences in his essay 'Virginia's Verger' published in 1625:

> But when Virginia was violently ravished by her owne ruder Natives, yea her Virgin cheekes dyed with the bloud of three Colonies . . . the stupid Earth seems distempered with such bloudy potions and cries that shee is ready to spue out her inhabitants.

The initial separation of land from inhabitants in the bestowal of the name Virginia pays handsome dividends here. Not only can the 'virgin' land be savagely raped by its own natives, but the blood thereby spilt onto its cheeks is that of the English colonies themselves, which are, in the process, identified with the Virginia that has been ravished. The Indians became satisfactorily 'unnatural Naturalls,' forfeiting any rights they may have had under natural law. In other words the 'massacre' has performed a miraculous reversal by which the settlers have become the natural inhabitants—identified with the land—and the original inhabitants have been discursively 'spewed out' by their own territories.

An even more immediate reaction came in the sermon addressed by John Donne at St. Paul's to the members of the Virginia Company on 13 November 1622, soon after news of the 'massacre' had reached

London. Donne took as his text Acts 1.8: 'But yee shall receive power, after that the Holy Ghost is come upon you, and yee shall be witnesses unto me both in Jerusalem, and in all Judea, and in Samaria, and unto the uttermost part of the earth.' He proceeded to speak not only of the Company's missionary duties, but also of the difficulties of gaining riches in that uttermost part of the earth: 'though you see not your money, though you see not your men, though a *Flood*, a *Flood* of *bloud* have broken in upon them, be not discouraged.'

Among Donne's audience that day was Thomas Hobbes. His 'warre of every man against every man' expounded in *Leviathan* (1651) comes complete with American references: 'savage people in many places of *America*' who 'live at this day in that brutish manner.' This pitiless account of the state of nature was not uninfluenced, it might be speculated, by the events of 1622, given Hobbes' own involvement, through Cavendish, his patron, with the affairs of the Virginia Company.

. . . The savagery of the state of nature is exemplified in Hobbes' writings 'in this present age' by American societies; but currently 'civil and flourishing' nations 'have been in former ages . . . fierce, short-lived, poor, nasty, and deprived of all that pleasure and beauty of life, which peace and society are wont to bring with them.' And what they have been, they can become again, very easily. In his 'Tripos' Hobbes lists the benefits of civilization, only to conclude with the question: 'all of which supposed away, what do we differ from the wildest of Indians?' The 'savages' hold a mirror up to the 'reality' of our human nature; they show a frightening image of a society bereft of those attributes which make it civilized. . . . In this way savagery is lodged disconcertingly close to the crust of civilization: America is allowed to provide a glimpse into the heart of darkness.

John Locke's argument in the second of his *Two Treatises of Government* (1690) might seem equally distant from both these traditions, the humanist and the Hobbesian. The 'Golden Age' does feature once in its pages as that time 'before vain Ambition, and *amor sceleratus habendi*, evil Concupiscence, had corrupted Mens minds into a Mistake of true Power and Honour,' but Locke's state of nature is as far removed from a land of milk and honey as it is from Hobbes' world of perpetual strife. It is rather a realm of positive achievements sustained in accordance with the Law of Nature, a state of perfect freedom and equality. The only one of the traditional negatives that applies to Locke's state of nature is 'without a common Superior on Earth.' And only the danger of the state of nature becoming a state of war explains the eventual acceptance of an ultimate earthly authority 'from which relief can be had *by appeal*.' This danger arises from the failure of a minority of human beings to conduct themselves according to natural law.

References to America might seem to bring Locke closer to Hobbes' chilling universalism: after all, 'in the beginning all the World was *America*.' . . . On closer inspection Locke's famous aphorism inserts an historical wedge of some size between the two continents. The implied relationship between Europe and America becomes apparent on that metaphorical map of the world unrolled a century later by Edmund Burke as the very map of mankind's history with all stages and periods of savagery and civility instantly under our view in different parts of that world. The language of development, here coming into being as an Enlightenment theory of history, is still very much with us, allowing our one world to be read through a metaphor of maturation in which some are—when not 'children'—always junior to the European standard.

Locke's argument in the *Second Treatise* can be seen in general terms as a radical attack on absolutism and its accompanying privileges, the most important of which is the control of land. The target of the book is, then, the practice of the unproductive land-owning aristocracy of seventeenth-century England. In the last analysis the book's complex argument, with its play of limitations and justifications, defends the principle of the enclosure of common land into private property and the accumulation of capital that results from a commitment to the improvement of that land. But private accumulation can, according to Locke, only be justified if its accumulation accrues—eventually—to the public good.

Locke's approach is to formulate what one critic has described as 'a statement of universal principle . . . completely independent of historical example.' In other words, an elaborate hypothesis is constructed based upon extrapolations from a supposed original condition, conventionally called the 'state of nature'; with key terms such as 'property' and 'labour' complexly and abstractly discussed, independent of any particular case that may be cited. . . . [T]he argument itself proceeds determinedly in the direction of general principles couched in the language of natural law. For these reasons the book is often seen as one of the founding texts of modern political philosophy.

However, despite the movement towards universal principles, most of the crucial steps in Locke's argument actually depend on references to America. Locke begins by affirming (on Biblical authority) that the state of nature is a state of equality with the earth given to mankind in common, and the taking of private property from the common stock only therefore warranted 'at least where there is enough, and as good left in common for others.' Seventeenth-century England could hardly be thought capable of supplying 'enough, and as good' to those without land, but this threatening limitation is overcome through a form of colonial calculus whereby private improvement of land has far-reaching *public* benefits:

> To which let me add, that he who appropriates land to himself by his labour, does not lessen but increase the common stock of mankind. . . . For I aske whether in the wild woods and uncultivated wast of America left to Nature, without any improvement, tillage or husbandry, a thousand acres will yeild the needy and wretched inhabitants as many conveniencies of life as ten acres of equally fertile land doe in Devonshire where they are well cultivated.

The equality existing under the state of nature was never likely to survive Locke's hypothetical reconstruction of the development of political society, but the resultant inequalities could still be defended if it were claimed that even the worst-off would have benefited—an argument that has become one of the planks of economic liberalism. The *Second Treatise* takes the worst case to be a day-labourer forced to sell his only property—his labour—in return for sufficient wages to keep him and his family alive. If the day-labourer were to question the improvement in his condition over what it had been in the state of nature when land was held in common, Locke's answer would again point across the Atlantic:

> There cannot be a clearer demonstration of any thing, than several Nations of the Americans are of this, who are rich in Land, and poor in all the Comforts of Life; whom Nature having furnished as liberally as any other people, with the materials of Plenty, i.e. a fruitful Soil, apt to produce in abundance, what might serve for food, rayment, and delight; yet for want of improving it by labour, have not one hundredth part of the Conveniences we enjoy: And a King of a large fruitful Territory there feeds, lodges, and is clad worse than a day Labourer in England.

If the best-off of the Indians is worse off than the worst-off of the English labourers, then Locke's extrapolations from natural law are vindicated. . . . And there is no doubt that the thrust of Locke's argument is towards the defence of a system in which the least well-off can be seen to have benefited from the 'improvements' accruing from a more 'rational' use of land.

However, neither can these references to America be without intended substance as is sometimes argued, since the edifice of Locke's argument would fall without the comparison between Indian king and English labourer. . . .

Locke himself had intimate connections with the developing project of colonial expansion, especially in North America and the West Indies. Shaftesbury, his patron and employer, was an active participant in this project—part-owner of slave-ships, leading member of the Committee for Trade and of the board of Lords Proprietors of Carolina; so much the progressive capitalist that his biographer speaks of him being regarded as 'a representative of the rising new capitalistic forces in society.' . . . Locke worked as secretary for these bodies, was involved in framing the *Fundamental Constitutions* for the new territory of Carolina, and invested capital in the Royal African Company and the Bahama Adventurers, a merchant company set up by Shaftesbury in 1673. In that year he also became secretary to the Council of Trade and Plantations, which emphasized English interests in tropical and sub-tropical colonies. And in 1697 he wrote about the continuing problems of Virginia for the Board of Trade, discussing the need for land reform.

Indeed the argument of the *Second Treatise* is implicated with that panoply of natural law theory (mainly Roman in origin) with which European occupation of American land was being justified. In his 1622 sermon, Donne had rooted the 'power' of his text from Acts in the law of nations by which 'if the inhabitants doe not in some measure fill the Land, so as the Land may bring foorth her increase for the use of men,' then the land 'becomes theirs that wil possesse it.' This argument, known as the *vacuum domicilium*, was much elaborated over the course of the seventeenth century, but its point was simple enough. As one European writer put it, with brutal succinctness: 'we rather than they being the prime occupants, and they only Sojourners in the land.' . . .

Logically, one might suppose that the deployment of the 'reason' given by God to men was responsible for all food production through the development of hunting, pastoralism, and agriculture. But, instead, Locke introduces a further distinction whereby originally—and still in certain kinds of society—food is provided 'by the spontaneous hand of Nature'; and appropriation out of this 'hand' is the first sign of how 'labour' intervenes in the process. Even the wild Indian—who still lives in a situation where land is held in common—makes a possession of what is to be his food by mixing his labour with it, even if that only involves picking the fruit off the branch. The Indian has used his labour—but not in the productive process, and so without, according to Locke, showing any exercise of reason.

What holds this argument together is the intervention of that 'spontaneous hand of Nature,' which enables Locke to separate the concepts of labour and reason. Without the spontaneous hand of nature there would be no explanation of how those who had not yet demonstrated their rationality had managed to survive with some degree of success. It is this idea of spontaneous food provision—prior to the exercise of reason—that underwrites the exclusivity of Locke's central category of fully rational human beings. . . .

So according to Locke humanity is defined by reason, and the exercise of reason demonstrated by improvement of land. The existence of food is not in itself sufficient proof of 'culture': labour sometimes merely 'collects' what nature has provided. Therefore the central division for Locke lies between those who 'improve' and those who merely 'collect': only the former are fully rational and therefore fully human. The argument from spontaneity is necessary to explain how the 'not fully rational' can manage to eat: it is this trope that excludes native American agriculture from consideration, and even from recognition.

As if in response to the significance of its references to America, Locke's *Second Treatise* was soon drawn upon to support one of the most extensive and sophisticated of the Puritan justifications for appropriation of Indian land, John Bulkley's long preface to Roger Wolcott's highly political *Poetical Meditations*, aimed at the group of European colonists called the 'native rights men' after their insistence on buying land from the Indians on the grounds that they did fully own it. Bulkley quotes extensively from the *Second Treatise*, making particular play of Locke's theory of labour, for which he finds support in Genesis:

> *And to this voice of the Law of Nature, viz. that* Labour in this State *shall be the beginning of Property, seems well to agree the voice of* God Himself *in the Gift or Grant he made of the Earth, the Creatures & productions of it to Mankind, Gen. I. 28 Where we find that* Cultivating and Subduing the Earth, *and* having Dominion *are joyned together: thereby assuring us that as in that Gift he then made of it in common to men, he did not design it should serve to their benefit & comfort only by*

> *its* spontaneous Productions, *but that it was his will that by* Art and In-
> dustry *in Subduing and Cultivating of it they should draw still more*
> *from it, so that this should be their* Title to it *at least during the contin-*
> *uance of* that State of Nature, *& till by positive Constitutions of their own,*
> *the matter of Property should be otherwise Determined and Settled.*

. . . Bulkley's enthusiastic explication of Locke highlights a peculiarity
about the spontaneous hand of nature which had remained invisible
in Locke's exposition. What supports the crucial distinction between
universal labour and the more restricted exercise of reason amongst
humanity is precisely the humanist language of the Golden Age from
which Locke — paradigm of the modern political philosophy — is supposedly so distant. . . .

Ovid's 'golden age' is a time of abundance and bounty, part of a
narrative of loss that was central to classical (and particularly Roman)
self-definitions. That narrative has a long discontinuous history. It had
provided a frame of reference for the humanism of Peter Martyr and
Montaigne; it is an ingredient in Diderot's Enlightenment story of the
noble Tahitian savage; and it would still, in the next century, be visible
in Karl Marx's theory of primitive communism. But the abundance and
bounty of a lost Golden Age can have no part to play in a political philosophy based on justifying the rational use of land previously allowed to
lie waste. For Locke, bounty has only ever resulted from improvements in
food production. Where land has not been improved the inhabitants —
reliant on the provisions of nature — are 'needy and wretched.' Or, as he
elsewhere has it, if it were not for the practical knowledge of some men
in the past, 'we should spend all our time to make a scanty provision for
a poor and miserable life,' such as that of the inhabitants of the West
Indies, who are 'scarce able to subsist.' . . . The trope of spontaneity itself
is a necessary component of Locke's argument, drawn from the repertory
of contemporary colonial discourse to hold apart 'labour' and 'reason':
but its Ovidian connotations work counter to the picture of deprivation
against which the promise of greater 'Conveniences' finds its justification.
It took Adam Smith, nearly a hundred years later, to clarify Locke's position for him in a paraphrase on the very first page of *The Wealth of*
Nations which equates the 'civilized and thriving' nations with their
technological superiority over 'the savage nations.' In the former

> *the produce of the whole labour of the society is so great, that all are*
> *often abundantly supplied, and a workman, even of the lowest and poor-*
> *est order, if he is frugal and industrious, may enjoy a greater share*

of the necessaries and conveniences of life than it is possible for any
savage to acquire.

Here 'labour' and 'reason' are unproblematically universal: it is just that
the level of skills is very different in 'savage' and 'civilized' societies. The
argument now has a satisfying circularity to it, its confident generaliza-
tions purged of the contradictions associated with the Ovidian reference
to spontaneity. . . .

It was only towards the end of the 'age of the Enlightenment' that a
scientific racism came to secure the distinctions between different groups
of human beings. For Locke—as for Descartes before him—the mono-
genetic tradition of Christian thought guaranteed the essential unity of
the human species, even unto the uttermost part of the earth. But Locke's
differential rationality with respect to cultural production, held in place
by that trope of the spontaneous hand of nature, still contained within it
a powerful set of consequences: the penalty for failing to see reason
could be severe. The earth produces fruits and feeds beasts. If the Indian
merely collects what is provided 'spontaneously' then it is not easy to see
how he differs from the beasts that are similarly provided for; except of
course that as a human being he is guilty of ignoring the law of nature
that is incumbent upon humans but not on animals. Here—in an almost
Hobbesian way—the boundary between animal and human is distinctly
permeable. Certainly those who can be seen as 'having renounced Reason' by shedding blood, or even those who have revealed an 'enmity'
towards a man of reason, may, under Locke's fiercesome gloss on the
law of nature, 'be treated as Beasts of Prey, those dangerous and noxious
Creatures,' destroyed 'for the same Reason, that he may kill a *Wolf* or a
Lyon.' This is not the war of all against all, but the war of the righteous
against those they perceive as attacking them: the language in which all
colonial wars against native Americans have been justified.

There are different narratives available to explain the presence of that
'spontaneous hand of Nature' in the *Second Treatise*. According to one
story it would be an unfortunate 'survival' from the language of classical
humanism, with Locke seen as a transitional figure in a gradual movement towards that 'purer' language of calculation only fully articulated
in *The Wealth of Nations*. Such stories of the progressive shedding of
earlier rhetorical encumbrances sit comfortably with the Enlightenment's self-image. The story told here has had a different accent: on
the implication of two discourses, the political and the colonial, both

with their foundations in theories of natural law, but here articulated around a single nodal point—the need to deny the existence of American Indian agriculture. The 'Enlightenment' argument of the *Second Treatise* is shadowed by that unconscious denial which serves to tether Locke's reasoning to historical and ideological circumstances beyond its conscious control.

David A. Hollinger

The Enlightenment and the Genealogy of Cultural Conflict in the United States

In 1969, Charlie Manson and his band committed the stylized murders for which they are still remembered. Several months after these grisly events, a faculty colleague of mine at SUNY Buffalo, where he and I had just begun our teaching careers, said to me in a sober voice that if Charlie Manson was what it truly meant to not believe in God—if this cult of murder was the culmination of the historical process of secularization, was what the Enlightenment had come to—he was glad to remain a Christian believer. . . .

I invoke here my memory of this private exchange because its dynamics are similar to many of the public conversations of our own time in which "the Enlightenment" is invoked. It is a discourse of warning and counter-warning, of morally portentous claims and counterclaims, a discourse in which episodes from intellectual history are manipulated and mobilized to discredit or to legitimate one program or another in contemporary struggles. . . .

So, on the one side, we are told that the Enlightenment project apotheosized individuality and has left us without means of acting on the elementary communitarian truth that selves are the product of social groups. The Enlightenment project denied the constraints and the enabling consequences of history by assigning to human reason the role of building life anew from a slate wiped clean of tradition. This project tyrannized a host of particular cultural initiatives and tried to make everyone alike by advancing universal rules for identifying goodness, justice, and truth. Politically, the Enlightenment promoted absolutist and imperialist initiatives. Above all, the Enlightenment project blinded us to the uncertainties of knowledge by promoting an ideal of absolute scientific certainty.

Meanwhile, others assure us with equal confidence that the Enlightenment recognized the limits and fallibility of knowledge to a degree that pre-Enlightenment regimes of truth simply did not. This Enlightenment project brought under devastating scrutiny the prejudices and superstitions that protected slavery and a virtual infinity of other injustices. It created the historical and social scientific inquiries that enable us to speak with such confidence about the social dependence of the self. The Enlightenment promoted religious tolerance against the imperialist ambitions of conflicting absolutisms. Above all, the Enlightenment was subversive of traditional political authority, and ultimately it gave us democracy.

. . . [W]e add the entire experience of the nineteenth and twentieth centuries to our inventory of historical vehicles that have transported things we like—or don't like—from the eighteenth century to the present. The Enlightenment led to Auschwitz, just as it had led to the Terror; or the Enlightenment led to the principles by which we judge the Terror to have been excessive, just as it led to the standards by which Auschwitz can be the most convincingly condemned today. . . .

The Enlightenment [is] blamed for what is said to be the excessive universalism and individualism that multiculturalists are trying to correct. The Enlightenment, it seems, has led us to suppose that all people are pretty much alike, thus blinding us to diversity. It is another mark of lingering Enlightenment assumptions, moreover, to focus on ostensibly autonomous individuals rather than the groups that provide individuals with their culture. And on the other side of the ideological coin, those who suspect multiculturalism of putting people into a small number of color-coded boxes and expecting them to stay there often voice their complaint in the name of the Enlightenment's revolt against the claims of blood and history. Yet some ideas that might be seen as extensions of an Enlightenment tradition—such as the right of an individual to choose his or her own cultural affiliations regardless of ancestry—are quite acceptable to the same audiences who will be suspicious of these same ideas if they are presented as Enlightenment ideas. A good rule of thumb in the multiculturalist debates is that a good way to get your ideas accepted is to conceal, rather than to emphasize, whatever ancestry those ideas may have in the Enlightenment.

The polemical use of history is common. It would be a mistake to suggest that the case I have described is unique. The legacy of the Enlightenment, in particular, has always been contested because so many enduring religious, political, and philosophical issues were engaged in the historic episode that bears its name. But during the last quarter-century, the Enlightenment has been an extreme case of this dynamic in the United States. Why this has happened is the chief question I pursue here. I want also to comment, more tentatively, on another question: where do we go from here? What are the prospects for an honest inquiry into the long-term historical trajectories in which the Enlightenment-invoking quarrels of our own time are embedded?

An answer to the first question requires an understanding of how the debate over the "modern" was transformed during the 1980s by historical claims offered under the sign of postmodernism. Among Anglophone intellectuals, the term modernism was long used to refer to a cluster of revolts against the Enlightenment. . . . The modern canon, in the arts as well as philosophy and social theory, was widely understood in the 1950s and 1960s to be the work of a heroic generation of late-nineteenth and early-twentieth century intellectuals who had challenged the epistemological and political traditions of the Enlightenment, and had seen the dark side of what came to be called the modernization process. What had happened during the very late nineteenth and early twentieth centuries, scholars agreed, was a revolt against the positivism, rationalism, realism, and liberalism that the Victorian intellectuals had refined from the Enlightenment of the eighteenth century. . . .

During the 1980s, however, Anglophone intellectuals attended to a formidable sequence of books and articles that used the word modernism very differently, to refer not to the revolt against the Enlightenment, but to the tradition of the Enlightenment itself. Modernism came to mean not Dostoevsky, but Descartes. . . .

This new sense of modernism was aggressively retailed in the United States under the name of postmodernism. Nietzsche, after his long career as founder of modernism, began a new career as a precursor, if not a founder, of postmodernism. . . . Nietzsche's ideas had not changed. . . . The only thing that had changed was the history in which Nietzsche was to be placed, or, more precisely, the movement to which he was assigned. . . . [M]odernism had become the Enlightenment and the revolt against it had become postmodernism. . . .

Hardly anybody, it seemed, had really seen through the illusions of the Enlightenment until the postmodernists came along. . . .

Entailed in this transformation in the Enlightenment's relation to modernism was the more widespread acceptance, by American academics, of a notion of intellectual modernity that had been popular in France, and that achieved currency in the United States along with the ideas of French theorists whose names were associated with postmodernism. Two autonomous revolts against two quite distinctive modernisms merged, apparently without anyone's planning it or negotiating it. The first modernism was that taken for granted when the term postmodernism was first invoked by Leslie Fiedler, Susan Sontag, and [Irving] Howe in the United States in the 1960s. The modernism against which these writers and their American contemporaries defined postmodernism was still the modernism of Eliot and Pound and Nietzsche and James; this was the modernism that entailed a critique of the Enlightenment and of the social and cultural processes of "modernization." . . . But a resoundingly different version of modernism, one associated with the Enlightenment, was the counter-referent for Lyotard's *Postmodern Condition*, translated into English in 1984. The French conversation that produced Lyotard had been preoccupied, moreover, not with the arts, but with ideas about language, power, and the human subject that had been developed by philosophers, psychologists, and political theorists.

. . . [T]hese two quite distinctive postmodernisms—an American, literary-artistic postmodernism defined against the canonical modernists of 1890–1930, and a French, philosophical-political postmodernism defined against the Enlightenment—might not have become part of the same discourse were it not for the quaint belief that there is but a single torch to be passed, requiring that each moment in the discourse of intellectuals be named. What is our moment? Why, the moment of postmodernism, of course. How do we know what it is? Well, we can start by scrutinizing the various things said and done under its sign. By the end of the 1980s the Anglophone world was awash with sweeping assessments of architecture, poetry, film, social theory, epistemology, fiction, and political economy, all of which were said to partake of post-modernism in the French sense of the term. Older critiques of the Enlightenment that had previously attained only a tiny constituency, such as Theodor Adorno and Max Horkheimer's *Dialectic of Enlightenment*, a book published in German in the 1940s but translated into English only in 1972, gained unprecedented currency.

Hence the Enlightenment made the historic transition from a distant episode long interrogated by the great modernists into a vibrant enemy of the newest and most exciting insights coming from Paris. The Enlightenment was dehistoricized, and made into a vivid and somewhat dangerous presence insufficiently criticized and transcended by previous generations of intellectuals. It was up to us, now in the 1980s and 1990s, to do the job right, to complete the anti-Enlightenment project. No wonder the tensions surrounding the name of the Enlightenment sharply increased. All of the historic layers of mediation between "us" and the Enlightenment had been put aside. The Enlightenment became more relevant to contemporary cultural conflicts because the discourse of post-modernism made it so.

Where do we go from here? One response to the ease with which discursive blacksmiths forge and shatter links between ourselves and the Enlightenment is to suspend, temporarily, at least, explicit assertions of the Enlightenment or counter-Enlightenment significance of contemporary debates. . . .

Yet this approach, tempting as it will be to anyone who has encountered the Enlightenment in its capacity as a conversation-stopper, runs into difficulties when enacted. Consider what happens when we try this in relation to a set of ideas that were widely adhered to by American intellectuals in the 1940s and 1950s, were then brought under severe suspicion at one point or other between the late 1960s and the 1980s, and have more recently been subject to critical revision and reassertion. . . . I call attention only to ideas that underwent all three experiences: popular in the 40s and 50s, then subject to widespread suspicion, and, finally, subject to critical reformulation and defense in recent years. Such ideas—argued about so earnestly, and subject to sharp reversals—are obviously important to the intellectual life of our own time. Any study of American intellectual life since 1950 needs an analytic language for interpreting these ideas.

What ideas fall into this distinctive class? Let me suggest seven, although the list could no doubt be extended:

- Nature has a capacity to significantly resist or respond to human efforts to represent it and to intervene in it.
- Humankind as a whole is a valid epistemic unit.
- Intersubjective reason has great emancipatory potential.
- Civil liberties formulated on the basis of rights ascribed to individual citizens are indispensable to a just society.
- Religion, whatever its role in past centuries, is now likely to be irrelevant, or even an obstruction, to cognitive and social progress.
- Physical characteristics such as skin color and shape of the face should not be allowed to determine the cultural tastes and social associations of individuals.
- The United States is potentially a world-historical agent of democratic-egalitarian values.

These ideas were affirmed with conviction by a great variety of voices during the 1940s and 1950s, when modernization theorists and positivists and behaviorists and liberals and integrationists of many kinds were in vogue. . . . Each of the seven was later brought under suspicion, often by persons identified with one or more of the following movements: communitarianism, feminism, neo-conservatism, poststructuralism, Marxism, postmodernism, and multiculturalism. These seven ideas are now situated in the classic baby-and-bathwater domain. Some say, in effect, "forget it, it's time we got beyond those ideas, let's talk about something else," and other people respond, "wait a minute, there's something here we can probably still use, if we are careful about it." And some who say "forget it" concerning one or another of the seven will switch sides about another of the seven, and say, "hold on, I like that one if we can make it non-racist, non-sexist, non-imperialist, non-universalist, non-logocentric, non-formalist, and, above all, non-European." . . .

Each of the seven ideas on my little list deserves its own history within the discourse of the American academic intelligentsia since 1950. I invoke these ideas here only to render concrete the challenge of dealing with recent intellectual history in relation to the question of the

Enlightenment's legacy. Are these seven ideas "Enlightenment ideas"?
. . . Does the critical revision and reassertion of these ideas in very recent years amount to a "neo-Enlightenment" of sorts? I state these questions not to answer them, but to suggest that if one wants to be historical
at all, it is difficult to analyze some central feature of recent American
intellectual life without making at least some use of the Enlightenment.
The universalism and individualism prominent in the list surely owe
much to Christianity, but so does the Enlightenment itself. The potential
connection between the Enlightenment and these seven energetic ideas
of our own time cannot be disposed of simply by pointing to a "more
complicated" intellectual ancestry. At issue, rather, is whether we can get
very far in explaining how these ideas have come to us, and how they acquired the hold they have on our conversations, without making extensive use of the collection of seventeenth- and eighteenth-century-centered
episodes that we continue to call "the Enlightenment."

This is to suggest that if we are going to make any use at all of
intellectual history in trying to understand where we are today, the Enlightenment is extremely difficult to avoid. The temptation to turn away
in disgust and frustration at the polemicism of recent uses of the Enlightenment should be resisted. To give in to this temptation would be
to deny our own historicity, and to shrink from searching for the sources
and sustaining conditions of the ideas that animate much of contemporary intellectual life. We might save the Enlightenment from polemicism,
but at a considerable cost: we might cut off too abruptly an opportunity
for the cultural self-knowledge that history is supposedly in the business
of providing. . . .

Biographical Sketches

The following sketches provide biographical information about the Enlightenment figures whose writings are included in this volume.

Jean le Rond d'Alembert (1717–1783). Born illegitimate of noble parents and abandoned at birth on the steps of the church of Saint Jean-le-Rond in Paris, from which he received his name, d'Alembert was raised in a family of modest means. With the financial support of his natural father, d'Alembert studied law and medicine at the Jansenist Collège des Quatre Nations, but his gift lay in mathematics, in which he was largely self-taught. At the age of 22, he was elected to the French Academy of Sciences based on his treatise on integral calculus. His *Treatise of Dynamics* (1742), in which he modified Newton's definition of force, established his reputation as one of the foremost mathematicians of his age. D'Alembert's contributions to the Enlightenment went well beyond mathematics, however. Co-editor with Diderot of the *Encyclopedia*, d'Alembert wrote the *Preliminary Discourse* to it and was responsible for the articles on science and mathematics until his resignation in 1758. Elected to the French Academy in 1754, d'Alembert was named its permanent secretary in 1772. Under his leadership, both the academy and the salon of his close friend, Julie de Lespinasse, became important institutions of the French Enlightenment.

Jean-Antoine-Nicolas de Caritat, Marquis de Condorcet (1743–1794). Descended from the ancient French nobility, Condorcet grew up on his family's estate and was educated first at the Jesuit collège in Reims, and later at the Collège de Navarre of the University of Paris. In 1765, he attracted the attention of d'Alembert with his *Essay on Integral Calculus,* and four years later was elected to the Academy of Sciences. He was also introduced into the circle that gathered in the salon of Julie de Lespinasse and to the political and humanitarian passions of d'Alembert's mentor, Voltaire. In 1776, Condorcet succeeded d'Alembert as permanent secretary of the Academy of Sciences, and six years later was elected to the French Academy. He contributed to the origins of social science by applying the mathematical theory of probability to social and political problems. Condorcet developed a political philosophy whose main features were rights, representation, and public instruction. He publicly supported the cause of the American Revolution and advocated human rights in France for women, Jews, and people of color. With the coming of the French Revolution, Condorcet attempted to put his ideas into practice. In 1789, he proposed several drafts of a declaration of rights to the new National Assembly; in 1791, he was elected to the Legislative Assembly, where he served as secretary and drew up plans for a state system of education. When the moderate republicans lost power to the more radical Jacobins, a warrant was issued for Condorcet's arrest. In October 1793, he went into hiding, where he wrote his final work, the *Sketch for a Historical Picture of the Progress of the Human Mind*, an eloquent final testament to the Enlightenment's optimistic belief in human progress. With the manuscript still unfinished, he was arrested in March 1794, and died in prison two days later.

Denis Diderot (1713–1784).   Diderot's most important contribution to the Enlightenment was his editorship of the *Encyclopedia*, which consumed more than 20 years of his life, brought him into conflict with the authorities of church and state, and forced him to demonstrate personal courage on many occasions. The son of a master cutler in the provincial city of Langres, Diderot was educated first by the local Jesuits, and then at the University of Paris, where he was sent at the age of 13 to study for the priesthood. After earning degrees in philosophy and theology, he abandoned his studies, ostensibly to apprentice for a legal career, but in reality to make his way as a man of letters. His early writings include pornographic novels that sold well and philosophical works that gave him a reputation for atheism and materialism. He was at the heart of a group of friends, which included d'Alembert and Rousseau (who later broke with him publicly), who would lead the French Enlightenment from the 1750s through the 1770s. With d'Alembert, he became editor of the *Encyclopedia* in 1747. While working on this project (directing it alone after d'Alembert's resignation in 1758), Diderot continued to write philosophy, art criticism, novels, and plays. Today he is most admired for the philosophical dialogues he circulated but did not publish during his lifetime: *Rameau's Nephew*, *D'Alembert's Dream*, and the *Supplement to Bougainville's Voyage*, above all. Diderot's humanitarian politics are best seen in his impassioned but anonymous contributions to Raynal's eight-volume *History of the Two Indies*, the Enlightenment's most important critique of colonialism and the slave trade.

Louise-Florence-Pétronile Tardieu d'Esclavelles, Marquise de Lalive d'Epinay (1726–1783). When she was orphaned young and left penniless, Louise Tardieu d'Esclavelles was taken in by rich relatives. She married one of the sons of this household in a love match that soon proved disastrous. After her husband spent his fortune on gambling and mistresses, she found love and companionship elsewhere, eventually with the philosophe Melchior Grimm, who was her lover from 1753 until her death 30 years later. Her house was a second home to Grimm, Diderot, the abbé Galiani, and other friends. Rousseau lived for more than a year in a small house she built for him on her estate so that he could escape Paris for the simple life. She won the first "Prize for Utility" given by the French Academy in 1774 for her *Conversations with Emily*, a pedagogical dialogue between a mother and daughter. Epinay was a major contributor to the *Correspondance littéraire*, a newsletter edited by Grimm and distributed to royal and noble subscribers mostly in central and eastern Europe. Her other major work was an unfinished autobiographical novel, *The Story of Madame de Montbrillant*, published after her death. When Galiani was recalled to Naples from his post as secretary to the Neapolitan ambassador in Paris, she began a correspondence with him that reveals her to be the important thinker and critic that her reluctance, as a woman, to publish, conceals.

Françoise de Graffigny (1695–1758).   Graffigny did not publish her first book until 1747, when she was in her fifties. *Letters of a Peruvian Woman* was an enormous popular and critical success and encouraged her to write for the theater. Two of her plays were performed by the Comédie Française in the 1750s, but her fame continued to rest on the novel, which was translated into several languages and reprinted many times until the 1830s. Her personal life took a similar trajectory. Born into local nobility in Nancy, capital of the then-independent duchy of Lorraine, Graffigny was married young to a man who abused her. After obtaining a legal separation, she found protection at the ducal court. In 1738, she left Lorraine for Paris, where her literary talents were nourished through conversations and correspondence with the men of letters of her day and extensive reading that took the place of the formal schooling she never received. That same year she spent two months at Cirey, the estate of Emilie du Châtelet, the translator of Newton and a notable scientist and philosopher in her own right, as well as the mistress of Voltaire. In Paris, she was part of the literary circle around the retired actress, Mlle Quinault, and became a mentor to a young cousin whose marriage to the wealthy philosophe, Helvétius, she facilitated. (Mme Helvétius became a notable salonnière.) Like other women of the Enlightenment, Graffigny's unpublished writing was considerably more extensive than the works she published. Letters she wrote to a friend during her stay at Cirey were published in the nineteenth century, but the rest of her 2500 letters and the 1500 responses to them are only now being published in a critical scholarly edition.

David Hume (1711–1776).   Born and raised in Scotland, Hume studied ancient languages and philosophy at the University of Edinburgh. His interest in philosophy continued through a brief stint working for a Bristol merchant and a much longer stay in France, where he entered into the culture of the local Republic of Letters and educated himself in the French skeptical tradition. A *Treatise of Human Nature* was published shortly after his return to England (1739–1740). The general indifference with which it was greeted persuaded Hume to adopt the essay form to reach a broad public. The *Essays, Moral and Political* (1741–1742) were highly successful and show his breadth, his wit, and his commitment to the Enlightenment project of teaching the public to think critically. The brisk sales of his next philosophical works, *Enquiry Concerning Human Understanding* (1748) and *Enquiry Concerning the Principles of Morals* (1752), attest to his success in reworking his philosophy for the reading public. Having failed twice to secure a professorship in Scotland over the opposition of the local clergy, Hume became a librarian to the Edinburgh law faculty, a post that allowed him to pursue his interest in history. His six-volume *History of Great Britain*, published between 1754 and 1762, was a bestseller well into the nineteenth century. Thanks to the fame and financial independence it gave him, he was able to return to Paris as secretary to the British ambassador in 1763. There he became a regular at the salons frequented by the French philosophes and became their ally and friend. In 1769 he retired to Edinburgh, where he enjoyed his literary reputation until his death. His most controversial work, *Dialogues Concerning Natural Religion*, was published posthumously in 1779.

Immanuel Kant (1724–1804).   Kant was born in Königsberg, then part of East Prussia. His father was a saddle maker whose Pietism exerted a lasting influence on his son. Kant attended the University of Königsberg, where he focused on philosophy, mathematics, and physics. He spent his entire career at this university, starting as a lecturer and ultimately becoming its rector. At the same time, he achieved a Europe-wide reputation as a philosopher through his published writings. Around 1769 Kant experienced what he called a great "upheaval" in his thinking, possibly from reading Hume's works of philosophical skepticism. His most important works of philosophy were the result of this "critical turn:" *Critique of Pure Reason* (1781), *Prolegomena to Any Future Metaphysics* (1783), *Foundations of the Metaphysics of Morals* (1785), *Critique of Practical Reason* (1788), and *Critique of Judgment* (1790). Kant's *Critique of Pure Reason* established the basis of knowledge claims now associated with the Enlightenment and modernity by working out a position that avoided both skepticism and determinism, but assumed universal human reason. Between 1784 and 1786, Kant's interventions in several public debates, including his response to the question, "What is Enlightenment," made him a prominent representative of the German Enlightenment. By the 1790s, however, a backlash against the Enlightenment had developed in Germany, and Kant's ability to publish freely was constrained by the order of his king. Thereafter Kant avoided the subject of religion but published on other topics until his death in 1804.

Jean-Jacques Rousseau (1712–1778).   Rousseau was born in Protestant Geneva and raised by his father, a well-respected but modest citizen of the city, after the death of his mother in childbirth. In his teens he ran away from home and, using his wits, sought asylum in neighboring Savoy by asking to be baptized into the Catholic faith. Rousseau stayed in Savoy for more than a decade, during which time he read widely and developed a deep interest in music and botany. In 1742, he went to Paris, where he quickly became part of a circle of friends that included Diderot and d'Alembert, who asked him to write the articles on music for the *Encyclopedia*. He made his name, however, with a pair of essays written for competitions sponsored by the Academy of Dijon. In his *Discourse on the Arts and Sciences* (1751), Rousseau took the position that culture corrupted human beings and that civilized society was a moral wasteland. In his *Discourse on the Origins of Inequality* (1754), he traced a conjectural history of humanity from a state of nature in which isolated men roamed the earth in perfect freedom and equality, to a modern world in which inequality was institutionalized in private property, and despotism loomed on the horizon. In 1758, Rousseau broke definitively with the Enlightenment, condemning it and the modern society in which it flourished on moral grounds. In Rousseau's view, education, society, and the state all worked to deprive men of their natural freedom and to corrupt women's natural goodness. In *Emile, or Education* (1762), he laid out an idealized plan for the education of a boy; in *Julie, or the New Heloise* (1761), he imagined an ideal community; and in *The Social Contract* (1762), he theorized the ideal state. In each case, the "natural" differences between women and men are strengthened so as to re-establish "nature." After the condemnation of *Emile* in both Protestant Geneva and Catholic France for its ideas on religious education, Rousseau resumed the wandering life of the exile—taking on the persona of a martyr persecuted for his truth-telling, as his popularity with the reading public throughout Europe and America grew. He devoted his later years to autobiographical writings that charted his inner state and turbulent life. Despite Rousseau's break with the philosophes in the 1750s, his relationship to the Enlightenment remains complex, such that many of his ideas are considered synonymous with it.

Antoine-Léonard Thomas (1732–1785).   Born in the French provinces, Thomas soon lost his father and was sent to Paris by his mother to study at the age of 10. He took up the law but soon abandoned it for the Republic of Letters, supporting himself with a teaching position at the Collège de Beauvais of the University of Paris. Eventually his success as a writer led to a position as secretary to the minister of foreign affairs. In 1759, Thomas published *Jumonville*, a patriotic poem that established him as a writer, but his gift was for the eulogy. Between 1759 and 1765, he won the French Academy's prize for eloquence five times. He was a regular member of all the major Enlightenment salons, including that of Madame Geoffrin, who remembered him in her will, and Suzanne Necker, whom he idealized in his *Essay on Women*. In his inaugural address upon being elected to the French Academy (1767), Thomas proclaimed the Enlightenment man of letters to be the model citizen in the face of attacks on the philosophes' patriotism in a time of war. Three years later, he ran afoul of the Catholic Church with a eulogy of Marcus Aurelius, but later retaliated with a speech delivered in the academy to the acclaim of his peers. Thomas is not much remembered today; his life does not conform to the image of the philosophe as daring radical or nonconformist, and his writings do not appeal to the modern reader. His membership in the community of philosophes, however, was based on his integrity as a writer, his willingness to defy authority, and his sociability.

François-Marie Arouet de Voltaire (1694–1778). Voltaire was the longest-lived and most prolific writer of the Enlightenment. The son of a rich Parisian bourgeois, he was educated at the most prestigious Jesuit collège in Paris. He became a poet against the wishes of his father, who wanted him to be a lawyer. At the age of 22, he reinvented himself as the noble-sounding "Monsieur de Voltaire." Voltaire's vision of the poet's life did not entail poverty; he sought fortune and status as well as fame through the glory of letters. Fame came with the success of his tragedy *Oedipus* (1718), and it grew with the publication of *Henriade* (1723), an epic poem glorifying Henry IV for the peace he brought to France through religious toleration. In 1745 Voltaire was named royal historiographer, and a year later he was elected to the French Academy. Despite public acclaim and official honors, however, Voltaire was a constant annoyance to those in power. In 1726, after a brief imprisonment for some impolitic words, Voltaire left Paris for a three-year stay in London that had a significant impact on his intellectual development, as seen in the *Philosophical Letters* (1734). For the rest of his life Voltaire lived and worked far enough from Paris and Versailles to be tolerated by the French government: for 20 years with his mistress, Emilie du Châtelet, with whom he shared an interest in philosophy and Newtonian science; for 3 years at the court of Frederick II of Prussia; and for the last 20 years of his life at his own estate on France's Swiss border. Voltaire's works reflect the critical spirit of the Enlightenment as well as the irreverence that both attracted the public and infuriated officialdom. Most of what he wrote was published outside France and smuggled in to a receptive public. He is best known today for the satiric novella *Candide* (1759) and for his anti-clericalism. In his own day, Voltaire was widely admired as the greatest dramatist of the century and for his personal campaign to *écraser l'infâme*, or "crush infamy," by using his celebrity to fight on behalf of victims of religious intolerance; his *Treatise on Toleration* (1763) publicized this injustice. By the time of his death at the age of 84, Voltaire represented for many the Enlightenment synthesis of writer and spokesman for the cause of humanity. In 1791, the French revolutionaries proclaimed Voltaire their heroic precursor by transferring his remains to the Pantheon.

Mary Wollstonecraft (1759–1797).   Wollstonecraft's most important contribution to the Enlightenment was written during and in direct response to the French Revolution. In A *Vindication of the Rights of Woman* (1792), she engaged critically the ideas of Rousseau, Adam Smith, Richard Price, and other Enlightenment writers to articulate modern, liberal feminism on Enlightenment principles. Raised on the edges of gentility in the English provinces, Wollstonecraft educated and supported herself within the limits available to a respectable, single Englishwoman of her day. After working as a companion and a governess, she opened a girls' boarding school in a London community of religious Dissenters. When the school failed, she penned her *Thoughts on the Education of Daughters* (1787) to pay her debts, and then took a post as a governess in Ireland. In 1787, Wollstonecraft returned to London with a contract for her first novel, *Mary* (1788), and a paid position with Joseph Johnson, the leading publisher of the English nonconformist Enlightenment. She became a regular member of Johnson's circle, which included the chemist and radical Joseph Priestley, political philosopher William Godwin, poet William Blake, and American patriot Tom Paine. Wollstonecraft wrote book reviews for the journals Johnson published and eventually became his (anonymous) collaborator and co-editor. In 1790 she published A *Vindication of the Rights of Men*, an immediate response to Burke's *Reflections on the Revolution in France*, but she achieved public prominence two years later with A *Vindication of the Rights of Woman*. In 1797, Wollstonecraft married Godwin, but she died later that year of puerperal fever after the birth of her daughter Mary, who would later marry the poet Percy Shelley and write *Frankenstein*.

Suggestions for Further Reading

This brief bibliography is restricted to literature available in English and does not include any of the works excerpted in this volume or any of the many studies of individual Enlightenment writers.

Reference Works

Michel Delon, ed., *Encyclopedia of the Enlightenment*, (Chicago, Ill.: Fitzroy Dearborn, 2001).

Alan Kors, ed., *Encyclopedia of the Enlightenment*, 4 vols. (New York: Oxford University Press, 2003).

Anthologies of Enlightenment Texts

Simon Eliot and Beverly Stern, eds., *The Age of Enlightenment*, 2 vols. (London: Ward Lock Educational, 1979).

Peter Gay, ed., *The Enlightenment: A Comprehensive Anthology* (New York: Simon and Schuster, 1973).

Isaac Kramnick, ed., *The Portable Enlightenment Reader* (New York: Penguin, 1995).

General Overviews

Norman Hampson, *The Enlightenment* (Harmondsworth, Eng.: Penguin, 1968).

Ulrich Im Hof, *The Enlightenment*, trans. William E. Yuill (Oxford: Blackwell Publishers, 1994).

Dorinda Outram, *The Enlightenment* (Cambridge: Cambridge University Press, 1995).

The Enlightenment and Its Practitioners

Daniel Brewer and Julie Candler Hayes, eds., *Using the Encyclopédie: Ways of Knowing, Ways of Reading* (Oxford: Voltaire Foundation, 2002).

Jonathan Israel, *Radical Enlightenment: Philosophy and the Making of Modernity, 1650–1750* (Oxford: Oxford University Press, 2001).

Margaret C. Jacob, *The Radical Enlightenment: Pantheists, Freemasons, and Republicans* (London: George Allen & Unwin, 1981).

Alan Kors, *D'Holbach's Coterie: An Enlightenment in Paris* (Princeton, N.J.: Princeton University Press, 1978).

James Van Horn Melton, *The Rise of the Public in Enlightenment Europe* (Cambridge: Cambridge University Press, 2001).

Roy Porter and Mikulas Teich, eds., *The Enlightenment in National Context* (Cambridge: Cambridge University Press, 1981).

Daniel Roche, *France in the Enlightenment*, trans. Arthur Goldhammer (Cambridge, Mass.: Harvard University Press, 1998).

Richard B. Sher, *Church and University in the Scottish Enlightenment: The Moderate Literati of Edinburgh* (Princeton, N.J.: Princeton University Press, 1985).

Franco Venturi, *Italy and the Enlightenment: Studies in a Cosmopolitan Century*, trans. Susan Corsi (New York: New York University Press, 1972).

Institutions of Enlightenment: Print and Sociability

Robert Darnton, *The Business of Enlightenment* (Cambridge, Mass.: Harvard University Press, 1979).

Elizabeth L. Eisenstein, *Grub Street Abroad: Aspects of the French Cosmopolitan Press from the Age of Louis XIV to the French Revolution* (Oxford: Oxford University Press, 1992).

Anne Goldgar, *Impolite Learning: Conduct and Community in the Republic of Letters, 1680–1750* (New Haven, Conn.: Yale University Press, 1995).

Dena Goodman, *The Republic of Letters: A Cultural History of the French Enlightenment* (Ithaca, N.Y.: Cornell University Press, 1994).

Daniel Gordon, *Citizens Without Sovreignty: Equality and Sociability in French Thought, 1670–1789* (Princeton, N.J.: Princeton University Press, 1994).

Jürgen Habermas, *The Structural Transformation of the Public Sphere: An Inquiry into a Category of Bourgeois Society*, trans. Thomas Burger and Frederick Lawrence (Cambridge, Mass.: MIT Press, 1989).

Margaret C. Jacob, *Living the Enlightenment: Freemasonry and Politics in Eighteenth-Century Europe* (New York: Oxford University Press, 1991).

James E. McClellan III, *Science Reorganized: Scientific Societies in the Eighteenth Century* (New York: Columbia University Press, 1985).

Patricia Selwyn, *Everyday Life in the German Book Trade: Friedrich Nicolai as Bookseller and Publisher in the Age of Enlightenment, 1750–1810* (University Park: Penn State University Press, 2000).

Science and the Enlightenment

William Clark, Jan Golinski, and Simon Schaffer, eds., *The Sciences in Enlightenment Europe* (Chicago: University of Chicago Press, 1999).

Christopher Fox, Roy Porter, and Robert Wokler, eds., *Inventing Human Science: Eighteenth-Century Domains* (Berkeley: University of California Press, 1995).

Thomas Hankins, *Science and the Enlightenment* (Cambridge: Cambridge University Press, 1985).

Jessica Riskin, *Science in the Age of Sensibility: The Sentimental Empiricists of the French Enlightenment* (Chicago: University of Chicago Press, 2002).

Jacques Roger, *The Life Sciences in Eighteenth-Century French Thought*, trans. Robert Ellrich (Stanford: Stanford University Press, 1998).

G. S. Rousseau and Roy Porter, eds., *The Ferment of Knowledge: Studies in the Historiography of Eighteenth-Century Science* (Cambridge: Cambridge University Press, 1980).

Mary Terrall, *The Man Who Flattened the Earth: Maupertuis and the Sciences in the Enlightenment* (Chicago: University of Chicago Press, 2002).

Anne Vila, *Enlightenment and Pathology: Sensibility in the Literature and Medicine of Eighteenth-Century France* (Baltimore, Md.: Johns Hopkins University Press, 1998).

Kathleen Wellman, *La Mettrie: Medicine, Philosophy and Enlightenment* (Durham, N.C.: Duke University Press, 1992).

Elizabeth Williams, *The Physical and the Moral: Anthropology, Physiology, and Philosophical Medicine in France, 1750–1850* (Cambridge: Cambridge University Press, 2002).

Women and the Enlightenment

Hans Erich Böedeker and Lieselotte Steinbrügge, eds., *Conceptualizing Woman in Enlightenment Thought* (Berlin: Berlin Verlag Arno Spitz, 2001).

Natalie Zemon Davis and Arlette Farge, eds., *A History of Women in the West: Renaissance and Enlightenment Paradoxes* (Cambridge, Mass.: Harvard University Press, 1993).

Nina Rattner Gelbart, *Feminine and Opposition Journalism in Old Regime France: "Le Journal des Dames"* (Berkeley: University of California Press, 1987).

Erica Harth, *Cartesian Women: Versions and Subversions of Rational Discourse in the Old Regime* (Ithaca, N.Y.: Cornell University Press, 1992).

Margaret Hunt et al., *Women and the Enlightenment* (New York: Haworth Press, 1984).

Rebecca Messbarger, *The Century of Women: Representations of Women in Eighteenth-Century Italian Public Discourse* (Toronto: University of Toronto Press, 2002).

Sylvia Harcstark Myers, *The Bluestocking Circle: Women, Friendship and the Life of the Mind in Eighteenth-Century Britain* (Oxford: Oxford University Press, 1990).

Londa Schiebinger, *The Mind Has No Sex?: Women in the Origins of Modern Science* (Cambridge, Mass.: Harvard University Press, 1989).

Samia I. Spencer, ed., *French Women and the Age of Enlightenment* (Bloomington: Indiana University Press, 1984).

Critiques of Enlightenment

Keith Michael Baker and Peter Hanns Reill, eds., *What's Left of Enlightenment? A Postmodern Question* (Stanford: Stanford University Press, 2001).

Daniel Gordon, ed., *Postmodernism and the Enlightenment: New Perspectives in Eighteenth-Century French Intellectual History* (New York: Routledge, 2000).

Reinhart Koselleck, *Critique and Crisis: Enlightenment and the Pathogenesis of Modern Society* (Cambridge, Mass.: MIT Press, 1988).

Sven-Eric Liedman, ed., *The Postmodernist Critique of the Project of Enlightenment* (Amsterdam and Atlanta: Rodopi, 1997).

Darrin McMahon, *Enemies of the Enlightenment: The French Counter-Enlightenment and the Making of Modernity* (New York: Oxford University Press, 2001).

James Schmidt, ed., *What Is Enlightenment?: Eighteenth-Century Answers and Twentieth-Century Questions* (Berkeley: University of California Press, 1996).